ARCTIC OBSESSION

ARCTIC OBSESSION
The Lure of the Far North

Alexis S. Troubetzkoy

Thomas Dunne Books
St. Martin's Press
New York

Thomas Dunne Books.
An imprint of St. Martin's Press

Copyright © Alexis S. Troubetzkoy, 2011

www.thomasdunnebooks.com
www.stmartins.com

Editor: Shannon Whibbs
Design: Jennifer Scott
Printer: Friesens

Library of Congress Cataloging-in-Publication Data Available Upon Request

ISBN 978-0-312-62503-0

1   2   3   4   5   15   14   13   12   11

Printed and bound in Canada.

To my former students at Bishop's College School,
Selwyn House School and Appleby College, in gratitude

Contents

The Song of the Siren

"And now they saw a firm island, Anthamaessa,
where the fair-voiced Sirens beguiled with their sweet songs
whoever cast ashore there, and then destroyed them …"
The Argonautica by Apollonus

Introduction

The Arctic: Who Is She?

ON BOARD THE RUSSIAN Arctic research vessel, *Akademik Fedeorov*, and the nuclear-powered submarine *Rossya* on that bright summer day in 2007, the moods were distinctly jubilant. And there was every reason to celebrate, for they were headed home to Murmansk; their mission completed.

Following weeks of planning and exhaustive trial runs, the expedition had launched the 18.6-ton submersible, *Mir-1* on its momentous underwater assignment in the high Arctic. Eight hours and forty minutes later, the tiny vessel returned to the surface, its task accomplished. After a fourteen-thousand-foot descent through inky darkness of those frigid waters, a "soft landing" had been made on the ocean's floor — a perfect landing at the precise terrestrial point of the North Pole.

With their vessel resting on the bottom, the crew went quickly to work scooping up samples of sand, collecting vials of water, and making observations of the rock formation. Artur Chilingarov, chief of the three-man crew, radioed the mother ship above. "It's lovely down here with yellowish ground all around us," he said, before adding, "there is no sign of sea dwellers." The most perilous part of the journey was the return to the surface. Had the navigation been even slightly off, the tiny sub might easily have missed the exact gap in the ice through which it had entered; possibility of entrapment in the Arctic ice sheet was real. All went well, however.

But the sensational aspect of this risky journey to "a point no one had so far been able to reach" was the planting of the Russian flag at the North Pole, a one-metre-high construction of corrosion-resistant titanium. "If in a hundred or a thousand years from now someone goes down to where we were, they will see the Russian flag," Chilingarov gushed enthusiastically. A symbolic claim had been made to that significant spot; insofar as the expedition's elated crew was concerned, the North Pole was now Russian.

The story of the underwater conquest on that August day made headlines around the world, creating a flurry of excitement in many capitals. Not unexpectedly, the most vociferous outcry came from Ottawa, where foreign minister Peter MacKay condemned the achievement. "This isn't the fifteenth century," he thundered. "You can't go around the world and just plant flags and say 'We're claiming your territory.'" In a more reflective moment he later declared, "There is no threat to Canadian sovereignty in the Arctic … we're not at all concerned about this mission. Basically it's just a show by Russia." Nevertheless, the true terrestrial pole had been reached.

The expedition was a costly venture for Russia, but the country was prepared to assume it in the interest of making a strong statement. Russia is a northern nation and the Arctic is an integral part of its inheritance — beware, those making claims there. Whatever the country's political and economic vicissitudes since the days of Sputnik, its scientific and technological capabilities remain robust. Russia is not only ineluctably wed to the Arctic, but it possesses the wherewithal to realize its full destiny in those far reaches.

But for Chilingarov, the passage to that unique dot on the earth's surface transcended any political statement. His voyage was a personal triumph, one for the record books; he had achieved what for centuries many had deemed improbable. The call of the North had been well and truly answered – the Arctic Siren had sung her beguiling song, as it were, and he had successfully ignored her. Not so, the scores of others who over the centuries found themselves lured by her call, drawn as if by a magnet into a deadly embrace.

The Arctic seems to forever cast a spell over man's imagination, with the North Pole being a particularly tantalizing draw. A corner of the world of ice-encrusted shores and unbounded frozen tundra, of endless days or continuous nights and of scarcity and want. A land that is as unpredictable and dangerous as it is alluring and wondrously beautiful.

Although barely populated, the Arctic is rich in history and tales of its explorers, adventurers, and competitive entrepreneurs are legion. Since early medieval times, man has ventured into those hostile expanses for one purpose or another. The outcomes for these early gallants invariably proved disappointing — mirages of sorts. The passage seemed just beyond the next point, but it wasn't there; the binding ice packs are certain to give way, but they only grow firmer; the objective will be reached tomorrow, but the tomorrows kept passing by — like chasing rainbows. Some survived to tell about it while others perished and left the telling to their chroniclers.

The early thrusts were ever plagued by defiant ice, deprivation, haunting solitude, and above all, by unimaginable cold. Listen to one nineteenth-century explorer, George Kennan:

> Our eyelids froze together while we were drinking tea. Our soup taken from a hot kettle froze in our tin plates before we could possibly finish eating it, and the breasts of our fur coats were covered with white rime while we sat only a few feet from a huge blazing campfire. Tin plates, knives and spoons burned the bare hand when touched, almost exactly as if they were red hot, and water spilled on a little piece of board only fourteen inches from the fire, froze solid in less than two minutes The warm bodies of our dogs gave off clouds of steam, and even the bare hand, wiped perfectly dry, exhaled a thin vapor when exposed to air ...[1]

What manner of persons were these early hardies — the likes of Sir John Franklin, for example? On his final quest of the elusive Northwest Passage, every sort of calamity befell him and his crew: exposure and hypothermia, starvation and scurvy, tuberculosis and lead poisoning. What force propelled him so resolutely to battle the formidable ice packs of the Canadian north in the first place? The draw of the Siren's "sweet song," possibly? "Nothing is dearer to my heart ... than the accomplishment of the Northwest Passage," he once declared. Twice he tried to break through the ice, and on the third attempt in 1845 he and his company simply disappeared, swallowed by the hostile expanses and "taken to their eternal rest."

A polar bear attack on one of Barents's crew members during his second expedition into Arctic waters. His frightened colleagues reacted at first by running away, but soon returned and found the animal "devouring the man ... the beare bit his head in sunder and sucked out his blood."

Consider also the likes of the Dutchman, Willem Barents, "the most distinguished martyr to Arctic investigation," who more than two centuries before Franklin set out no less determinedly in the opposite direction, to uncover the Northeast Passage. And like Sir John, he too made three journeys, on the last of which his small vessel became decisively ice-bound. The crushing packs continued to press, and eventually the vessel was heaved up like a toy and broken beyond repair. Barents and his tiny crew came ashore and with no small effort constructed a shelter from material of the wrecked ship. They thus become the first Europeans to pass an entire Arctic winter — long, dark days in constant fear of intruding polar bears. Once, the horrified crew witnessed such a beast attacking and killing one of their numbers and then gorging itself on brain matter that spilled from the split skull. Some of the crew returned home to tell the tale of the incredible adventures, but others, Barents included, forfeited their lives in futile missions.

One of the most compelling tales of man's resourcefulness and endurance in the Arctic is that of the four Pomori hunters who in 1741 found themselves accidental castaways on one of the Arctic's most inhospitable islands, in Spitzbergen. For *six years* they managed to survive in isolation on what little they happened to have carried originally: the clothes on their backs, a musket and twelve rounds of ammunition, a knife, an axe, a small tea kettle, a tinderbox, twenty pounds of flour, and a pouch of tobacco. That and later, a hunk of driftwood which had washed ashore — providentially, with a spike driven through. What sort of men were these, and what force was within them that allowed for survival?

Franklin, Barents, and Kennan: three among scores of others who over the centuries answered the call of the North. These valiants came from England, Russia, United States, and Denmark, from Norway, Sweden, and Canada, from Germany, Italy, and Hungary. Most were spurred on in search of fame and fortune while others, by hopes of discovery or simply through a sense of adventure. However one might view them, they were all outsiders not belonging to the Arctic, interlopers really. These Europeans form one of two stout threads that are woven into the fabric of Arctic history. The other thread finds its strength in the scattering of indigenous peoples who arrived to those far northlands centuries before any European and settled there — the Inuit of Canada and Greenland, Aleuts of Alaska, Yakut and Chukchi of Siberia or Lapps of Scandinavia, to name but a few. It was their homeland that suffered European incursion, but it was they who ultimately showed many of the outsiders how to cope with those inhospitable environs. These were the children of the Arctic Siren, who smiled benevolently upon them. Two distinctive threads that share a commonality — their histories are equally framed in display of courage and stubbornness, in conquest and failure, and in death and survival.

So, for starters, how to define the region known as the Arctic? Where does it begin and end and what exactly is the North Pole, the so-called "top of the world"? Simply put, the pole is that point on the surface of the northern hemisphere through which passes the tilted axis of earth's rotation. This geographic North Pole is not to be confused with the magnetic North Pole, the globe's constantly-moving point where the earth's magnetic field tips vertically downward and from which the compass finds its bearing.

Strictly speaking, anyone laying claim to having stood at the pole is in error for, as we have seen, such person was positioned some four kilometeres *above* it, on the ice-covered ocean surface. Of the world's five oceans, the Arctic is the smallest, yet in linear terms from one shore to the opposite, distances exceed 3100 miles. The nearest landfall from the pole is the obscure island of Kaffeklubben 440 miles away, off the coast of Greenland. Had the same claimant been challenged to point east or west, he would have been unable to do so, for at the pole all directions point south. Had the adventurer looked directly above at the night sky, he would have found the most telling celestial body in the northern hemisphere, *Polaris*, or the North Star. From ancient times, astronomers and navigators took their bearings from this apparently stationary star, around which the night sky seems to revolve. The star is also known as "the Great Bear," and the word for bear in Greek is *arktos* — hence, "arctic".

The term "arctic" has two commonly used, varied definitions, neither of which is 100 percent satisfactory. The neatest, less amorphous demarcation has it in terms of earth–sun relationship: the Arctic Circle at latitude 66°33' N is the clearly drawn boundary. Here on one day of the year (about June 21) the sun does not set, and on one day of the year (about December 21), it does not rise — the summer and winter solstices. The second definition is rooted in terms of climate and vegetation. The Arctic is delineated by the irregular and shifting 50°F July isotherm — the line closely corresponding to the northern limit of tree growth: to the south, taiga and low-lying trees, and to the north, the treeless tundra.

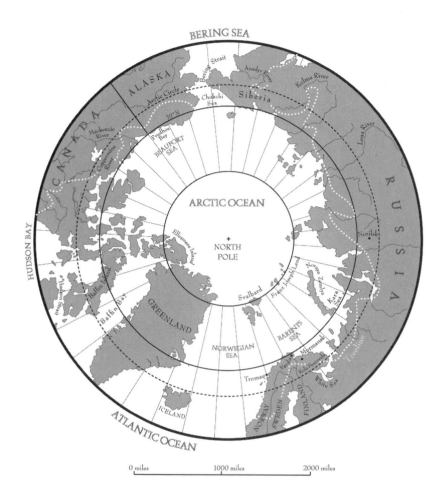

The circumpolar region with the Arctic Circle. The irregular dotted line indicates the approximate treeline.

Map by Cameron McLeod Jones.

By accepting the latter definition, it must be appreciated that much of what is called "the sub-Arctic" falls within these parameters. This book's purview is framed by that second definition, for within the broader bounds are found the majority of the Arctic's indigenous population, which today is being dramatically affected by climatic change. The canvas before us therefore is sizeable and broad brushstrokes are required to come to terms with it.

Amid false hopes and mirages, early explorers competed as much for glory and kudos as for discovery and territorial claim. But for today's explorers and entrepreneurs the mirages are a thing of the past — scientific and technological advances have written an end to them with unsettling rapidity. Pressures wrought by climate change and environmental concerns, the dogged quest for fresh sources of energy and political jockeying of nations for strategic positioning have brought fresh realities to the North. The principals in the continuing rivalry are the five prime Arctic nations: Russia, Canada, United States, Norway, and Denmark — all taken up in the whirlwind of transformation of which the greater public generally is imperfectly informed.

Beneath the Arctic landscape lies a vast wealth of hidden treasures — gold, silver, copper, lead, zinc, uranium, cobalt, titanium, and platinum. But it is oil and gas that attracts most attention. Estimates of the region's oil reserves are wild, with some figures running as high as 40 percent of the world's total. If such is the case, the Arctic's potential eclipses those of Saudi Arabia and Iran combined. The challenges of exploration and extraction are one thing, getting it all to the markets is quite another matter. But with global warming and the retreat of the ice caps, the promise of an open shipping channel is an eminent reality. An ice-free Northwest Passage will not only permit the transport of Arctic riches to the markets, but would unlock a trans-polar route for east–west shipping, cutting some sailing times by 40 percent or more. Not surprising, therefore, that interest today in that distant reach of our planet is as great as ever; the place that "God had secreted all for himself" is being ruthlessly penetrated. My hope for this volume is that it will stimulate a greater appreciation for this wondrous and fragile part of our world. As a friend adroitly put it, "The Arctic today is tomorrow's hot spot."

Some years ago I was invited to join a group of businessmen flying to Resolute, Canada's second-most northern settlement at 74°43' N. The place continues as the springboard for scientific research stations and polar expeditions. During the five-day visit, I was invited to accompany a couple of supply flights to isolated meteorological stations, one at Mould Bay in the western Arctic not far from the Beaufort Sea, and the other to Eurika, just north of 80° N, a mere 460 miles from the North Pole (and, it may be noted, 2,581 miles from Canada's southernmost point).

At seven thousand feet, our ancient DC-3 seemed to skim over the landscape with unreal rapidity. Clear blue skies and the midnight sun made for perfect visibility. Mountains, dark crevasses, moraines, ancient glaciers, snow — all blended the unfolding landscape into a barrenness of dynamic beauty. Here, melting snow fed streams that cascaded through ruts and gullies; there, stands of dark silt contrasted with sparkling white ice. Expanse, expanse, and on and on ... a panorama of pristine landscape and perfect solitude. It's as though God had indeed secreted this awesomely magnificent place all for himself ... and here we were — trespassers.

On the return flight from Mould Bay, the RCMP constable sitting in the adjacent seat let fly with an idle reflection. "An Arctic expert," he mused, "is someone who has peed above the Arctic Circle." Were one to take this definition to heart, I qualify, but to lay serious claim to such is no small presumption. I'm merely one of the Arctic's countless lovers and my fidelity to her remains constant. Above all, I stand in wonder of the indigenous peoples who for millennia have been at home in those distant and inhospitable reaches. I'm equally awed by tales of the early Europeans who brought the Arctic into our world — be they stories of courage and conquest or of folly and error, they were all men of high resolve and wondrous strength of character.

Pausing for a moment at my work, here in our Laurentian cottage, I gaze out the frosted windows at the winter countryside. Snow and ice mercilessly blanket the slumbering landscape while overhead an inverted bowl of darkened sky hangs heavy. Communities of skeletal birches blend effortlessly into the white panorama while pines, heavily burdened by season's weight, sag in welcome contrast. Gusts of wind give rise to wispy billows of snow. Far out on the frozen lake, two tiny figures on snowshoes plod along doggedly. Outside, the thermometer reads -21°F; inside, it's warm and cozy. Uncanny stillness envelopes the room, broken only by the gentle flickering from within the wood stove; I'm bathed in silence. Then the soft sound of the wind outside. It seems more like a drone, an enticing sound — perhaps not the wind at all. Is it possible that what I'm really hearing is the soft hum of the Arctic Siren's beguiling song?

A.S. Troubetzkoy
Labelle, Québec

I

Earlies· Explorations

THE EARLIEST WRITTEN record of possible Arctic exploration is that of Pytheas, a fourth-century B.C. Greek astronomer and geographer from Massilia (Marseilles) — "one of the most intrepid explorers the world has seen." Without a doubt, this was a scientist of notable accomplishments, not the least of which, it is thought, was an estimation of Great Britain's circumference to a 2.5 percent accuracy of twentieth-century figures. Additionally, he calculated the distance from Marseilles to northernmost Britain as being 1,050 miles, a figure 6 percent off modern calculations. Among his earlier discoveries was a method for the determination of latitude, and many credit him for having been the first to define the relationship of tides to moon phases.

In his book Περίτ ου Ὠκανοῦ (On the Ocean), he recorded the events of a voyage undertaken by him to the far North around 325 B.C. Regrettably, the volume was lost in the seventh-century burning of the Library of Alexandria and all that has come down to us are garbled quotations and commentaries by Greek and Roman scholars. Pytheas's account has it that he sailed out of Massilia (Marseilles), bypassed the blockades set up by the Carthaginians of the Straits of Gibraltar, circumnavigated Great Britain, and reached a place called "Thule," or *Ultima Thule*, a six-day sail north of Britain. What the place actually was continues to baffle scholars, but a number of possibilities present themselves: the coast of Norway, the Shetlands, the Faroe Islands, or possibly Greenland. The most probable guess is that Pytheas reached

Iceland, and if he did not actually penetrate the Arctic, he certainly attained a high latitude. His descriptions of the midnight sun and the "congealed sea" indicate that he might well have gotten to, or closely reached, the Arctic Circle.

What are we to make of Pytheas's journey, particularly as scholars and commentators of the ancient world seem divided on the veracity of his account? The Greek geographer Strabo, for example, made no secret of his contempt for his countryman and he poured derisive scorn on the claimed voyage — jealousy, perhaps? In his seventeen-volume *Geographica*, penned some three centuries after the voyage, he writes, "Pytheas, by whom many have been misled ... asserts that he explored in person the whole northern regions of Europe as far as the end of the world — an assertion which no man would believe, not even if Hermes made it." As for Thule, he went on to comment:

> [O]f all the countries that are named, [it] is set farthest north. But that the things Pytheas has told about Thule, as well as the other places in that part of the world, have indeed been fabricated by him ... any man who has told such great falsehoods about known regions would hardly, I imagine, be able to tell the truth about places that are not known to anybody.[1]

Pliny the Elder, the Roman naturalist and encyclopedist, on the other hand, endorsed Pytheas positively and he wrote of him as an authoritative figure. The commentary in *Historia Naturalis* is illuminating:

> The most remote [point] of all is Thule, in which as we have pointed out there are no nights at midsummer when the sun is passing through the sign of the Crab, and on the other hand no days in midwinter. Indeed some writers think this is the case for periods of six months at a time without a break ... Pytheas of Marsailles writes that this occurs in the island of Thule, six days voyage

north of Britain ... One day's sail from Thule is the frozen ocean called by some the Cronian Sea ...[2]

That Pytheas appears to have experienced the midnight sun is one
thing — the phenomena is universal of Arctic regions and affects all of
Thule's nominated locations. Of the place he writes that there is "neither
sea nor air but a mixture like sea-lung ... binds everything together," a
reference perhaps to the ice packs or possibly to dense sea fog. All told,
it is likely that the explorer had come in contact with drift ice, if not
icebergs, and this gives Iceland greater credibility in the search for the
real Thule. It cannot be discounted, furthermore, that Pytheas sailed
the ice-strewn waters of Greenland's east coast. An impressive journey
it was, made all the more so by the primitiveness of the vessels at the
time. The explorer's broad-beamed, wooden boat of two, possibly three,
masts could not have been more than 150 tons. Whether he had came to
Iceland or not, the point is that the first Europeans apparently reached,
or nearly reached, the Arctic Circle as early as about 325 B.C.

It may be supposed that Pytheas's book and the commentaries on him
were sufficiently controversial to discourage further interest in Arctic
exploration for quite some time. Subsequent texts by Roman and early
medieval scholars for the most part speak of the Arctic in speculative or
fanciful terms. A widespread ocean surrounded the habitable world —
beyond that, nothing. The polar region was the kingdom of the dead. It
was a bottomless pit where perpetual darkness reigned. It was the dwell-
ing place of the Cyclops. The pole was a gigantic magnetic rock rising out
of the ocean. It "is a place of chaos, the abysmal chasm." A place inhabited
by people with swine heads, dog's legs, and wolf teeth. And so on.

One tradition has it that the first of the medievals to venture into
the far northern waters were Irish monks and it is they who discovered
Iceland — or, if you want, rediscovered it. One such monk, Dicuil by
name, in his book *De mensura orbis terrae* (*Concerning the Measurement
of the Globe*), written in 825 A.D., tells of meeting up with fellow monks
who claimed at one time to have lived in that same unidentified spot
called Thule. Their descriptions of the place are vivid, for example:
darkness reigning throughout the winter day, and summer nights being

A fanciful 1606 map of the greater Arctic region produced by the Flemish cartographer, Gerhard Mercator. The North Pole is shown as a vast rock surrounded by open seas, while the magnetic pole is pictured as a mountain protruding through the waters separating Asia and America. The Northwest and Northeast Passages are clearly visible.

bright enough "to pick fleas from my shirt." While the veracity of Dicuil's report is open to question, it is more than probable that the monks of Ireland and Britain did know of some large land mass far to the north. After all, the Faroe Islands, which they had visited in the sixth century and were settled by the Norse a hundred years later, are a mere 280 miles from Iceland — a relatively short sail even for early medieval mariners. Whichever way one looks at it, the possibility is real that these intrepid monks may have set foot on Iceland before any Norseman.

The Norsemen, or Vikings, stemmed from the Teutons, whose ancestors migrated north through Denmark into Norway and Sweden, a part of the world until then outside European history. The new arrivals took up settlements along the *viks*, or bays of the rugged coastlines and their populations swelled. These were pagans whose ideas of conscience and sin were in direct variance to Christianity. Drink, women, and song were embraced with the same fervor as war, pillage, and slaughter. Such was the disposition of the "Northmen," but additionally, these people were creative craftsmen and hard workers. Their structured society was based on a divinely ordained class system, within which prevailed a curious blend of monarchy and democracy. Kings were selected from royal blood; landowners acted as legislators and judges. The laws were strict and harsh punishments helped to keep law and order — a parricide, for example, would be suspended by the heels side by side with a starved wolf similarly hung. Literacy was not universal, but it was highly respected and a rich literature came to be written. A vast collection of sagas has been bequeathed us — narratives written on sheepskin that detail heroic episodes of Norwegian and Icelandic history, accounts considered among the finest of medieval literary achievements.

Vikings were polygamous, which only exacerbated the high birth rate. With the rapid growth of settlements, the limited agricultural possibilities of the coastlines were insufficient fully to meet community needs. Hunger eventually became a fact of life in many parts of the regions — or as one historian put it, "the fertility of women ... outran the fertility of the soil." The Vikings were master woodworkers whose talents were brilliantly reflected in the construction of sturdy sea-going vessels. Shipbuilding and accomplished seamanship were essential for the maintenance of intercommunity contact along the vast coastlines, made difficult otherwise by generally high mountains. Those who now found themselves in want, or simply the young and restless, took to their boats to forage for sources of food farther afield.

The hunt for food, coupled with the seemingly insatiable thirst for plunder expanded into a pursuit of slaves, women, and gold. Accounts of Viking invasions of the nearby British Isles and of continental coastal towns are legion, and within a century the scourge of the Norsemen was

The art of Viking shipbuilding produced the finest vessels ever to that time. Their slender and flexible boats were capable of withstanding the roughest North Atlantic seas, and at the same time of navigating rivers and shoals. The drawings are of two freight ships, one fifty-three feet in length and the other forty-five feet.

strongly felt in most coastal parts of northern Europe. The rich monasteries of nearby Britain and Ireland, with their gold chalices and silver plate, offered especially attractive targets for plunder; the depredations wrought by the Viking invaders were horrific.

Around 890 A.D. one Viking expedition sailed to the northernmost reaches of Scandinavia, and rounding Lapland it passed the North Cape at 71°N, the Kola Peninsula, and penetrated the White Sea. One of its stated objectives was "desirous to try how far that country extended north," while another was to hunt for walrus whose ivory tusks were greatly valued throughout Europe. Heading the expedition was a Norwegian nobleman called Othere and since the North Cape and most of the Kola Peninsula are well above Arctic Circle, to him falls credit for being the first European to explore the Arctic in that part of the globe. Othere found himself not only at the backyard of the Slavs — soon to be overcome by his kin— but at the mouth of what was to become known as the Northeast Passage, or the Northern Sea Route.

Fatalism was as much a part of the Norse character as tenaciousness and daring. Their gods would attend them one way or another, for they were allies and companions in adventure and battle, not paternal guides to behaviour and right conduct. It is unsurprising, therefore, that in the quest for food and plunder these fearless seamen eventually braved the open waters of the Atlantic, westward and to the north, into the unexplored where others had feared to sail — into the "bottomless pit where perpetual darkness reigns."

Credit for the penetration of the Atlantic's Arctic regions and for the discovery of the "New World" is popularly given to the Viking chieftain, Erik the Red, of whom much is written. Erik did indeed uncover the New World, but his springboard was the already discovered and populated Iceland, lying in mid-Atlantic at the Arctic Circle. If claims to earlier discovery of Iceland by Irish monks are discounted, the credit undoubtedly falls to the Vikings, and in particular to a certain Floki "of the Ravens." It is this bold seaman who first ventured into the far reaches of northwest Atlantic and who in 870 made landfall in Iceland two centuries before Erik's arrival. Floki was pleased to find that sections of the land's coastline were cultivatable and suitable for cattle grazing, and he also judged the climate hospitable. (Climatic conditions were at the time more clement than they are at present.)

Within a few short years of Floki's landing, Viking settlers arrived in numbers and successfully established themselves at Reykjavik and along the island's western and northwestern coasts. These were not the hungry nor the restless; these were political refugees who quit their Scandinavian homes to escape the tyrannical hand of King Harold, "The Fairhair." Harold, having "murdered, burnt and otherwise exterminated all his brother kings who at that time grew as thick as blackberries in Norway," went on to abrogate the udal rights of landholders and to impose every sort of restriction on the population. The landowners were men "with possessions to be taxed, and a spirit too haughty to endure taxation" — individuals who cherished liberty and for whom freedom of possession and of movement was a sacred birthright. Lord Duffern describes an aspect of these astonishing early settlers:

> They were the first of any European nation to create for themselves a native literature ... almost all the ancient Scandinavian manuscripts are in Icelandic. Negotiations between the Courts of the North were conducted by Icelandic diplomats. The earliest topographical survey with which we are acquainted was Icelandic ... The first historical composition ever written by any European in the vernacular was the product of Icelandic genius.[3]

And what was this land that beckoned to the Norwegian emigrants? Iceland continues today as a country of startling contrasts — a geologist's paradise. The irregularly shaped island is home to rugged mountains, roaring rivers and waterfalls, subterranean thermal springs, geysers, and sparkling glaciers. With the exception of a small island off the north coast, the entire country lies just below the Arctic Circle, but in structure, relief, and climate, the land is definitely sub-Arctic. The settlements then and now are found along the island's periphery where conditions are quasi-maritime and where farming is possible with careful cultivation.

Iceland is one of the few Arctic territories in which no indigenous population existed at the time of European discovery.

Within seventy years of Floki's arrival, the population of Iceland had blossomed from naught to forty thousand, and the figure doubled in the century that followed. In that lawless society the need for some form of political organization became apparent, and in order to attain this, the resourceful citizens established the *Althingi*, the world's first parliament. The "Thing" lasted for over three centuries until 1262 when the island's unique status as an independent republic was lost by a Norwegian takeover. It remained under the colonial rule of Norway until 1944 when it regained its independence, at which time the Althingi was re-established. (As an aside: if the British Parliament founded in 1295 is regarded as the "Mother of Parliaments," surely Iceland's Althingi may legitimately lay claim to being its godmother.).

The thirteenth-century *Saga of Erik the Red* tells us that Erik's family had been forced to flee Norway on account of "some killings," and that they fled to Iceland where the boy was raised. In 980, Erik became involved in a heated dispute with a neighbour — over a shovel, of all things. One confrontation led to another and the short of it is that Erik killed his antagonist just as he had earlier murdered a second neighbour in another dispute over slaves. Convicted of the killings, he was declared an outlaw and sentenced to banishment for a three-year period. But where to go? A return to Norway was not possible, so the only alternative was to move farther west where, he was certain, other lands would offer refuge. (It might be noted that on exceptionally clear days, Greenland is visible from the mountaintops of western Iceland, a distance of 175 miles.) Thus it was that around the year 982 that the hot-blooded exile sailed off on what must be regarded as one of the most notable voyages in the Arctic's biography. A thirty-three year-old, accompanied by his young family and some retainers, set sail in an open boat with no compass and scant provisions into unknown Arctic waters — quite literally "into the setting sun" — propelled only by courage, determination, and a promising wind.

His vessel eventually reached Greenland, the landfall being made near Julianehaab on the southwest coast. The bay and the surrounding coastline were ice-free, groves of stunted birch dotted the area, and the summer vegetation seemed plentiful. Since topographic and climatic conditions appeared promising and closely resembled those of Iceland, Erik determined to establish his party at that spot.

Barns were erected, hay was made, and the group took to their new surroundings. Three years passed and with his sentence of banishment completed, Erik returned to Iceland to gather more settlers for the land he had uncovered. Erik was a sharp salesman, for in his call for colonists he cunningly named the place Green Land, thus colouring it in significantly more alluring tones than Ice Land. Twenty-five shiploads of emigrants signed on to sail west — men, women, and children, who for the most part had been living on the poorer tracts of the Icelandic coast. Horses, sheep, cattle, serfs, and every sort of household goods and building material were loaded onto the ships before heading out to sea. And then disaster hit. A vicious storm arose and the small flotilla was walloped by three gigantic waves — "taller than mountains and they are like lofty pinnacles" — that slammed the heavily laden ships with particular force. Nine of the vessels foundered or returned to Iceland, but fourteen succeeded in making it to shore and discharged 350 colonists.

"Green Land" proved to be something of a misnomer; life was seriously more difficult than anticipated. Sufficient tracts of arable land were few and far between, the soil was generally inferior to that of Iceland, and wood was hard to come by. Of necessity they resorted to fish which were abundant in the local waters. In summer months the colonists regularly travelled 625 miles north along the coastline as far as Disko Bay at latitude 70°, well above the Arctic Circle. Here they hunted for walrus and seal, not only for the blubber content, but for ivory and sealskin, which they used to fashion rope. A saga written in 986 relates that "they found many settlements, toward the east and west, and remains of skin boats and stone implements, which shows that to that place journeyed the kind of people ... whom the [Norse] called Skrælings [Inuit]."[4] It was not long thereafter that the colonists came face to face with the indigenous people, who, much to their surprise, proved welcoming and hospitable. Initial relations between the two peoples were warm, but friction was not long in coming and lamentably the relationship soon deteriorated, eventually growing so antagonistic that bloody encounters became common.

A rendering of the ninth-century Viking village at Hedeby at the southern reaches of the Jutland Peninsula. By the eleventh century, the settlement had developed into Denmark's largest at the time.

Despite the challenges of the harsh life, Greenland's Norse population continued to swell, and by the thirteenth century it numbered 3,500 inhabitants. Christianity came to the land at the time that the Norwegians converted, and by 1125 a bishopric had been established, having within it sixteen separate churches, a monastery, and a nunnery, all of which, incidentally, contributed — rather, were levied — funds for the Crusades. Following Icelandic and Greenlandic acceptance of Norwegian rule in 1262, the king granted a trade monopoly to a coterie of Bergen merchants, who in quick time demonstrated indifference to the far-off island by imposing such extortionate terms upon the Greenlanders that commercial relations withered and all but died. Records indicate, for example, that at one time seven or more trading vessels arrived from Norway *each* year. In the six-year period following the takeover by the Norwegian merchants, only *one* ship entered Greenland waters. As the island's traders suffered, so did the farmers. For centuries, these stalwart tillers of the soil had worked the coastal lands, but then a severe worsening of climate set in, bringing exceptional cold — the "New Ice Age." For the people, the entire way of life had become altered.

The short of it is that by the early 1500s, settlements on eastern and western Greenland ceased to exist. The people had quite simply vanished, and what it was specifically that befell them remains a mystery. Quite possibly it was the worsening of climate that caused a disruption in the food supply and brought famine to many parts. Perhaps the tyranny of the Bergen merchants impacted the Greenlanders more severely than acknowledged — their denial to the island of an adequate supply of essential goods. Disease in one form or another was unquestionably a factor in the population's decimation, with one hypothesis stating that the Black Plague that so devastated Europe at the time eventually hit Greenland. And undoubtedly, the deterioration of relations with the Inuit had become so severe that many European settlements were simply exterminated by them. A saga written in 1379, for example, mentions an incident when "Skrælings assaulted the Greenlanders, killed eighteen men and captured two swains and one bondswoman."[5] But most probably the disappearance of the early Greenlanders was a result of all these factors.

For over two hundred years Greenland lay barely inhabited. The Europeans were gone, and for whatever reason the Inuit who at one time had been scattered along the central and southern coastlines, migrated to the far north, with a goodly number crossing the sixteen-mile strait to Ellesmere Island in Canada.

The country to which Erik enticed settlers and called home is a unique corner of the globe. Greenland is the world's largest island with a coastline of some twenty-five thousand miles — nearly the same length as the equator — and in area it is approximately the same size as Mexico or Saudi Arabia. Its northernmost point is less than five hundred miles from the North Pole, and the southernmost is on the same latitude as St. Petersburg, Oslo, and Churchill, Manitoba. North–south it stretches 1,700 miles or a distance equal to that of New York to Miami. As part of the Laurentian Shield, the island structurally is part of the North American continent, but historically and politically, it is European, while geophysically and in ethnicity it is undeniably Arctic — virtually all of it lies above the Arctic Circle.

For the most part, the island is bordered by mountains and fjords, although in some places the coast rises straight up to considerable heights; the highest elevation is 12,200 feet. A vast, asymmetrical, dome-shaped glacier covers 80 percent of the surface, extending over seven hundred thousand square miles, in some places reaching depths of ten thousand feet. It is of such massive weight that a depression has been created in the central part of the island, forming a basin one thousand feet below sea level. Little wonder that the sixteenth-century explorer, John Davis, called the place "the land of desolation."

The first Vikings reaching Greenland had travelled west from Iceland; the first reaching Iceland had travelled west from Norway. For the Norse, the lure of the west seems to have been no less strong than for many restless Americans of the nineteenth century — "Go west, young man, go west!" — some irresistible force tugging. The first Greenlander heeding the call was the eldest of Erik the Red's four children, Leif Eriksson. His boyhood friend, Bjarni Herjolfsson, had once been severely driven off course while sailing from Iceland to Greenland, and in the process he spotted in the far distance an unfamiliar mountainous land, one that was forested and ice-bound. It was an intriguing report, and word of trees was particularly tantalizing as Icelanders were wood-starved. Curiosity got the better of Leif and about the year 1000 he persuaded his elderly father to lead an expedition in search of the mysterious place. Erik agreed with some reluctance, but as preparations for the journey got under way, he tumbled from his horse and sprained an ankle. Deeming this to be an ill omen he begged off the voyage, leaving Leif on his own. Thus it was that the restless young man, accompanied by thirty-five others, sailed from home to explore the prospects of the viewed, but untouched land. The congenital need of Vikings for fame and posthumous reputation was unquestionably as much a motivation for the quest as any.

Steering by the sun and stars, Leif headed in the direction indicated by his friend and in time a barren country came into view, largely covered by glaciers, "but from the sea to the glaciers was, as it were, a single slab of rock." The ice-bound land bore little resemblance to Bjarni's description, for it was neither mountainous nor forested. This disappointing place Leif called Helluland, or "the Land of Flat Rocks," reckoned to be the southern reaches of Baffin Island. Three more days of sailing brought him to a place that "was flat and covered with forest, with extensive white sands wherever they went and shelving gently to the sea," and this he named Markland, thought to be southern Labrador.

Continuing south along the coastline, Leif finally came to a point of land with rolling grassland, spruce forests, and a stream "that glistened with salmon." So pleasing was this discovery that he determined to winter at the spot, and with no small delight the party set about constructing houses and barns. As they were settling down, one of the crewmembers, thought to be a Hungarian or a German, came upon "wine berries" growing freely. It's popularly believed that these were grapes, but caution must be exercised here for the Norse called most berries *vinbery*. Most likely the discovered were cranberries, but be that as it may, Leif called the place "Vinland." And here the first European settlement in the New World came to be established, nearly four centuries before Columbus "sailed the ocean blue" to America. The life of Leif's settlement was short-lived, for within two years the would-be colonists forsook the place and returned to Greenland. A further attempt was made by the Vikings to establish in the New World, but here again it was met by failure. The sagas tell us that in both cases fighting broke out with the hostile "Skærlings," which simply proved too much for the Norse. Today the remains of Leif's site have been preserved by the Canadian government at L'Anse aux Meadows, at the northernmost point of Newfoundland nearly across from Labrador.

At about the time that Erik and Leif were planting footprints in the Arctic regions of the New World, other Norsemen were pressing east and infiltrating the territory soon to become known as Russia. Othere's penetration of the White Sea had been made nearly a century-and-a-half earlier. In the decades that followed, his countrymen arrived in numbers not only into Arctic regions, but into more southern areas below Kola and the White Sea. This was the land of the Slavs, a semi-Asiatic people scattered about in small settlements within an unframed world of endlessly stretching spaces, a harsh land of empty plains, miasmic marshes, forbidding forests, parching summers, and arctic snows. So focused were these people on coping with hostile nature that little energy remained for more refined activity or for the development of social organization. While the

Latin and Teutonic peoples were developing dynamically in the west, the Slavs, as one historian put it, "slumbered in oriental seclusion … and pursued their way without Latin or scholasticism, without parliament or university, without literature or political debate, or a sustained challenge to religious belief."[6] The Slavs were in Europe without being European. ,[

It was in this land, where abundant river systems offered ideal avenues for trade, that the Norse merchant-warriors focused their energies. Trading posts were established, the natives engaged, and with the passing of time a burgeoning commerce developed with Novgorod serving as the pivotal point. This city is one of Russia's oldest and at its height, along with Kiev in the south, it was the richest. From this eastern-most outpost of north Europe's Hanseatic League, goods were shipped to the Black Sea and the Mediterranean along the connecting river system, to places as far away as Sicily. Furs, amber, wax, honey, and slaves streamed south in return for spices, wines, silk, and gems, which were then forwarded on to northern European markets.

Novgorod expanded rapidly from a prosperous commercial hub into a flourishing independent city-state that reached far out into neighbouring territories. By the thirteenth century, its expansionist-minded merchants found themselves hemmed in. To the west the threatening Swedes and the Teutonic knights were well entrenched. To the south and east, the fierce Mongols had established themselves — Genghis Khan's "Golden Horde" in the world's largest empire ever. The only direction remaining for Novgorodians to expand was north into the Arctic.

Thus it was that a migration of sorts got under way with merchants, peasants, and churchmen leaving the city to plant themselves on the shores of the White Sea or along the banks of the numerous rivers flowing into it. For the most part these pioneers were experienced rivermen and now they adeptly navigated the waterways pushing ever north and creating settlements. By late fourteenth century, most of the Arctic regions west of the Urals had come under Novgorod's control — a continuation of Russian expansion.

Of Arctic coastal nations today, Russian territory extends along the longest global spread of any — nearly half the world, across ten time zones from the Norwegian border to the Bering Sea. Twenty percent of that immense country is situated in the Arctic with over 10 million Russians calling it home. It has always been the most populated of Arctic lands, not only with indigenous peoples, but with Europeans. The city of greater Murmansk at 68°30' N boasts a population of 850,000.

The medieval pioneers arriving in those parts were inexperienced in the ways of the Arctic, but they managed masterfully, enduring all the adverse conditions the pitiless Arctic threw at them. Winter temperatures steadily reading -40°F were one thing, but psychologically, imagine the isolation: "As far as the eye could see in the gathering gloom, in every direction lay the barren steppe. There was not a tree nor a bush … only silence and desolation. The country seemed abandoned by God and man to the Arctic Spirit …" It was the early hunters and trappers who penetrated that "gathering gloom," paving the way for others, and it was they who most forcefully coped with the early challenges of daily life — shelter, food, clothing, firewood, and transport. Lessons were learned through trial and error and one might well wonder why it took these hardies decades to adapt to the ways of the indigenous peoples, the Nanets, who for millennia had been surviving brilliantly in the same demanding conditions. All the while that the trappers and hunters suffered at their tasks, Novgorod merchants, comfortably ensconced in the warmth of their homes, toyed with bottom-lines and hatched fresh schemes for further development and deeper thrusts into the Arctic.

The Arctic, however, did smile upon these arrivals, and she showered them with rich rewards of luxuriant furs. The exceptional cold of the place is such that fur-bearing animals like ermine, marten, fox, and hare develop thicker coats than those of their southern cousins, therefore making them more desirable and valuable. In addition to furs, walrus tusks were harvested, as well as polar bear skins and the occasional nugget of some esoteric mineral, all in high demand in the parlours of Novgorod, Moscow, and throughout Europe.

With the impetus of Columbus's discovery in 1492, the "Age of Exploration" quickly got under way. No seafaring nation of importance failed to dispatch one explorer or another to seek out fresh channels to fabled Cathay (China) or Cipango (Japan), or to claim new lands. Relying mostly on the talents of Genoese navigators, Spain and Portugal grabbed the early initiative and before long the two countries had claimed vast areas of South America and Africa. And it was upon these two countries that Pope Alexander VI lavished his munificence in 1494. With a stroke of a pen on a primitive map, he divided the world into two parts, allocating the western hemisphere to Spain and the eastern hemisphere to Portugal — the Line of Demarcation. To these kingdoms now fell the onus of bringing Christianity to the indigenous of lands discovered and uncovered, but in return the two countries were accorded exclusive rights to trade and commercial development in their respective parts. With their advanced fleets and determination of purpose, the Spanish rapidly established supremacy over South America and the Portuguese over Africa — as the navies of the two patrolled the coasts guarding Vatican-granted monopolies.

Aspiring maritime nations of Northern Europe — England, France, Holland, and Denmark — found themselves locked out from trade as well as exploration in southern regions. If a trade route to the east was to be had, it could only be via a northern passage. The sixteenth-century historian Richard Hakluyt declared, "Beside the portion of land pertaining to the Spaniards ... there yet remaineth another portion of that main land reaching toward the northeast, thought to be as large as the other, and not yet known ... neither inhabited by any Christian man ..."

Thus a fresh chapter in the biography of the Arctic came to be written as a series of explorations got under way with the English, French, and Danes knocking at the gate of the Northwest Passage, and the Dutch (and later, the Russians) pressing the portals of the Northern Sea Route.

2

Eastern Thrusts to Cathay

BY LATE MIDDLE AGES, merchant guilds had come to dominate commerce in most parts of Europe, and in Britain they had developed into a way of life, with most trades being organized — goldsmiths, shoemakers, dyers, stonemasons, bakers, and the like. In 1407, Henry IV approved the formation of a guild to oversee and control overseas trade, particularly in cloth. The Company of Merchant Adventurers, it was popularly called, but its precise name was "Mysterie and Companie of Merchant Adventurers for the Discoverie of Regions, Dominions, Islands, and Places Unknowen."

The guild flourished and in time it spawned a number of ancillary organizations, including the establishment of the Muscovy Trading Company, the first major English joint-stock company. By its royal charter, the new entity was granted a monopoly of trade between England and Russia, a privilege it enjoyed for 150 years (ceasing operations in 1917 with the Russian Revolution). Impetus for the organization's formation came from a trio of adventurous entrepreneurs: Richard Chancellor, Sir Hugh Willoughby, and Sebastian Cabot, son of John Cabot, who was the first European to have set foot in North America since the Vikings.

Sebastian Cabot, appointed by the king as "Grand Pilot of England," held but one searing ambition — to secure the passage to Cathay through the "impassable waters" of northern Russia. He successfully persuaded his fellow merchants to finance an exploratory expedition, and in 1553 three ships were procured, outfitted in Bristol, and launched on their journey:

the *Bona Esperanza* of 120 tons, the 160-ton *Edward Bonaventure*, and the *Bona Confidentia*, the smallest of the lot at ninety tons. So confident were they of success in reaching the east, India in particular, that the hulls were coated with lead as protection against infestation of worms, which they understood were common in tropical waters. Commanding the whole was "Admiral of the Fleet" Willoughby on board the *Esperanza*. A dubious appointment made, we are informed, because he was "preferred above all others, both by reason of his goodly personage (for he was tall of stature) as also for his singular skill in the services of warre."[1] Height and service as a cavalry officer was all very well and good, but the ships might have been better served had Sir Hugh "taken to the sea" earlier in his career. With a mere three years of sailing experience, his navigation and piloting skills were anything but developed. At his side was a crew of thirty-eight that included a master gunner, a couple of surgeons, and six merchants. Richard Chancellor, the expedition's chief pilot, was on board the fifty-crew-member *Bonaventure*, commanded by Stephen Borough.

The sixty-four-year-old Cabot judged himself too aged to join the expedition, which promised to be lengthy and arduous. He did, however, oversee every facet of outfitting and provisioning of the small fleet and he also provided detailed "ordinances, instructions and advertisements of and for the intended voyage to Cathay." Every aspect of the undertaking was touched upon by the comprehensive orders, including exhortations on personal behaviour. When making contact with the locals of the Far East, for example, Cabot instructed that no native was to be trusted and that every effort had to be made to give the impression that nothing in particular was being sought. He enjoined the expedition's leaders to treat natives courteously and hospitably, suggesting that they be invited on board and offered beer or wine — a bit of drink was a legitimate bargaining tool. Details of the expedition are vividly related by Richard Hakluyt in a book published in 1599, the remarkable title of which runs 123 words — the short title being, *The Principall Navigations, Voiages, and Discoveries of the English Nation: Made by Sea or Overland to the Most Remote and Furthest Distant Quarters of the Earth*. In this singular account, Hakluyt observes that unlike Spanish and Portuguese explorers who were obligated to engage in missionary work, Cabot's expedition was "not to disclose to any nation the state of our religion, but to pass over in silence, without any declaration of it, seeming to beare with such lawes and rites, as the place hath, when you shall arrive."[2]

Cabot firmly ordered, however, that prayers be had every morning and every evening on board the ships. Additionally, he directed that there be no swearing, dirty stories, or "ungodly talk to be suffered in the company of any ship, neither dicing, carding, tabling nor other devilish games ..." And harking back to his early North American experience with his father, Hakluyt tells us, he gravely warned of certain dangers:

> [T]here are people that can swimme in the sea, havens & rivers, naked, having bows and shafts, coveting to draw nigh your ships, which if they shal finde not wel watched, or warded, they wil assault, desirous of the bodies of men, which they covet for meate; if you resist them, they dive, and do well flee, and therefore diligent watch is to be kept both day & night, in some Islands.[3]

Great excitement prevailed as the ships set out to sea from London. As the small fleet passed Greenwich Palace where Edward VI was residing at the time, "the courtiers came running out and the common people flockt together, standing very thicke upon the shoare; the Privie Conssel, they lookt out at the windows of the court, and the rest ranne upto the tops of the towers." On board the *Esperanza*, in the strongbox of Willoughby's cabin, lay letters of recommendation, which His Majesty had graciously provided, introductions to "the Kings, Princes, and other Potentates, inhabiting the Northern parts of the Worlde, towards the mighty Empire of Cathay."[4] As the vessels passed the palace, gun salutes were exchanged, with everyone on the decks and many ashore resplendent in blue uniforms. By mid-July the ships were off the west coast of Norway, well above the Arctic Circle and in fine weather they made steady progress toward the North Cape.

On the night of August 2, a violent storm struck that the ships barely managed to ride out. In the mayhem, however, the little fleet became dispersed, never fully to reunite. The *Edward Bonaventure* made its way to the Danish fortress-settlement of Vardø at Norway's extreme northeast tip, forty-five miles from Russia. Chancellor thought to await the hopeful reappearance of the other two vessels, but after a week of idleness and no sight of the other ships, he moved on. Rounding the Kola Peninsula, he made his way into the White Sea and eventually reached the mouth of the Dvina River, near the settlement of Arkhangelsk. Winter arrives early to those parts, and with the markedly deteriorating weather and the start of ice formation, it was decided to take up winter quarters ashore.

In the meantime, the *Bona Esperanza* and the *Bona Confidentia* sailed right by Vardø without stopping, and continued east, eventually coming to Novaya Zemlya (Russian: "New Land"). This vast archipelago is an extension of the Ural Mountains and it consists of two major islands and scores of lesser ones, stretching northward over a distance of 375 miles. The islands were familiar to Novgorod hunters as early as the eleventh century, but shortly after Sir Hugh's efforts, they became known to Western Europeans. For the most part the archipelago is a mountainous place with some peaks reaching heights of 3,500 feet. Over a quarter of the thirty-five thousand square miles of territory is permanently ice-covered. In early days, the attraction of Novaya Zemlya was the abundance of walruses, seals, Arctic fox, and polar bears that inhabited the islands — particularly rich fare for hunters resolute enough to carry on their work in dismal winter days when the furs grew especially thick. The modern reader may be familiar with Novaya Zemlya for the nuclear testing ranges the islands housed during the Cold War. It was here that the Arctic suffered her most grievous incursion ever when in 1961 the Soviets detonated "Tsar Bomba" in a massive fifty-megaton atmospheric blast — the largest, most powerful nuclear weapon ever detonated. That detonation was followed twelve years later by an underground blast that recorded 6.97 on the Richter Scale — nearly the same strength of force that devastated San Francisco in 1906. It precipitated an avalanche of 80 million tons of rock that blocked two glacial streams, causing a vast lake to form.

With landfall denied and the *Confidentia* leaking badly, Willoughby decided to turn about and head back whence they had come. As they approached the shores of the Kola Peninsula, one storm after another battered the small vessels — "very evill weather, as frost, snow and haile, as though it had beene the deepe of winter." The tired and dispirited Willoughby was simply unprepared to continue battling the hostile elements, and he set his sights on securing a safe anchorage in some sheltered harbor. This he found at Nokujeff Bay, a body of water surrounded by barren land, and here he dropped anchor.

Three scouting parties were sent in different directions to scour the area for signs of native settlements, but all to no avail; they returned "without finding of people, or any similitude of habitation." Days shortened, bitter cold set in, and before long the thick snow of early winter blanketed the ships' decks.

At the time the gallant little fleet had set out from London, three months earlier in the balm of England's late summer, no thought had been given to the possibility of becoming ice-locked or of having to winter in the Arctic. Little did they know. The expedition's chronicler drew a pathetic picture of what unfolded next:

> ... the days became shorter and shorter, and after 25th of November our voyagers saw no more of the sun even at mid-day. No one was aware of any means of guarding against the cold, and, indeed nothing had been brought for the purpose; for at that time they had no idea in England what a winter in Russia, or in the northern regions in general, was; moreover, the country surrounding Nokujeff Bay was quite bare of wood, so that at that spot were frozen to death, with Sir Hugh Willoughby, the strong crews of both vessels, consisting of sixty-five men. Most of them may have commenced their eternal sleep during the night of more than a month's duration, from the 25th of November to the 29th of December. But from a signature of Willoughby, it is certain that he was still alive at the end of January, 1554.
>
> Probably before his decease he was even several times rejoiced by a sight of the sun at mid-day; but what a sense of horror it shone upon! Two frozen-up vessels

full of stiffened corpses, and only partly discernable through the snow which had drifted over them, towards which the looks of the remaining unhappy voyagers, now but half live, were involuntarily turned, as, hopeless, and deprived even of the comforts of religion, there were despairingly awaiting the same fate.[5]

In the early summer, Russian fishermen came across the two ghostly vessels, and they reported finding Sir Hugh "congealed and frozen to death," sitting in his cabin making an entry into his journal. Others of the crew, seemingly like a tableau in a wax museum, were described as being frozen with plates in hand or spoons to the mouth, with one man standing opening his locker and "others in various postures like statues."

Willoughby had elected to winter on board the frozen-in ships; Chancellor chose to establish quarters ashore. It is argued that had Willoughby wintered in snow houses within a protected space he might have survived, whereas others contend that Sir Hugh and his sixty-five companions were doomed from the start, whatever the shelter. As one historian has it, the expedition's leader suffered from "want of skill and inconstancy of purpose that had led him into difficulties; want of adaptability made the difficulties fatal." Chancellor's chronicler concludes, with characteristic British understatement, "One must say they were men worth of a better fate."[6]

Chancellor and the crew of the *Edward Bonaventure* fared better than their ill-fated companions on the sister ships. Archangelsk at the time had grown into a substantial Russian settlement, and on his arrival to the area the inhabitants, who were awed by the great size of the English ship, met him with curiosity, warmth, and above all, with reverence. Chancellor seized the moment and in a lordly fashion greeted the awed visitors warmly — taking "them up in all loving sort from the ground." When news of the Englishman's landing eventually reached Moscow, the exotic visitor was invited to visit the capital as an honoured guest, so great an impression he had created. Within a few weeks of coming ashore, Chancellor had subtly morphed from an unlucky mariner into a figure of highest consequence — His Majesty's unofficial envoy to the court of Tsar Ivan IV, "The Terrible."

On November 23, accompanied by two of the merchants voyaging with him, Chancellor set off by sleigh to Moscow, a distance of 625 miles. Twelve days later, he arrived at the capital and the small party was received by the tsar, who gave them a warm reception and graciously accepted the open letter — credentials, as it were — that Edward VI had supplied to each of the three ships, a message written in many languages:

> We have permitted the honourable and brave Hugh Willoughby, and others of our faithful and dear servants who accompany him, to proceed to regions previously unknown, in order to seek such things as We stand in need of, as well as to take to them from our country such things as they require.[7]

Ivan was delighted with the Englishmen and with their opportune visit to his capital. Russia at the time had not yet extended its empire to the shores of the Black Sea, and the Baltic Sea was firmly closed to Russian shipping for that "window to the West" was under the disputed control of two hostile powers: the Lithuanian Commonwealth and the Swedish Empire. The very presence in Moscow of the tsar's distinguished and genial English guest, however, demonstrated that an open sea route to the west was available to Russia through the Arctic. Furthermore, the Muscovy Company gave every indication of being an ideal trading partner. Ivan was well pleased and he sent Chancellor back to England with promised trade privileges. Thus rooted a long history of Anglo–Russian trade and friendship.

Chancellor, alas, did not survive long enough to enjoy the fruits of his initiatives. In 1556, as a follow-up to his initial trip to Russia, he undertook a second such voyage, and accompanying him on the return home was the tsar's first ambassador to England. It was a rough passage and as they neared the Scottish coast, an "outrageous tempest" struck the ship. The vessel was driven ashore and Chancellor, hauling the Russian onto a lifeboat, barely managed to escape the condemned ship. He successfully got the envoy ashore, but in the process the boat was swamped and he perished along with much of the crew.

Chancellor's groundwork in Russia resulted in a period of intense activity for the Muscovy Trading Company and notable successes were achieved, particularly in the Arctic fur trade. These developments did not escape the covetous eyes of the Dutch, who within the decade formed the Dutch White Sea Trading Company, the purpose of which, as the name indicates, was to do business in that region. In 1565, the firm charged Oliver Brunel to establish a trading post at Archangelsk, and to develop his country's presence in the Arctic. This resourceful and quick-witted individual wasted little time in getting on with it. Within months he had charmed his way into the local society and in the process mastered its language, thus enabling him to deal directly and more advantageously with the hunters. No small-time apparatchik was he — now a growing threat to the hitherto virtual trade monopoly enjoyed by the Muscovy Company. The enraged English managed craftily to persuade Archangelsk officials that the Dutchman was a spy, and the authorities reacted by arresting and imprisoning him. Brunel eventually gained parole, and exiting from jail he fell into the waiting arms of the enterprising Strogonoff family, a Russian merchant clique that eventually came to control Siberia's entire fur industry — the country's nineteenth-century Astors. Brunel mustered all his persuasive skills and convinced his benefactors to bypass the British by directing the fur trade of the greater White Sea area through the Dutch. A *coup* of no small significance.

Successful as he was in matters of trade, Brunel was driven by the burning ambition of laying bare the Northeast Passage, a cause that shaped his life for the following two decades. In those years under a succession of sponsors — the Strogonoffs, Dutch merchants, the Danish King, English fur barons — he undertook five expeditions into the Russian Arctic, one of which was by land to the Ob River in central Siberia, the first European to reach those parts. And then, on his final journey in 1584, he and his ship vanished mysteriously without a trace, never to be seen or heard from again — victim of the Arctic's beguiling song.

Brunel's early success on the White Sea, however, and his subsequent thrusts into the frozen east served to enflame further Dutch interest in the elusive eastern passage. The most renowned of the country's ensuing explorers was "the prudent, skillful, brave and experienced [Willem]

Barents — the most distinguished martyr to Arctic investigation," who, at the close of the sixteenth century, undertook three successive journeys into the northeast. The first two expeditions returned home with nothing more than colourful tales of adventures in the frozen North, but the report of the third journey stands high in the literature of Arctic survival. As one nineteenth-century historian put it, Barents was the first European "to winter amid the horrors of the Polar cold; deprived of every comfort which could have ameliorated the sojourn; dependent even for vital warmth on the fires which are kindled in indomitable *heart*; and uncheered from the beginning to the end by the sight of, or intercourse with, any human visitors ..."[8] It's a tale that is vividly recorded by Gerrit de Veer, one of the seventeen-man crew who survived the ordeal.

The first of Barents's journeys took place in 1594. Four ships put out to sea from Zealand on Denmark's shores, he on board the *Mercury* and his partner, Corneilius Nai, on board the *Swan*. After a month's sail they reached the west coast of Novaya Zemlya, where the group split up. Nai set course with two ships for the archipelago's southern tip with the goal of securing the passage to Cathay from that direction, while Barents moved north to do the same on the opposite end. Nai successfully navigated through the southern strait and after working his way through the ice packs he reached a vast expanse of open water. "We met with no more ice, nor any sign of it," the record for August 9 tells us, "... only a spacious open sea with a swell such as oceans have everywhere, and a great depth, for which we could not touch ground with the lead ..."[9] There was no doubting it: they had at long last pried open the coveted northern door to Cathay — success at last. One can imagine the euphoria that must have descended on the ships' crews ... and the foaming tankards that no doubt were raised to celebrate their victory. With mission accomplished and the season rapidly advancing, Nai found no need for continuing farther east, and he ordered a turnabout and a course for home. Little did the poor man know that the "spacious open sea" with swells and depths were in no way a key to any doorway; it was an illusion, a mirage of sorts. Had he sailed east a few more days into the Kara Sea, he would have encountered the same irresolute ice barrier that would stymie more than one future traveller.

In the meantime, Barents was making his way up the coast, pressing ever more north. One highlight of that passage seems to have been their stumbling upon a herd of walrus — some two hundred of them. Knowledge of these "wonderfull strong sea monsters"[10] was already had, but now they came face to face with these "sea-horses … with two teeth sticking out of their mouths, one on each side, each being about halfe an elle long [fourteen inches]." We are told of a close encounter with one such animal, which, having "cast her young ones before her into the water," attacked their ship's boat … "the sea-horse almost stricken her teeth into the sterne of the boate, thinking to overthrow it." The crew barely managed to ward it off with oars and "the great cry that the men made."

Barents's expedition proved inconclusive and on the whole uneventful. The vessels completed the passage to the most northerly point of Novaya Zemlya, where they were battered by a strong gale and where their progess was barred by thick ice packs. Unable to proceed farther and with the exhausted crews in a mutinous mood, there was no alternative but to return home. Whatever disappointment Barents may have suffered for his part of the venture, certain satisfaction was taken in the charting of much of the archipelago's coastlines. All in all, he regarded the expedition as a glorious success — his partner travelling in the south, after all, had uncovered the elusive passage to the Far East, in the words of one contemporary, "a very broad claim."

In the earlier part of the voyage, as the ships followed the Siberian coastline eastward, they made first European contact with "the strange people called 'Samoyeds.'" Word of the existence of these primitive "wilde men" had already filtered to Europeans. Their culture was based entirely on reindeer — draught animals were reindeer; boats were of reindeer hide; their semi-underground homes were covered by reindeer hides; parkas were of reindeer (with the skin on the outside); their gloves and hoods also of reindeer, and their crudely carved idols were of reindeer skulls and bones. The other news of these people was not good: it was said that they engaged in cannibalism. One staggering Russian report of 1560 tells of a feast offered a visiting merchant in which a roasted child was the centrepiece. The same report asserted that should the merchant have died among them his body would also have been eaten — small wonder that the literal translation of Samoyed is "self-eater." Barents's chronicler makes only passing comment on the exchanges that took place between the Dutch and these singular natives. Today the descendents of the Samoyeds are called Nenets. In the 1870s the Russian government forcibly relocated some of them to Novaya Zemlya in a successful effort to wrest claim of the land from Norway.

Word of Barents's success spread quickly through Holland. Prince Maurice, son of King William I, was particularly encouraged by the fruits of the initiatives and he became filled with "the most exaggerated hopes." In his enthusiasm he caused a fresh expedition to be mounted which he, himself, helped to finance. Barents was awarded the title, "Chief Pilot of the States-General and Conductor" and urged to prepare promptly for a return to Siberia, this time with an enlarged fleet … and hopes assured.

Bathed in optimism and good cheer, six ships set sail in June 1595, heavily loaded with an array of goods for trade with the peoples of Cathay. They were accompanied by a seventh vessel, which was to return home to report on the expedition's progress after it had rounded the Taymyr Peninsula, the massive body of land that serves as the Arctic Ocean's east–west divide in that part of the globe.

In nearing 75°N the ships came across an unfamiliar island sided by high cliffs rising from the sea. An exploratory party was sent ashore to search out the place and as the men moved inland they were ambushed by a polar bear. The animal had snuck up stealthily behind them and grabbed a hapless sailor by the neck. The victim's panicked companions ran for their lives, but shortly thereafter turned back "either to save the man or else to drive the beare from the body."[11] As the group approached the animal with pikes and oars they were horrified to find the animal "devouring the man … the beare bit his head in sunder and sucked out his blood." The feasting animal spotted the approaching party and charged. Again, the sailors scattered, but as they ran, one of them was caught by the enraged beast and killed by a single blow of a massive paw. From the deck of one of the nearby ships, the unfolding drama had been observed and boats were quickly lowered with reinforcements. The well-armed party engaged the "cruell, fierce and ravenous beast;" and after a frantic struggle managed to kill it without further casualty. Barents gave the name of Bear Island to the place where this fatal encounter occurred.

At this point it might be appropriate briefly to digress by putting Barents aside, and make a few introductory remarks on the polar bear in general. It is after all *the* iconic animal of the Arctic Ocean and sub-Arctic regions, and, given the rapidity of environmental changes, anxiety exists as to its future. The polar bear is the world's largest land predator, reaching heights of as much as ten feet and weights of 1,500 pounds. Its preferred world, however, is the ice packs and the open waters where seals flourish, its principal source of food. Land becomes attractive in the absence of seals, and it is on land also that the female bear passes through her final stages of gestation and where, after burrowing into the permafrost, she delivers her newborns.

In addition to an exceptional sense of smell, the polar bear possesses a remarkable ability to hunt out its next meal by stealth; it approaches a target seemingly cloaked by invisibility, so well does its white coat blend with the terrain. It then usually seizes the victim's head and crushes the skull with powerful jaws, the strength of which is capable of killing a mature walrus or a beluga whale. Although seals are undeniably the dietary preference, the bear's tastes are remarkably eclectic with reindeer, rodents, birds, and shellfish acceptable substitutes. (In the garbage dumps of Churchill, Manitoba, bears have been observed ingesting Styrofoam, plastics, and a car battery.)

In bygone days, native bear hunters were handsomely rewarded for their successes for every part of the felled animal found use: food for nourishment, fur for trousers and footwear, sinews for thread, fat for lamp oil, bones for tools, and the heart and gallbladders for their medicinal qualities. Only the highly toxic liver was discarded. So valued and revered were the beasts that in certain societies — the Chukchi of eastern Siberia, for example — that they took on religious significance and their skulls and body parts were used in shamanistic rituals.

Today's polar bears have fallen mightily from their lofty pedestals, and they are viewed in diverse terms — as tourist attractions for the curious, as parents of cuddly cubs, as the dream quarry of recreational hunters, and as scavengers of garbage dumps or unwelcomed, dangerous interlopers. The impact of global warming is proving calamitous for these noble animals and the possibility of extinction hovers ominously, as will be explored more fully in the final chapters.

Returning now to Barents. His expedition continued east from Bear Island and eventually arrived at Novaya Zemlya. He rounded the southern tip at the point where Nai was pleased to make his "very broad claim," but, alas, he found no sign of the "spacious, open sea." The Kara Sea was frozen solid, a smooth sheet of thick ice that made further passage impossible. The disappointment must have been palpable, but with the season advancing rapidly and a restless crew clamoring for a return home, there was no option but to do so.

Despite frustration at having failed to confirm a gateway to the East, the undaunted Barents once more lobbied Dutch authorities for funds to launch yet another exploration. The Estates General, however, had had enough and it balked at acquiescing to the explorer's demands. It did, however, post a reward of 25,000 guilders to any association or individual who would successfully navigate the Northern Sea Passage. Even before that announcement was formally made, the steadfast Town Council of Amsterdam took up the challenge and, raising 12,000 guilders, they outfitted two small vessels. This time the practical precaution was taken to engage only bachelor seamen, so that "they might not be diswaded by means of their wives and children to leave off the voyage."[12] Overall charge of the enterprise was given over to Barents with Jacob van Heemskirk commanding one ship and Jan Rijp the other.

Setting out on May 18, 1596, the vessels reached the Shetlands within a fortnight and by early June they were well above the Arctic Circle with course set for east. Excitement was had when the ships came across a floating carcass of a massive whale that "stouncke monsterously," and later even more was generated when an enormous polar bear was spotted swimming across the bows of the lead vessel, which the sailors chased and hunted down. On June 17 they reached 79°49′ N, arriving to a snow-covered land, which they initially assumed to be part of Greenland, but quickly realized otherwise. A landing party was sent ashore to explore the place, and it was richly rewarded by the discovery of countless bird nests, from which hundreds of eggs were harvested for the ships' larders. During that brief

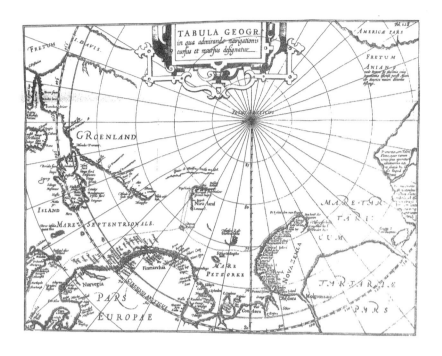

A map "closely agreeing with Barents' own original Map, 1598," which depicts the explorer's third voyage into the Arctic.

Taken from J.I. Pontani, Rerum et Urbis Amstelodamensium Historia. *Amsterdam. 1611.*

foray, a plaque bearing the Dutch coat of arms was ceremoniously erected and the new land claimed in the name of King Willliam I. They named the place "Spitzbergen" (sharp mountain), as it is known today.

At this point a serious disagreement took place between Rijp and Heemskirk as to the direction to be taken next. In those days it was commonly believed that water did not freeze at a distance from land — even in the highest latitudes — a belief that persisted well into the nineteenth century. Rijp therefore insisted on a return due north while Heemskirk argued for a sail northeast toward Novaya Zemlya for another try via the islands' north. Barents sided with Heemskirk. Since both parties held firm in their stubborn convictions it was decided to split up — one to pursue a course due north, the other to head for Novaya Zemlya.

The record of Rijp's further sail is incomplete. Suffice to say that his tiny vessel did press on and in following Greenland's coastline north it eventually became obstructed by dense ice floes that made further progress impossible. Weary and disheartened, he returned home with little to show for his efforts. Of Barents's voyage, on the other hand, much is known thanks to de Veer, the diarist. His writings provide one of the more compelling tales of Arctic winter survival — the first such by Europeans.

Proceeding northeast as argued, Barents arrived at Novaya Zemlya and followed its coast to the northern tip at Mys Zhelaniya (Russian, meaning *Cape Desire*). The promontory was rounded and the vessel continued to parallel the coastline, which, to universal disappointment, was found to be unfolding in a southerly direction, rather than eastward. Contrary to expectations, furthermore, the Kara Sea was cluttered with formidable ice packs. The weather initially was "mistie, melancholy and snowie," but then strong northeasterly winds developed that grew into gale force. Not only was the ship being systematically driven toward the rocky shore, but the ice was being pushed in the same direction. Heemstrick had his hands full trying to forcefully twist and dodge the menacing floes. Some sixty miles south of Mys Zhelaniya, ice and wind conditions deteriorated further, so much so that it was decided to find refuge in some coastal haven and wait out the fierce weather. The unabating east wind made it impossible for the ship to retrace its route A hurried search for suitable harbourage along the unpromising coastline brought the little vessel to a place they called "Ice Haven." It was August 26, late in the season, and they were at 70°45' N.

That night the winds grew more forceful and so pressed the ice packs in the shallow cove that Barents's vessel became tightly pinned. The relentless pressure of the floes increased alarmingly, and, in the somewhat fanciful 1857 words of the Dutchman de Peyster, the vessel, like a child's toy, was "raised up to the top of the constantly-increasing ice-elevation, as if by the scientific application of machinery ..." [T]he "cabined, cribbed and confined" crew was overwhelmed by "the thundering crashes of the icebergs outside their frail bark ... with a din as if a whole mountain of marble had been blown up by some internal explosive force." And the cracking and groaning of the ship, itself, "was so dreadful ... that the crew were terrified lest their ship should fall in pieces with every throe, which seemed to rock it from deck to keel."

The precariousness of their situation became abundantly clear, so much so that Barents ordered most of the ship's cargo be taken ashore, with just enough left on board should the ship survive. In the days that followed, the wind died down and hopes were raised that the ice might retreat. But that was not to be, and after the brief respite the bluster resumed, causing the ice to squeeze and smash the trapped vessel even more. From the shore, the crew watched the unfolding spectacle with horror, making "all the hairs of our heads to rise upright with fear."

Days passed with the weather vacillating from fair and sunny to cold and snowy, all the while the badly scarred ship remaining firmly locked in an icy grip. On September 5, a scouting party sent out into the island's treeless interior returned with welcome news that not only had a vast deposit of driftwood been discovered but also a source of fresh water. By the 11th the stark reality was accepted that the group would be forced "in great cold, poverty, misery and grief to stay all that winter." In preparation for the grim prospect, it was decided to begin without delay the construction of a suitable shelter ashore, "to keep us therein as well as we could, and so to commit ourselves unto the tuition of God."

Parties were sent inland to scout out the most suitable place "to raise our house, and yet we had not much stuff to make it with … there grew no trees nor any other thing in that country convenient to build it with." They did, however, receive "unexpected comfort" in locating another large deposit of driftwood and that "wood served us not only to build our house, but also to burne and serve us all winter; otherwise without doubt we had died there miserably with extreme cold."

De Veer's diary is an interesting read for the telling vignettes he offers on the day-by-day existence of the stranded party. His September 13 entry, for example, read: "It was a calm but very misty weather, so that we could do nothing because it was dangerous for us to go inland, because we could not see the bears; and yet they could smell better than they see." And then the laconic entry for the 23rd in its entirety — and here one might well ask, what manner of men were these? "We fetched more wood to build our house, which we did twice a day, but it grew to be misty and still weather again, the wind blowing east and east-northeast. That day our carpenter (being of Purmecaet)[13] died as we came aboard about evening." And then, the totality of the following day's entry: "We buried him under the sieges [shale] in the cleft of a hill, hard by the water, for we could not dig up the earth by reason of the great frost and cold; and that day we went twice with our sleds to fetch wood." Void of emotion, almost heartless in delivery.

The construction work was wrought with difficulties, despite the abundance of driftwood and quantities of planks scavenged from the ship. The undertaking had now to be done without the professional oversight of the deceased carpenter. Extreme cold hindered rapid progress — "it froze so hard that as we put a nail in our mouths, there would ice hang there on when we took it out again, and made the blood flow." Work on particularly misty days had to be suspended for fear of marauding bears that seemed constantly about. For the hauling of wood, a sled had been fabricated from some planks taken from the stranded ship. The distance from the driftwood quarry to the site was four miles and bears were periodically encountered on the long haul. Once a particularly threatening beast suddenly appeared and the frightened men panicked. Heenskirk's level-headedness and power of command saved the situation. He ordered the men to form a tight circle, threatening to kill anyone who ran, and, by uproariously shouting and waving arms, they intimidated the animal sufficiently to scare it away.

It took nearly a month to complete construction, and on October 24 the sixteen men moved into their new quarters. The building measured thirty-two feet by twenty, constructed of driftwood and ship's planking; with the roof covered by slate gathered from nearby. As the men were making the final run with the sled carrying supplies from the stranded ship to their new quarters, they were attacked by three bears. While Heemskirk and de Veer fought the beasts with halberds, the remainder of the party ran for the ship. The distracted animals paused long enough for the men to make a goodly head start, but quickly gave chase. The sailors made it safely to the vessel and a lively battle ensued with the animals, soon joined by Heemskirk and de Veer. The sole means of defence

In 1596, William Barents's third expedition in search of the Northeast Passage became ice-locked off Novaya Zemlya. A contemporary sketch shows "the exact manner of house wherein we wintered."

at hand was the two halberds and an abundance of fireplace logs that were hurled at the marauders, "and every time we threw they ran after them, as a dog [might] do at a stone cast at him." The struggle came to an abrupt close by a well-placed halberd blow on one animal's delicate snout. The pained bear ran off with the other two closely behind. "We thanked God that we were so well delivered from them."

With the passing of time, the bears seemed to have migrated out of the region and, in their wake, white fox appeared in large numbers. One such animal was killed with a hatchet, skinned, and roasted on a spit. It was found to taste like a rabbit, and "its skin served us for a good defense [against the cold]." The lamps at the dinner table were fuelled by melted bear fat and outside the shelter lay the frozen carcasses of beasts that had been hunted earlier.

October 28: "Three of our men went to the place where we had set the bear upright and there stood frozen, thinking to pull out her teeth. But it was clean covered over with snow. And while they were there it began to snow so fast, that they were glad to come home as fast as they could. But the snow beat so sore upon them that they could hardly see their way, and had almost lost their way."

November 4: "It was calm weather, but then we saw the sun no more, for it was no longer about the horizon. Then our surgeon made a bath for us to bathe in, of a wine pipe,[14] wherein we entered one after the other, and it did us much good and was a great means of our health." By mid-November the clock ceased ticking and all sense of time was lost; was it day or was it night? Dark inside, dark outside. Men crawling out of their bunks "to make water" outdoors could not discern "whether the light they saw was the light of day or of the moon."

By then, they became conscious of the diminishing supply of bread — "we shared our bread amongst us, each man having four pounds and ten ounces for his allowance in eight days ... whereas before we ate it up in five or six days." Traps set for fox proved effective and the animals became an important food source, that and plentiful fish. The store of beer was also a concern for not only was the supply lessening, but the stuff "was for the most part wholly without strength, so that it had no flavor at all." Wine was rationed — "every man had two glasses a day, but commonly our drink was water which we melted out of the snow."

As for successive weather notations of late November and early December : "foule weather," "faire weather," "darke weather," "still weather," "indifferent weather," but for the most part it was "foule," with a continuous blow of east winds. It was "so cold that when we washed our sheets and wrung them, they froze so stiff that, although we laid them by a great fire, the side that lay next to the fire thawed, but the other side was hard frozen." Boots turned "as hard as horns upon our feet, and within they were white froze." Indoor it was not only dark, but the quarters were smoke-filled for lack of sufficient draw by the primitive chimney. And it was bitterly cold — "we could hardly sit by the fire because of the smoke, and therefore stayed in our cabins [bunks]. We heated stones which we put in our cabins to warm our feet, for both the cold and the smoke were insupportable." Sleep often proved impossible because of the thunderous cracking of ice in the nearby sea.

At one time the cold became so bitter that they decided to burn some coal brought from the ship. The satisfying intensity of the fire "cast a great heat" and the men gathered happily about the table. Soon, however, poisonous fumes overcame one of them and the others found themselves developing nausea and headaches. The nearly asphyxiated man was hustled out-of-doors, had vinegar sprinkled on his face, and in the cold, bracing air he soon came around. Barents "gave every one of us a little wine to comfort our hearts."

By mid-December the checking of fox traps became a grim task because of the excessive cold and wind for "if we stayed too long there arose blisters upon our faces and our ears." The plentiful fox provided not only sustenance, but their skins were fashioned into snowsuits. Christmas Day came and went as any other day with no mention of the occasion — "it was foule weather with a northwest wind." It had been snowing steadily and the house had become literally snowed in. On the 28th one of the men thought to explore the outdoors, but to do so he had first to pry open the frozen door and then dig a passage through the wall of blocking snow. "He found it so bad weather that he stayed not long and told us that the snow lay higher than our house."

New Years' Day, 1597. A ration of wine for every man, sipped sparingly for the depleting stock. "We were in fear that it would still be long before we should get out from thence." The cold and wind were so bad that days passed without anyone venturing outside — "in four or five days we durst not put our heads out of doores," writes de Veer. Little wonder at the uncertainty of days: with no clock or view of the outside world, how could the incarcerated crew determine a day's beginning or end? Finally, to check the wind, a pike was thrust through the chimney opening "with a little cloth or feather upon it," but the improvised vane froze instantly and proved useless.

And so the days and weeks dragged into April. During that time food stores diminished, especially store of bread, which was a cause for alarm. Men weakened as illnesses of one sort or another seemed constantly to plague them with one death being recorded. The appearance of scurvy was particularly concerning — these pioneer Arctic explorers had not yet learned that fresh bear meat was an effective counteragent. The gathering of wood became a task beyond endurance, for in the passing of time the search had to be made farther afield. The valued fox population petered out and the bears reappeared. A particularly close call was had when one threatened entry into the house through the chimney — it was killed.

The days eventually grew longer and the sun's rays not only warmed the spirits of the closeted men, but brought about changes to the stark Arctic landscape. Where before there was only rugged ice on the nearby sea, now more and more open water became visible. Barents's broken ship, however, continued in its firm ice-bound captivity. The inspections that had been carried out periodically during the winter had long revealed that the vessel was probably beyond repair, and now the accumulated frozen waters within the hold confirmed the worst: the ship would never sail again. All hopes of the despairing men to return home appeared to have vanished and only miraculous intervention by the Almighty could save them.

Great as the anguish no doubt was, Dutch willpower and resourcefulness ultimately prevailed: the men determined to hazard an escape on the ship's whaleboat and the tiny yawl. To do nothing was certain death; a try, however challenging and unlikely, offered a modicum of hope. In anticipation that the sea would open completely in the coming weeks, they set to work refurbishing and supplying the two small boats. The highest quality of seamanship would be required with every man having to be totally alert and pulling his weight. But then, an unexpected turn: as preparations were nearing completion, the work party was attacked by bears. Not without difficulty, one animal was killed and the other scurried away. A fire was kindled and the hungry men indulged in fresh roasted meat with three of them unknowingly consuming the liver, the toxic bit of the carcass which under no circumstances was ever to be consumed — within hours they fell gravely ill. Worrisome days passed with the three being ministered to as well as circumstances permitted. Thankfully, they recovered, "for which we gave God thanks," writes de Veer, "for if as then we had lost these three men, it was a hundred to one we should never have gotten away, because we should have had too few men to draw and lift at our need."

While the men worked on the boats, Barents was ashore, prone on his back suffering from advanced scurvy and a helpless invalid. On June 14 the sea opened sufficiently and with the vessels fully loaded, he and another sufferer were carried by stretcher to the shoreline and gently placed on board, one in each boat. They then sailed away, "committing ourselves to the will and mercie of God, with a west north-west wind and an endifferent open water, we set saile and put to sea." Left behind was the lovingly constructed house that had sheltered them during that dark, savage winter. A letter written by Barents was nailed on the chimney relating the tale of the expedition's adventures and survival and signed by every member of the crew. The document told "how we came out of Holland to saile to the kingdom of China, and what had happened unto us being there on land, with all our crosses, that if any man chanced to come thither, they might know what happened unto us and how we had been forced in our extremity to make that house and had dwelt 10 monthes therein." The two tiny crafts put out to sea and headed north. Their plan was to round Mys Zhelaniya, proceed south, hugging Novaya Zemlya's west shore and make contact with Russians or Samoyeds on the mainland coast.

On the third day out they found themselves in a narrow channel with thick ice buffeting them about. With action of the floes growing increasingly rough and threatening to the insubstantial hulls, Heemskirk gave orders for the vessels to be hauled out of the water onto a large stable floe. Supplies were unloaded, the sick men laid out on piles of clothing, and the boats were duly dragged to safety. From time to time faults in the ice opened and a number of containers disappeared into the sea, including casks of bread, trunks of clothing, and the boxed astrolabe.[15] One sharp-eyed sailor, however, managed to grab hold of the ship's moneybox just in the nick of time as it was about to be swallowed up — Dutch blood spoke.

Repairs were carried out on the hulls, "much bruised and crushed with the racking of the ice." On the third day of their self-imposed idleness as they awaited the clearing of a passage, Barents suffered his last and died. His body was gently lowered into the water. "The death of Willem

Barents put us in no small discomfort, as being the chief guide and only pilot on whom we reposed ourselves next under God ..." writes de Veer. Shortly after the leader's death, the other critically ill man also died.

On the 22nd, the waters cleared sufficiently for the boats to move on and after a few days more sail through ice, contrary winds, and then fog the two vessels managed to clear Novaya Zemlya and eventually reached Siberia where they were greeted by native fishermen. After days of rest and with strength renewed, they continued their two-hundred-mile passage, rounded the Kola Peninsula and arrived safely to a Lapland fishing village. The Russians received them with every sort of hospitality, taking them into their homes and offering them dry clothing. "We ate our bellies full which in long time we had not." Then in early September, eleven weeks after setting out, they came across by pure serendipity their colleague from whom they separated in Spitzbergen on the outbound passage. The survivors reached Holland on November 1, eleven months after leaving.

Reflecting on this remarkable tale of endurance and survival, one stands in awe at the Dutchmen's force of character. Imagine setting out on a sixty-foot wooden boat into unknown and uncharted reaches of the high Arctic, provisioned and equipped with four-hundred-year old technology. Imagine standing on a barren, bear-infested island in bitter cold and snow and watching your vessel being heaved up by ice and broken. Then, with little likelihood of rescue, being cloistered for over half a year with seventeen others, freezing in a gloomy, acrid shelter inexpertly constructed of planks and driftwood (your share of the floor space is forty square feet). And in that isolation: sickness and death, pitiable diet, dangerous bears, extreme monotony, and a profound sense of isolation and abandonment. One wonders at the mould from which these early Arctic intrepids were formed — exceptional people they were. Eighteen men had been drawn by the beguiling song of the Arctic Siren. Twelve returned home, six became enveloped in her deadly embrace.

3

First Western Thrust

A T THE TIME THAT the Muscovy Company and the Dutch were pushing eastward into the Arctic, the English sought the elusive passage to Cathay through the Arctic regions of the western hemisphere.

It was an Italian navigator in the service of King Henry VII of England, Giovanni Caboto — John Cabot — who was the first to follow upon Columbus's initial voyages to "the Indies" half a decade earlier. Armed with the royal commission from His Majesty awarding him "full and free authoritie, leave, and Power, to sayle to all Partes, Countreys and Seas of the East, of the West and of the North under our banners and ensigns with five shippes ...,"[1] Cabot set off in 1497 from Bristol, England's second-largest seaport.[2] The voyage was short-lived. He made landfall in Iceland, which in itself was of no major significance since English fishermen had already been harvesting those rich waters and the island was familiar to them. Details of this particular voyage and the subsequent one are not known, and much of what has come down to us is speculation. In Iceland some sort of critical dispute took place between Cabot and the crews, which sadly resulted in an empty-handed return home.

In May of the following year, Cabot set off again, this time with only one vessel, the fifty-ton *Matthew*. We know that the ship reached Dursey Head in southernmost Ireland, that they pressed on, that the ship's crew was deeply frightened by icebergs, and that they landed somewhere in North America on June 24, 1497. But where, exactly? Possibly Cape Breton or Labrador or even in Maine, and conflicting claims are made on the matter. The most likely landing spot was Cape Bonavista in eastern Newfoundland. But what matters is that John Cabot is acknowledged as being the first European to have set foot in North America since the Vikings a half millennium earlier — of whom nothing had been known at the time. Back in England, the delighted king received the explorer enthusiastically and awarded "to him that founde the new isle, £10," a princely sum in those days. The prize was bestowed with no regard to the protestations of the Spanish Ambassador, who complained bitterly that in entering western hemisphere waters Cabot had trespassed illegally, for this was an allocation assigned to Spain three years earlier by His Holiness.

The significance to Arctic history of Cabot's second voyage lies in the interest it generated for further search of a passage to Cathay. Hard on his heels, a series of explorers prodded the western hemisphere, seeking the riches of the East. In the south, there were such notables as Vespucci, who in 1499 landed in Guiana, Bilboa, and Panama; and Magellan, who landed in Brazil. In the north, Estevan Gomez explored the Maine coast in 1519; five years later, Giovanni da Verrazano became the first to sail north along the American coast exploring New York harbour, in the process. Jacques Cartier made three journeys to the New World and in 1541 planted the first European settlement in North America at Quebec City. These were Spaniards, Portuguese, and Frenchmen; the Dutch and the English all that time were focused on the Northern Sea Route.

In 1566, the soldier and academic, Sir Humphrey Gilbert[3] effectively argued before Elizabeth I that exploration of a northeastern route to Cathay was too dangerous — "the air is so darkened with continual mists and fogs so bar the pole that no man can well see either to guide his ship or direct his course." He persuaded Her Majesty that the passage laid west and he urged that England should not to be outdone by its European rivals in the business of North American exploration. The queen's interest piqued, she agreed — in principle — to sponsor an exploration. The proposal received exhaustive study and then at last the required funds were raised and ships made ready. But by then ten years had passed and

Gilbert's personal interests had shifted elsewhere — to soldiering, the acquisition of land, and raising a family of six children.

Eighty years had passed since the pope divided the world between the Spanish and Portuguese. During that remarkable time a whirlwind of change had enveloped Europe — with global ramifications. Seeded by the Renaissance and Reformation, humanism and secularism had taken spectacular root, and the pervasive influence of the one Church was no more. Although God created the world, it was humans who had developed it. Man, it was now held, is master of his own destiny. Emphasis shifted from God and afterlife to the world of today — the world that was to be enjoyed. Things spiritual found themselves secondary to the things material.

Commerce and trade blossomed throughout Europe, with the dockyards of London and Amsterdam being particularly busy. Demand burgeoned for silks and fine textiles, for ebony, spices, and other exotic commodities of the east. The wharfs and quays of European harbours teemed as never before with merchants and enthusiastic buyers clamouring for such items as nutmeg, cloves, cardamom, ginger, peppers, and cinnamon. The spice trade soon came to dominate the marketplaces and in England, it's fair to say, spice became the business of the nation.

By the mid-sixteenth century, the overland free flow of goods from the East had long been staunched by the Ottomans. With the conquest of Constantinople in 1453 and the fall of the Byzantine Empire, the Turks virtually closed the vital Silk Road — traders could pass only by paying exorbitant taxes. Da Gama's voyage around Africa into the Indian Ocean, and Magellan's expedition around South America into the Pacific offered fresh avenues for eastern trade. The passage around Cape Horn and across the Pacific was inordinately long and expensive, while and the route around Africa was equally arduous as well as dangerous — Portuguese and Spanish warships patrolled the waters and Barbary pirates delighted in capturing English sailors, whom they sold as slaves.

Little wonder that Gilbert was successful in tweaking the queen's interest in another expedition to America. A Northwest Passage for the traders would indubitably prove more efficient, less hazardous, and less expensive. In view of Gilbert's lack of enthusiasm in leading the expedition, Martin

Frobisher was commissioned to take command — an appointment that became the opening salvo of a series of Arctic explorations by England in America. In the forty-year period, 1576–1616, fourteen English explorers sailed into those distant reaches, some undertaking more than one voyage — the siren song of the Arctic had unquestionably resonated.

Sir Martin Frobisher explored the Canadian Arctic Archipelago and penetrated Baffin Island's Frobisher Bay. An explorer and venture capitalist, his hopes of great wealth were falsely placed in the tons of "wonders stone" believed to contain gold.

Frobisher, one contemporary wrote, was "an eminent seaman and a great discoverer," while another called him "a knave and a scoundrel." Both were probably right. An adventurer and fortune-seeker he certainly was, whose early career progressed from trade in West Africa to privateering in the Mediterranean. Thrice he was arrested and charged with piracy, but never brought to trial. But he finished his career with distinction as a vice-admiral and had fought side by side with Sir Francis Drake in helping to defeat the Armada, for which he received a knighthood. Following that decisive battle, he continued to harass and engage the Spanish until his death in 1594 of a gunshot wound received off the coast of Spain.

From boyhood, Frobisher had dreamed of establishing a trade route to India and China through the North; speculation and rumour had long been had that the entrance to the waterway through the Arctic was there, awaiting discovery. A Portuguese mariner by the name Martin Chacque was said to have sailed west to east through Arctic waters in 1556, emerging into the Atlantic at latitude 59°N (northern Labrador). A certain Salvaterra, "a gentleman of Victoria in Spain," landed in Ireland in 1568 en route home from the West Indies, affirming the existence of the passage. He subsequently informed Frobisher of a Mexican friar, Fra Andrea Urdante, who claimed to have sailed from the south seas to Germany via the Northwest Passage, also from west to east. Such were the tales circulating of the elusive route that enflamed Frobisher's determination to penetrate the Arctic waterways. He noted reassuringly that Salvaterra "offered most willingly to accompany me in this discovery, which it is likely he would not have done, if he had stood in doubt thereof."[4]

For Frobisher it was not merely the kudos of successful discovery that motivated him. His entrepreneurial self was conscious of fresh market potential for English woollens and of untapped sources of furs and minerals. All this was wildly enticing, and the potential returns, he calculated, would far exceed anything that piracy or the slave trade could bring. While still in his twenties he began seeking financial backing for an exploration, but that was long in coming; it took fifteen years. In 1574, he managed to catch the ear of the Earl of Warwick, who exerted sufficient political pressure on the Muscovy Company to have it endorse the project and raise the required capital. So it was that Frobisher found himself in charge of a fleet of three small vessels being made ready to sail out of London's shipyards — the three-mast, twenty-five-ton *Gabriel*, the twenty-ton Michael, and a nameless pinnace, together bearing a complement of thirty-five men.[5]

The expedition set off down the Thames on July 7, and in sailing past Greenwich, Her Majesty honoured them by a gracious wave of the hand from a palace window. Within days of passing the Shetlands, the little fleet was hit by an uncommonly fierce storm, fierce enough to sink the tiny pinnace with its four-man crew. Days later near Greenland, the crew of the *Michael* became so terrified by the threatening ice amassing about them that they simply refused to sail farther and forced a return home. Frobisher aboard the *Gabriel*, however, pressed forward and on the 28th he sighted the north coast of Labrador. Paralleling the coastline in a northerly direction, the shores of Baffin Island eventually loomed into view. In following its coastline west, Frobisher found himself sailing for a long spell in a broad channel and here the explorer's heart no doubt beat faster — surely this was the start of the waterway of their search. The disappointment must have been palpable when after some fifty miles into the channel he came to a dead end. The channel in fact proved to be nothing more than a fjord — Frobisher Bay, some thee hundred miles south of the Arctic Circle, at the head of which today stands the town of Iqaluit.

Despite the sail's anticlimactic dead end, one notable outcome of the foray was the first post-Columbian European encounter with Arctic natives. The initial meeting with these natives was friendly, with the Inuit readily coming on board the *Gabriel* where they were entertained cordially. "They be like Tartars," reported the ship's captain, "with long black hair, broad faces and flatte noses, and taunie in colour, wearing seale skinnes, and so do the women, not differing in the fashion, but the women are marked in the face with blue streekes down the cheeks and round the eyes."[6] Meat and furs were traded for knives and bells and so amiable were these exchanges that five of the crew volunteered to row their newfound friends back to shore — not, however, before being strictly admonished by the captain that they on no account find themselves out of ship's sight. The men never returned.

For three days Frobisher lingered in the area, hoping that the missing men would reappear. As for the Inuit, they too seemed to have disappeared until, on the fourth day, at a far distance, a native was spotted in his kayak. With the rigorous tinkling of bells and welcoming waving of arms, the unsuspecting fellow was lured alongside the *Gabriel*. As he stretched up to receive a proffered bell, the sailors "caught the man fast and pluncked him with maine force, boate and all, into the ship out of the sea."

With no sign of his lost men, the season rapidly advancing, and with "the strange infidel" safely stowed away, Frobisher ordered a return home. Weeks later, the *Gabriel* sailed into London amid much joyous acclaim. Frobisher was greeted as a hero for not only had he and his ship survived, having been taken earlier for lost, but carrying with them a "strange man and his boate, which was such a wonder onto the whole city and to the rest of the realm ... [Frobisher] was highly commended ... for the great hope he brought of the passage to Cathay." His unfortunate prisoner, however, "had taken a cold at sea, soon died."

And then, a sensational turn of events. The returning sailors had carried home souvenirs of their adventurous journey, and among them one Seaman Hall brought an unusual black stone. His wife inadvertently cast it into the fireplace, but soon spotted, it was withdrawn and doused with water. It now "glistened with a bright marquesset of golde." The wondrous stone was taken to three assayers, two of whom thought it to be white pyrites, whereas the third convincingly pronounced it to contain gold.

The rush was on. Within five months of Frobisher's return, he was off again to the Arctic, this time not so much to seek the way to Cathay, but to mine more black rock. Funding for this second expedition had been gathered effortlessly; the queen herself subscribed £1,000, having received the hero "with gracious countenance and comfortable words." His backers directed him strictly to search "for the Gold Ore, and to deferre the further discoverie of the passage until another tyme." On May 31, 1577, the 120 men of the four heavily equipped ships, having "received the Sacrament and prepared themselves as good Christians towards God," sailed forth. On July 4, Frobisher reached Greenland's mountainous coast at 60°30', where the icebergs they had been encountering appeared larger than ever. He marvelled at the size of these "islands of ice," some he reckoned to be a half-mile in circumference. Mostly, however, he was stunned to find that they were of fresh water, which led him to believe that they "must be bredde in the sounds or in some land neere the pole." He concluded, furthermore, that if such were the case, the "maine sea freeseth not, therefore there is no *mare glaciale*, as the opinion hitherto hath been."

The ice prevented a landing and the small fleet continued on until it arrived to its destination, the strait on Baffin Island where Hall's black stone had been found. While the party of miners accompanying the expedition oversaw the excavation of the esteemed ore, Frobisher launched a search for his five missing sailors. The men were not found, but they discovered remnants of English shoes and clothing, some with arrow holes in an abandoned Inuit camp — foul play seemed obvious. One search party encountered a party of natives who initially appeared welcoming. The face-to-face encounter seemed friendly enough, but then it soured and became increasingly heated. Finally, the "savages ... so fiercely, desperately, and with such fury assaulted and pursued our generall and his master ... that they chased them to their boates, and hurt the generall in the buttocke with an arrow."

The search for ore on the north side of the bay proved disappointing, so it was moved to the south side. On that shore, much excitement was generated by the discovery of "a great dead fishe, twelve feet long, having a bone of two yards long growing out of the snoute or nostril" — a narwhal. Shortly after they established themselves and began the search in earnest, another party of natives was encountered, and these Frobisher determined to capture. In the ensuing melee, five Inuit were killed and the rest ran away. Two women, however, were captured, "whereof the one being old and ugly, our men thought she had been the devil or some witch, and therefore let her goe," but the other one was retained, an attractive young mother with a howling baby on her back. During the struggle, an arrow had pierced the infant's arm and "our surgeon meaning to heale her child's arme, applied salves thereonto." The frightened woman grew suspicious of the medication, brushed it off, and "by continuale lickng with her owne tongue, not much unlike our dogs, healed upthe childe's arm."

Using the mother and child as hostage, a parlay was successfully established with the natives, during which Frobisher was given to understand that the five missing men were alive, but were located at some distance. He penned a letter to them, which the natives were instructed to deliver on pain of the mother and child's death. The reassuring preamble is notable [spelling, in modern English]:

> In the name of God, in whom we all believe, who, I trust, has preserved your bodies and souls among these infidels, I commend myself to you. I will be glad to seek by all means one can devise for your deliverance, either with force, or with any commodities within my ships, which I will not spare for your sakes, or anything else I can do for you.

The letter goes on to explain that his men are to inform the "savages" that unless they are immediately and safely delivered, mother and child would die and that "I will not leave a man alive in their country." The natives were dispatched, but alas without result — they neither returned nor did the Englishmen reappear.

The mining operation had been progressing satisfactorily, but the season was rapidly advancing. Apart from not finding his missing men, it had been a successful mission and since Frobisher had been ordered "to deferre the further discoverie of the passage till another tyme," he ordered preparations for a return home. For the next twenty days every person present was put to work loading onto the vessels two hundred tons of the sought-after ore, and on August 22 they set sail, not however, before taking a third native hostage.

In England, samples of the ore were delivered to experts, but no consensus was reached on their value. Investors and refiners were at loggerheads, but the queen and her officials remained firm in their convictions that a unique source of gold had in fact been uncovered. So delighted was Her Majesty with prospects of "great riches and profit, and the hope of the passage to Cathay," that a fleet of fifteen ships was made ready for yet another expedition to the recently discovered land, which the Queen had named *Meta Incognita*. Frobisher was made an admiral and had a gold chain planted about his neck by his monarch.

On May 31, 1578, the fleet put out from England, with a twofold purpose: first, to return with a substantial cargo of ore, and second, to establish a mining colony in the new land — a hundred men had signed on to spend a winter on *Meta Incognita*, mostly miners, carpenters, and soldiers. Stowed in the ships' holds were all the material and equipment required for the building of a walled fortress-like shelter of 9,500 square feet, complete with bastions. On arriving at Frobisher's strait, they found it nearly chockablock with icebergs, one of which was fatally encountered by the one-hundred-ton bark *Dennis*. The ship sank, but its crew was saved. The unfortunate aspect of the loss, however, was that the vessel carried most of the expedition's construction supplies. Following this critical setback, further bad luck befell the ships. A brutal storm hit the anchored fleet and the vessels were dispersed, some driven farther into the strait, others were swept out to sea by drift ice, with most sustaining damage. Once reassembled and repaired, a period of fogs, heavy mists, and snows brought work to a stop, all this resulting in time lost.

With the loss of the building material it was deemed impractical to pursue the colonization project — something perhaps for the future. But the mining proceeded. Much to their satisfaction, an especially bounteous amount of the black ore was found on "a great black island … as might reasonably suffice all the gold gluttons of the world." Work on excavating the rock got underway in earnest with vast quantities of the stuff being loaded on board the vessels — nearly two thousand tons of it.

On August 31, the ships set off for home and after fighting their way through a series of storms — "many of the fleete were dangerously distressed and were severed almost all asunder" — they made it back. Prior to departing "the black island," Frobisher ordered the erection of a small house of stone and mortar, fourteen feet by eight complete with a wooden roof, an experiment to see how such a structure might weather an Arctic winter. Three hundred years later, it was discovered still standing.

All attempts to find gold in the mass of stone carried home came to naught. Five long years passed before the specialists investigating the material reluctantly agreed that the black rock contained no gold. So disheartened was everyone with the disappointing results — investors, refiners, the queen and above all, Frobisher — that further expeditions to the Arctic came to a temporary halt. The vast heap of Baffin Island stone was crushed and put to use in the construction of country roads. A princely sum totalling £20,160 had been spent on Frobisher's three attempts — an enormous amount when one considers that the cost of building the *Gabriel* was £83. And such was the disappointing conclusion to the earliest European effort to exploit the Arctic's natural resources. All the while, the veil of the Arctic Siren continued to envelop the coveted Northwest Passage.

The three Inuit hostages brought to England by Frobisher — a male, a female, and an infant — created a sensation. Londoners flocked to view "the savages," and their every aspect was enthusiastically commented upon and discussed. The pathetic captives, however, were not long for the world; all died within months of landing in the strange land. An autopsy on the man showed that two broken ribs had punctured a lung, which "had excited inflammation and the condition of the lung had, in the course of time, become putrified as a result."[7] Their misfortune was to have fallen into Frobisher's hands all because of the enmity that had coloured the exchanges following the disappearance of the five crew members. What had happened to the lost shore party? Did the sailors go astray on their own, perhaps jumping ship? Or had the men been kidnapped by "the infidels"? Whatever the case, the Baffin Island natives were believed to have been involved.

And what of the natives — whence had these people come and who were they? How did these tenacious folk manage life along the ice-encrusted shores of the Arctic's frozen expanses, in that harshest of all climates?

For starters, it should be noted that in bygone days all peoples of those regions were called *Eskimo* or *Esquimaux* — literally, "eaters of raw meat." The term, however, was found to be pejorative, and today the native people of northern Canada, Greenland, and the north slope of Alaska are referred to as *Inuit*, the native word for "men." The other group of Eskimos, the peoples of Siberia and the Pacific shores of Alaska, falls under the name *Yupik*.

Frobisher's Inuit were descended from settlers who had migrated to Alaska from Siberia after the end of the Ice Age eleven thousand ago. At the time, the Bering Strait separating North America from Asia continued to be bridged by glacial ice. Solid evidence shows that today's Inuit share a common ancestry with the Mongols and quite likely with the Koreans, as well. Around 1000 A.D., a migration of the peoples inhabiting western Alaska took place — a movement east with an eventual fanning out to various parts of the Canadian Arctic and Greenland. These people of the so-called *Thule* culture displaced those already there, a distinctive tribe of large, strong, and innocent peoples called *Tuniit*, identified by archeologists as being of the Dorset culture. The origins of the Tuniit are not understood, but artifacts have been uncovered in the Canadian Arctic that are nearly identical to those found near Lake Baikal and elsewhere in Siberia. Since the Russian finds are eighteen thousand years old, Canadian archeological evidence points to the Tuniit as appreciably predating the incursion of the Inuit. (The oldest settlement in North America today having a continuous history of unbroken human habitation is the Alaskan village of Port Hope, 150 miles north of the Arctic Circle on the Chukchi Sea — some two thousand years old.)

Tuniit survived over the millennia into the nineteenth century with numbers beginning to diminish in early medieval times due to the infiltration of the Inuit into their lands. The Tuniit were a relatively peaceful people disadvantaged by not possessing heavy weapons such as the new arrivals had, like sinew-backed bows and harpoons. The less culturally advanced Tuniit, furthermore, did not have dogs, which the Inuit possessed in numbers, thus holding an advantage in long-distance travel and haulage. With the arrival of Europeans to their shores in late medieval times, the Tuniits were exposed to and ravaged by imported diseases. Their immune systems were insufficient to withstand smallpox, in particular, and this scourge exacted heavy tolls. The nineteenth century wrought dreadful havoc on the settlements — 90 percent of the Tuniit population is estimated to have been decimated by measles, tuberculosis, influenza, and smallpox. By the end of that century only a handful of Tuniits remained and record has it that the last of them died in 1902 from a flu epidemic transmitted by visiting whalers. The Inuit, however, survived, and today an estimated sixty thousand inhabit the Alaskan north slopes, Canada, and Greenland, a sparse population indeed, no more than might fit into a good-sized football stadium.

The culture of the Inuit, and of all Arctic peoples, for that matter, has been shaped by the ecosystem, in which scarcity continues to prevail. Scarcity of lifegiving solar energy, for example. In winter, the sun disappears for weeks or months at a time, depending on latitude, and in summer, the rays of the midnight sun shine brightly, but are slanted and insufficiently strong to thaw or melt the permafrost, although global warming is rapidly changing this. The climate is characterized by long, cold winters, therefore, and short, cold summers. There is also a scarcity of precipitation — some parts of the Arctic are almost desert-like.

The first European contact with Inuit since the days of the Vikings was made by Frobisher. This 1574 sketch by one his party depicts an Inuit hunting scene. The kayaks and weapons are authentic representations, but the tentlike structure is fanciful.

Agriculture, therefore, is non-existent and people are dependent on animal life for subsistence: eating whales, polar bears, seals, walruses, caribou, muskoxen, birds, and on rare occasion fox or some other less common animal. As one Mackenzie Delta Inuit put it, "the land is just like our blood because we live off the animals that feed off the land."

In bygone days Inuit diet was solely meat supplemented by fish, as in certain remote parts it continues today. Not surprisingly, the protein content of their diet was highly elevated and rich in energy creating fat. For vitamin C, the Inuit relied on seal liver or whale skin, and in the more temperate areas of the Arctic, summertime grasses, roots, berries, and seaweed supplemented their daily needs.

But animals were not hunted exclusively for food. Every bit of the kill was valued and put to use — furs for clothing, hides for tents, sinews for thread, bones for tools, sealskins for kayaks, walrus tusks for knives, fat for light and heat, and claws and teeth for amulets to ward off evil spirits. It was believed that animals possessed souls like humans. An Inuit once remarked, "The great hazard to our existence lies in the fact that diet consists entirely of souls." A hunter who failed to show proper respect or to make the customary supplication before the kill was in peril of being avenged by the quarry's liberated spirit.

One animal never killed, barring dire life-and-death circumstances, was the dog. Man and husky lived together, worked together, and hunted together; for many Inuit they were considered family. This remarkable wolf-related breed, one of the world's oldest, is found in virtually every corner of the Arctic and sub-Arctic. It survives well in the brutal freezes because of its double-layered fur. The soft downy hairs of the inner lining serve to trap body heat while the longer and stiffer outer hairs prevent heat from escaping, at the same time blocking water penetration to the skin. With its remarkable strength, resilience, and energy the husky is ideally suited for Arctic life and for service to the people. Harnessed together, a dog team of eight is capable of pulling a winter sled bearing a 1,200-pound load many miles a day. As a summer pack animal, it is capable of carrying weights of some forty pounds.

The rich spiritual life of the Inuit was fundamental to their existence. Animals with spirits and the landscape with spirits — the visible intertwined with the invisible. Life was one of constant awareness of the invisible — ghosts, mystical apparitions, and fantastic creatures. Spirits of dancing ancestors were perceived in the *aurora*; long hours of waiting at a seal's breathing hole conjured ghostly apparitions; the surrounding waters contained deities, the principle one of which was an old woman residing in the far depths. Inuit spiritual life was focused on harmonization with the unseen; to offend a soul or a spirit was a risk to be avoided at all costs.

Until recent times, the Inuit were semi-nomadic, moving from summer camps to winter quarters in the continual pursuit of animals. In Frobisher's day, in summertime they lived in tents made of animal skins, driftwood, and bones, but in winter "snow houses" were constructed, the iconic *igloo*. Blocks of snow were cut from the ground and placed to form a domelike structure with an entrance opening at the base. Most often a short tunnel was added leading to the opening for additional protection from the wind. Temporary igloos of varied sizes and shapes met the needs of the travelling hunter, but the more permanent structures were "family size" or greater, capable of accommodating five, ten, or even twenty people. The abundant wind-blown snow provided readily available building material. Because heat gets trapped in the compact air pockets sitting between the snow's interlocking crystals, the material acquires substantial insulating qualities. The snow construction blocks out the Arctic winds, which can make it feel colder than the actual ambient temperature. Outside the igloo it might be -50°F while the temperature within could reach an overwhelming high of +55°F, with the heat being generated by the occupants' bodies and lamps fuelled by animal fat.

The Inuit concept of family was fluid — it might have consisted of a husband and wife plus children, or it might have included more than one wife or adopted children or possibly have incorporated one set of parents-in-law or both. Everything was shared, and the idea of personal wealth was non-existent. Every household had an elder and it was he who oversaw orderliness, made the important decisions of the day, and, in company with other elders, judged those who transgressed the established way. Until recent times, the Inuit knew nothing of laws and government, and the community abided by three governing principles long established by tradition: *maligait*, what has to be followed; *piqujait*, what

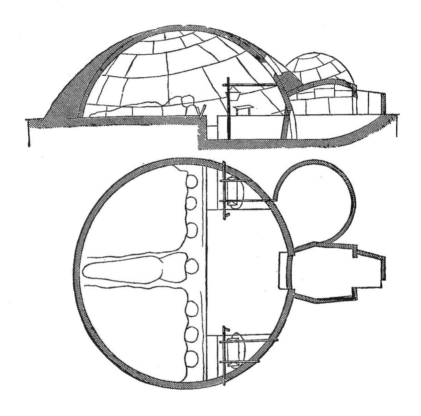

A cross-sectional view and a floor plan of an Inuit igloo, this one accommodating seven people. Heat was generated by the occupants' bodies and by lamps fuelled by animal fat.

has to be done; and *tirigusuusiit*, what must not be done. An individual transgressing any of these principles might find himself before the council of elders, whose intervention was deemed appropriate lest the community be harmed. The justice meted out could prove harsh in extreme cases and capital punishment was sometimes practised.

It is untrue, however, that the Inuit killed their elderly and unproductive people as many Europeans have historically claimed. Indeed, elders were revered as guardians of tradition and valued for their knowledge and memory. Suicide, though, was not unknown and if an elderly person felt him/herself to be an undue burden on the family or community, such a person might well resort to it — in times of extreme famine, for example, when it was clear that the hunter could provide only so much for the family. An open declaration of intention not uncommon, with the family then gathering about the individual to observe him donning his clothes inside-out, then exiting the igloo and disappearing into the barren wilderness, there to await death by freezing.

Europeans coming in early contact with the Inuit viewed the people as primitive savages in need of civilization. In time, however, it was they who took from the indigenous for it was the ingenuity of the native that permitted an adaptation to the singular environment of the Arctic. Native clothing, tools and diet, native habitat, transport, and social structures were all logical responses to those daunting conditions, a response that had been developed over the centuries and that worked well. Over the centuries, more than one European succumbed to the Arctic by failing to acknowledge the wisdom and inventiveness of "the primitive savage," the same people Frobisher encountered on his journeys into the Arctic.

The three Frobisher expeditions continued to generate interest among the merchants of London and Devon. A certain William Saunderson of the Fishmongers' Guild of London proved to be a particularly enthusiastic advocate for continued search of the Northwest Passage, and through his efforts a substantial sum was raised by the business community to launch yet another voyage of exploration in northern America. John Davis was selected to lead the fresh initiative, "a man very well grounded in the principles of navigation."

Davis was a childhood friend of Humphrey Gilbert and the half brother to Sir Walter Raleigh. Born on the seacoast of Devon and brought up amid sailing ships and fishermen, it was natural for the young man to take to the ocean. By the time he died in 1605 at age fifty-five, he had sailed the waters of Greenland, Canada, the Pacific, and the South Atlantic, where he discovered and laid claim to the Falkland Islands. In addition to being a brilliant navigator and expert seaman, he had a scholarly bent; in 1599 he authored *Seaman's Secrets*, a mariner's handbook of navigation that became an instant success.

The three successive expeditions undertaken by Davis into Arctic waters were inconclusive, with the elusive passage remaining uncovered. The significance of his work, however, lay in the meticulous records and detailed charts he offered the world of science, and to future explorers. Coastline details of Greenland, Baffin, and Labrador were faithfully documented, as well as observations on ice conditions, weather, terrain, rock formations, vegetation, and animal life. The Inuit especially intrigued Davis and he provided the earliest and most accurate observations of them and on their way of life — their dress, religion, customs, and their physiognomy. One curious detail he noted was, "[T]hese people are much given to bleed, and therefore stop their noses with deeres hair." The relationship he and his crew developed with the natives was conflicting — one day, all smiles and friendly trade; on another, antagonism and bellicose exchanges.

On Davis's second voyage to Greenland, a happy reunion took place with "the people of the countrey." The Inuit, having spotted the ships from afar, were at first reluctant to approach closely, but when they recognized some familiar faces among the crew of the earlier expedition, they happily brought their kayaks alongside the ship. Davis proceeded ashore accompanied by a small crew and eighteen natives "came running to mee and the rest and embraced us with many signes of heartie welcome." Each of the natives was given a gift of a knife. On the following day the "gentle and loving Savages" returned with the obvious purpose of trading. They brought with them sealskins and caribou skins, rabbit and seal meat, plus salmon, cod, and "other fish and byrdes such as the country did yielde." In return, knives, mirrors, bells, and glass beads were offered and enthusiastically accepted. Englishman and Inuk traded happily — the natives shed their surplus skins and stores of food, and the visitors surrendered a few modest trinkets, each no doubt pleased that the other was the lesser for the deal.

The pleasing relationship blossomed. On one occasion in the tiny Inuit settlement, Davis's men engaged their hosts in sport. Englishmen won the jumping contests — "our men over-leaped them" — but Inuit beat them at wrestling. "We found them very strong and nimble, and to have skill in wrestling; for they cast some of our men that were good wrestlers." A misunderstanding took place when one Inuk demonstrated the making of fire by rapidly twirling a "round stick like unto a bedstaffe" within a hole drilled in a piece of board, and "by his violent motion doeth very speedily produced fire." So shocked was Davis by this phenomenon that he ordered the fire immediately stamped out and the ashes thrown into the sea, "which was done to shew them that we did condemne their sorcery." (In this instance, one might ask, who was the primitive?)

Helpful and good-natured as the Inuit were, they soon "showed their vile nature" by stealing items from the ships, with objects of iron being of special interest. On one particularly audacious visit the natives were found helping themselves to spears, oars, laundry, a sword, and "diverse other things." A round of gunfire scared the raiders away, but within hours "in their simplicitie" they were back, grinning, merrily waving hands, and signalling for peace. The fractured relationship healed and before long the two parties were teaching rudiments of their languages, thus further cementing relations. In his diary, Davis offers a list of forty Inuit words, including *canyglow*, or "kiss me." On his previous year's voyage to Greenland's southern tip, it might be noted, Davis had acquired yet another word — *musketa*. "We found it very hot, and we were troubled with a flie which is called Musketa, for they did sting grievously."

The agreeable relationship that had prevailed to that point soured rapidly. The theft of laundry and oars was one thing, but now it was discovered that a ship's anchor went missing as well as a length of cable and one of the ship's boats. All a bit much. And then, quite without provocation, "they began to practice their devilish nature, and with slings threw stones very fiercely." The boatswain received a particular nasty blow, which so angered the sailors that they gave chase, but to no avail. Shortly thereafter, as with the first altercation, the Inuit indicated that they sought a truce, and one of the representatives waved a pair of gloves as an invitation to trade. Davis reciprocated by holding up a knife. Two natives then came on board the ship, and were immediately seized. One was kept and the other was set free with instructions to arrange for the return of the recently stolen items within an hour or his friend would never again be seen. An hour passed, and then another and another, but no result. Unprepared to linger longer, the ships weighed anchor and sailed away, quitting Greenland and bound for Newfoundland with the hapless Eskimo in tow. Unlike Frobisher's Inuit, this one acclimatized rapidly to his new situation and prospered — "at length he became a pleasant companion among us."

European fishermen and whalers had been harvesting the waters off Greenland and Labrador for generations before the voyages of Frobisher and Davis. It would be incorrect, therefore, to claim that they discovered these places, which they clearly did not. Their passages to Greenland and Baffin Island, however, are legendary and from the viewpoint of Arctic exploration, these two voyagers stand among the foremost. They opened a new world to navigators, cartographers, and historians and thus prepared the way for those who followed in unlocking the Arctic.

4

The Hudson Tragedy

WILLOUGHBY, CHANCELLOR, BRUNEL, and Barents — all met failure in uncovering an eastern passage through the Arctic. Cabot, Gilbert, Frobisher, Davis, and others met with equal disappointment in the West. The financial losses of their sponsors were profound; the Muscovy Company, the Dutch government and merchants, British traders and investors suffered severely, and their enthusiasm for a continued pursuit was badly shaken. Yet the challenge endured. An Arctic route to the East was undoubtedly there and only a systematic probe of every likely path could prove otherwise. The reports of Frobisher and Davis were tantalizing; dreams of the pot of gold at the end of the rainbow were slow in dying.

The East India Company, royally chartered in 1600, now grasped the baton of exploration. At the time the newly founded entity had been focused on trade in cottons, silks, spices, saltpeter (essential for gunpowder), and opium. A more direct and less costly route to suppliers in the East was distinctly advantageous, and the unexplored strait discovered by Davis was intriguing and sufficiently promising to launch a new expedition. To lead this new voyage of exploration, the company appointed Captain George Weymouth from Devonshire, a student of mathematics and shipbuilding, as well as an accomplished seaman, and offered him an inordinately generous reward of £500 if he succeeded.

On May 2, 1602, two ships sailed out of London, the solidly built fifty-five-ton barque, which within a decade was to become one of the most famous of all Arctic vessels, Henry Hudson's fatal ship the *Discovery*, and the smaller *Godspeed*. Weymouth carried with him a personally signed letter from "Elizabeth, by the Grace of God Queen of England, France and Ireland, Defender of the faith &c."[1] addressed "To the great, mighty and Invincible Emperour of Cathaia." In it she advises the invincible one that "we have set fourth two small ships under the direction of our subject and servant George Weymouth, being the principal Pylott of the present voyage a man of his knowledge and experience in navigacon specially chosen by us," and she requests that every courtesy be extended him.

Her Majesty's lengthy missive is perhaps more impressive than the results of Weymouth's actual voyage. The journal he kept was unfortunately far from fulsome and it is difficult to reconstruct the precise route he took. Suffice to say that having sighted Greenland on June 18, the vessels moved on and touched American shores ten days later. Weymouth entered, but did not explore Kennebec Bay on the coast of Maine and he probably spotted the White Mountains of New Hampshire. He then continued north and eventually came to Labrador where, doubtlessly amid much excitement, he discovered a new and promising channel leading west — without recognizing it as being the already-explored Hudson Strait. Storms, thick fog, and ice now plagued the *Discovery*. Despite it being mid-summer, the cold was so intense that the men complained they could not cope with the hard-frozen sails, ropes, and tackles. The overwhelmed crew simply refused to sail farther and with the chaplain urging them on, they rebelled and demanded a return home, to which Weymouth reluctantly agreed. The two vessels reached Gravesend at the mouth of the Thames on August 5. Disappointed as his London backers were, they were heartened by the report of another open body of water leading west — if not the strait discovered by Davis, then this new one might offer the long-sought passage East.

Undeterred, the East India Company teamed up with the Muscovy Company in partnership to form a new entity, the "Company of English Merchants Trading in the North West," and the search for the Northwest Passage went on. Captain John Knight, recently returned to England after service with the Danes, was engaged as the leader of a fresh search. In April 1606, four years after Weymouth's aborted voyage, Knight sailed west on board the fifty-five-ton *Hopewell*, with the specific intent of passing through the "unknown" strait discovered by his predecessor. Two months after departing from Gravesend, the ship made landfall in Labrador amid heavy ice floes, some of which caused damage to the hull. Repairs were required, and so Knight, accompanied by five others, went ashore to scout out a likely location to carry out the work. Leaving two of the men on the shore with the ship's boat, he and the other three climbed the nearest elevated point with the intention of viewing the surrounding countryside. The scouting party never returned, and what came of them is a matter of conjecture. A popular theory of the time was that they were attacked by natives, who were said to be "a very little people, tawnie coloured, thin or no beards, flat-nosed, and man-eaters." After a brief wait for the missing men, the build-up of ice conditions forced the *Hopewell* to move out to sea. It made its way to Newfoundland, where the necessary repairs were carried out, and then it returned to England, reaching Dartmouth on Christmas Eve. Nothing was again heard of Knight.

Disappointing as the failed expeditions of Weymouth and Knight had been, those who had sponsored them continued in their determination to reach the East through the Arctic. By then a new element had crept into the equation: contact had been made with the Inuit, and from them furs could be had for easy trade — lots of them and of excellent quality. The northern road to the Orient now gave promise of being paved with furs — all the more reason to give the New World one more try. Enter Henry Hudson.

Little is known of Hudson's early life and nothing of his death. The pages of his remarkable history seem narrowly restricted to one four-year period — 1607–1611 — and they centre on his explorations of three different regions of the North Atlantic. Hudson was a driven man, obsessed by the mission of sailing from England to India and the Spice Islands through the Arctic. As noted before, conventional wisdom at the time had it that ice forms only in the proximity of land, and given an absence of land, there is no ice buildup in open waters. A wide channel over the top of the world would therefore be navigable, and it was precisely this

Henry Hudson, an Englishman in the service of the Dutch. A number of alleged portraits of the explorer such as this exist, but all were executed after the explorer's death. Engraving based on John Collier's painting The Last Voyage of Henry Hudson.

Library and Archives Canada/Illustrated books, albums and scrapbooks/C-002061.

conviction that propelled Hudson and others. It was an ideal partnership: the Muscovy Company sought someone to take charge and Hudson was anxious to lead an expedition over the pole.

Thus on May 1, 1607, this passionate navigator set sail from Gravesend in the *Hopewell*, the same ship used by Knight a year earlier. Accompanying him was the eldest of his three sons, fourteen year-old John, the youngest of the eleven-man crew. The vessel proceeded directly north, and with favorable winds they managed to clear the Shetland Islands in four days. Variable winds slowed further progress, but on June 11 they finally crossed the Arctic Circle, where they were greeted by a pod of six whales that frolicked about the ship, causing fear and wonder among the crew, but no damage. A couple of days later they were off the coast of Greenland, battling a fierce storm and doing everything to avoid being driven onto the brutal coastline. Having won that battle, they moved on, but their progress was impeded by fog, drizzle, and bitter cold, plus the occasional encounter with ice. With the heavens consistently overcast, accurate navigation was impossible since the astrolabe was useless without a clear sky.

On June 20, the skies opened briefly and Hudson was able to get an accurate positioning, which he reckoned to be 72°38' N. On that same day, land was sighted for a few moments, a high mountain jutting out from the sea, but then the fog set in once more and the land disappeared from view. The breaking of the waves ashore, however, was soon heard, but they didn't attempt landfall because of the dangerous conditions; the *Hopewell* pressed on. Throughout the journey, Hudson made meticulous additions and corrections to the available charts and he painstakingly logged details on weather, sea conditions, and land formations, as well as on whatever flora and fauna he encountered. In attending this he was abiding to the long-standing tradition among scientists, seamen, and travellers of committing to paper anything that would enhance knowledge of the world. At one spot he notes, for example, that the seabed at sixty fathoms was found to be "black, oozy, sandy, with some yellow shells." And on one island, "we saw many Birds with black backs and white bellies in form much like a Duck."

One July day Hudson was able to confirm that they were at 81°N, the most northern latitude reached by any European. Pity that the crew was not to know that they were a mere 520 miles from the North Pole. Nor would they learn that their notable achievement was a record that would remain unbroken for two centuries. But the weather at this point was rapidly changing and the season drawing nigh; Hudson reckoned that they had come as far north as prudence allowed. Furthermore, leaks were developing in the *Hopewell* and her bilges were taking on more water than usual — battering ice floes had made life gruelling for the sturdy little ship. It was time to return home, and they turned south.

The Faroe Islands were reached on August 15, and a month later the vessel made its way up the Thames into Gravesend. Other than the notable record-setting and the wealth of practical information gathered on the Arctic, little had been achieved by the explorer. Though disappointed, his enthusiasm for continued exploration remained unshaken.

Within weeks of his return home, Hudson was again knocking on investors' doors in search of fresh funding for a follow-up northern voyage. Try as he might, however, the London business community was in no mood to sink more money into such projects; investor fatigue had set in. Frustrated, but undaunted, Hudson took his case to Amsterdam where the Dutch East India Company received him warmly and raised the required capital. Despite disappointment over Barents's inconclusive attempts, the Dutch continued in the conviction that the Northern Sea Route was there, perhaps via the pole, waiting only for the right person to knock at the right door. It seems that by that time Hudson had accepted the futility of another polar push and that he had became equally attracted to the possibility of a Northeast Passage. Returning home, he wasted little time in refitting and stocking the *Hopewell*. A crew of fourteen was gathered that included many of the same men who had accompanied him in the previous year, including young John.

Hudson sailed from Gravesend on April 22, 1608, one year to the day of quitting the place on his earlier exploration. In the four weeks that followed they ran into the all-too-familiar gamut of fog, drizzles, rains, contrary winds, and latterly, gusts of snow. By the time they rounded Nord Cap, at Norway's northernmost tip, the crew began to suffer from the cold, which was frigid enough to form ice on the upper decks and masts. Battling obdurate ice floes, Hudson managed to reach Novaya Zemlya where Chancellor had been a half century earlier, but at this point he was halted by a barrier of insurmountable ice and could progress no farther. Nothing was to be done but to return home. "By now having spent more than half the time I had, and gone but the shortest part of the way [because of] contrary winds, I thought it my duty to save victual, wages and tackle, by my speedy return…"[2] The *Hopewell* turned about and made for the south, arriving at Gravesend on August 26.

In his journal entry of August 7, after the decision to abandon further exploration had been made, Hudson made a curious entry in his journal: "I gave my companie a certificate under my hand, of my free and willing return, without persuasion or force of any one or more of them …" The document was nothing more than exoneration from possible accusation that the bearer had been party to the use of force in the decision to return home. It was an irregular thing to have done and it shows that Hudson's relationship with the men under his command was clumsy at best. He is seen as failing to establish a sympathetic and trusting rapport with his men; for all his prowess as a seaman and navigator, he lacked people skills. The journal entry is an ominous portent of things to come.

Among Hudson's dreary daily reports on weather, position, and ice conditions, one colourful account stands out of a meeting with a "mermaid" spotted by two of the crew: "She was come close to the ship's side," he writes, "looking earnestly on the men. A little after, a sea came and overturned her: from the navel upward, her back and breasts were like a woman's, as they say that saw her; her body as big as one of us; her skin very white; and long hair hanging down behind, of color black; in her going down they saw her tail, which was like the tail of a porpoise, and speckled like a mackerel." (In all probability what Seamen Thomas Hilles and Robert Rayner saw was a seal, whose underwater appearance and movements in some people's minds resemble those of a human).

Insofar as we are concerned, the account of Henry Hudson's third attempt at finding a direct route to Cathay is of tangential interest since most of it passed well south of Arctic boundaries. We might nevertheless pause for a brief glimpse at it — it tells much of the man. On March 20, 1609, the forty-ton *Halve Maen* (*Half Moon*), sailed away, bound for Novaya Zemlya for a fresh try at the Kara Sea. This time Hudson was financed entirely by a determined clique of Amsterdam merchants and he went out in the name of Dutch King Maurice. Rounding Norway's Nord Cap, he continued along the coast to the White Sea, passed it, and sailed on, only to be confounded by the same severe ice conditions that had halted his previous year's attempt. A cul-de-sac it was, and one can only imagine Hudson's chagrin at the disappointing development. At this point he appeared to have accepted the fact that a northern sea route through the east was not to be. Dispirited, but undaunted, he abandoned all hopes of finding such, and decided to redirect his efforts west to America.

The *Half Moon* about-turned and under favourable winds proceeded whence it had come. After a brief stop at the Faroe Islands, it made its way across the Atlantic and on July 8 it reached Newfoundland's Grand Banks. It then quickly passed Nova Scotia, Maine — where the crew feasted on thirty-one lobsters and two jugs of Hudson's personal stock of wine — and Cape Cod. By early August, the explorer was off the coast of Virginia not far from Jamestown, the colony founded three years earlier by his friend Captain John Smith. Hudson probably would not have aimed to reach those parts had Smith not informed him earlier that local Indians told of a great body of water opening to the west laying to the north of Jamestown. Near as he was to his friend's colony, Hudson felt he could not spare the time for a visit; he turned north and moved on with the intention of examining all promising coastal waterways leading inward. Interesting details of the explorations are given by Robert Juet, Hudson's second-in-command (who on the ensuing and final voyage fell out with his master and played a critical role in the infamous mutiny). His published account of 1625 is hardly a record of an illustrious expedition — quite the contrary. Not only did it fail to achieve its purpose, but it left behind a lamentable record of bloody encounters with the natives, of killings and kidnappings, and of drunkenness and looting. Inglorious, indeed.

In progressing up the coastline, Hudson explored Chesapeake Bay, Delaware Bay, and every other likely-looking body of water. By early September he had reached Staten Island, where doubtless there must have been a rush of adrenalin as the vast mouth of the Hudson River burst into view — might this be the gateway of which the Virginia natives spoke? The *Half Moon* entered the river and embarked on a six-week

Henry Hudson's Half Moon (Halve Maen *in Dutch*), *built in 1608 by the Dutch East India Company. The vessel met its end in the Dutch East Indies when it was attacked and sunk in 1618 by the English Navy.*

exploration of the waterway. Travelling seventy-five miles upriver, it reached a point slightly north of Albany, where the waterway narrowed dramatically and became shallower, making further passage impossible. (At one point his ship found itself in seven feet of water.) Yet another dead end had been reached and another about-turn executed. After a series of adventures and encounters with the natives, they were back at the river's mouth, where a stop was made at *Manna-hata*, an impressively lush, green island with massive oak trees facing *"Hopoghan"* (Hoboken). As he stepped ashore, Hudson was greeted by friendly natives who presented the Europeans with their first taste of corn, which the sailors called "Turkish wheat." Here Hudson, the Englishman, laid claim to the area by ceremoniously posting on a tree the royal arms of the House of Orange — the Dutch, after all, sponsored him. Relationship with the natives soured and at one point a flotilla of canoes bearing a hundred natives attacked the *Half Moon*, but were repelled by volleys of gunfire.

By then the expedition had been away from home for nearly a half year, virtually all of it under hard sail and without adequate rest stops. Hudson had knocked at a handful of possible gateways to Cathay, but all for naught; it was time to return to the Old World ... and he did. The expedition reached Europe on November 7 and put into Dartmouth rather than Amsterdam. In three years Henry Hudson had made three consecutive thrusts into the Arctic, and although each one added to the body of knowledge of the remote region, none had justified his mission.

English authorities were sufficiently displeased with Hudson's service to the Dutch that at first they imprisoned him. His incarceration was short-lived and once he was set free, he soon found himself heading a fresh expedition to the New World. On April 17, 1610, the *Discovery* put out from out of London, made its way down the Thames, and sailed on to what was to become one of the world's most notorious voyages. The Henry Hudson who commanded the ship was no longer the same man who three years earlier had navigated the *Hopewell* to Novaya Zemlya. Now, heading toward America for a third time, he had developed into "an old hand" at dealing with the demanding conditions of Arctic sailing and navigation. The experience he had gained amid the ice floes and weather conditions of northern Greenland and the Russian Arctic were inestimable. Additionally, Hudson had prepared himself well by exhaustively studying every available diary and log offered by previous explorers, not only the likes of Drake, Raleigh, Frobisher, and Davis, but of Spanish, Portuguese, and French voyagers. If a way to the Indies through the Northwest Passage did exist, none was better qualified to search it out than the driven Hudson.

Experienced and sea-wise as he may have been, Hudson had a difficult personality that many found grating. He was stubborn and frequently unpredictable; one moment he would show consideration and generosity, and in the next, thoughtlessness and harshness. Before having even cleared the Thames, for example, he became angered for some unrecorded reason with a certain crewman named Coleburne. The poor fellow was summarily dismissed and ordered ashore, bearing a note to the expedition's sponsors explaining the circumstances. Hudson, for all his attributes, was a weak judge of men and he brought onto himself much of the dissention and mutinous behaviour he encountered on his journeys. Simply put, he lacked leadership skills, a defect that lead to his death and that of others, including his son, John.

The account of Hudson's fateful expedition into the western Arctic was best made by an enigmatic individual who accompanied the voyage as the representative of the sponsors, a defrocked priest. The title of his narrative is *A large Discourse of the said Voyage, and the Success thereof, written by Abacuk Pricket, who lived to come Home.* Hudson's own record of the journey's early weeks is sketchy, and at one point the record stops abruptly. (Might it be that at some point the log's pages were deliberately removed?)

Within a month of quitting London, the *Discovery* had reached Iceland where "we saw the famous [volcanic] Mount Hecla, which cast out much fire, a sign of foul weather to come." Off Greenland's east coast "we saw great store of whales, some of which came about and under the ship, but did no harm." As they rounded Cape Farewell at Greenland's southern tip and entered Davis Strait, "proceeding betwixt ice and ice, we saw a great island of ice tumble over, which was a good warning to us not to come near them." They then entered Hudson Strait, the 450-mile length of water separating Baffin Island and Labrador, at the time called

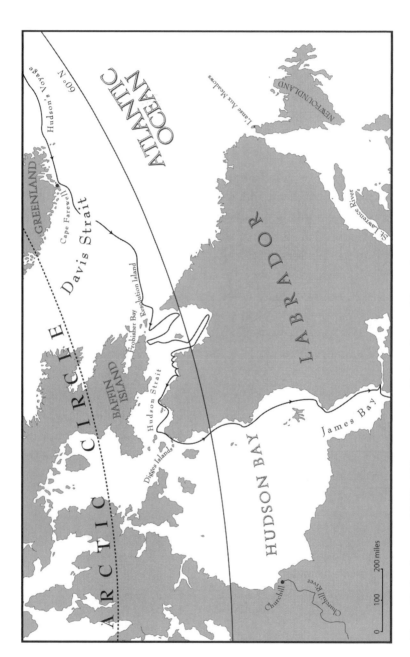

Henry Hudson's route of 1610–11 in penetrating Hudson Bay and James Bay.

Map by Cameron McLeod Jones.

"Frobisher's Straite." Even in summer the waters are not free of ice and great chunks are pushed to and fro by swift currents and turbulent tides, which make any passage hazardous. The *Discovery* once became "fast enclosed by ice and we began to despair, and (as the Master afterwards told me) he thought we should never have got out of this ice, but there have perished." The ice eventually loosened its grip, allowing the vessel to move on, but the experience of being bound by the floes, albeit briefly, weighed heavily on all members of the crew. As the vessel neared the Magnetic North Pole, the compasses performed erratically and direction location became problematic. The appalling sight of the vast iceberg recently toppling over had been indelibly impressed on everyone and the waters in which they now found themselves were perilous. What further surprises lay ahead could only be guessed at. The restlessness and fear of the weak-hearted became infectious and before long a certain disquiet began to envelope the *Discovery*.

Hudson summoned his men together and, opening up a chart, explained that they "were 100 leagues [approx. 300 miles] further than any English man was before us in this place." He then asked whether or not they were prepared to continue on, and the reaction was instantaneous. "Some of our people wished themselves at home; others wished themselves anywhere else so long as it was away from among the ice." The seemingly innocent call for opinion developed into a debate; and "in this perplexity there passed hot words between some of the people, which words were thought upon a long time after." It was evident even at this early stage of the passage that Hudson commanded a divided, opinionated crew with a number of men openly arguing for a return home. After all was said, however, the men did return to their posts and the *Discovery* sailed on, amid rocky shores, shards of icebergs, and all the discomfort the Arctic could provide.

The unsatisfactory state of affairs was compounded by a critical error in judgment made by Hudson, one that he lived ultimately to regret. He demoted his second-in-command, Robert Juet, and in his stead promoted a certain Robert Bylot. As early as Iceland, Juet had been openly critical of Hudson's leadership and had been passing remarks that bordered on mutiny. He had "threatened to turn the head of the ship home from action," said one sailor. Another of the crew reported that Juet at one time had warned shipmates to keep loaded muskets in their cabins, which would be "charged with shot before the voyage was over." What precipitated this disloyalty is a matter of conjecture — Juet and his captain had been long-time shipmates and presumably they were aware of one another's foibles. Hudson's action was highly irregular, exceptional for a ship at sea, and it sent a clear message of non-confidence in his long-time mate. Shunted aside in disgrace, Juet seemed never to have recovered from the galling insult. The sensational demotion only exacerbated the developing divisions among the *Discovery*'s crew.

In their progress westward along the strait's southern coast, Hudson periodically halted for quick explorations of the countryside. At one stop, vast flocks of partridges, ducks, and other birds were found, as well as grasses such as sorrel. The crew was especially pleased to discover an abundance of so-called "scurvy-grass."[3] A herd of sixteen "deere" was spotted — probably caribou — but the animals were out of musket range. The party was surprised to come across a cluster of man-made structures resembling haystacks — the first indication that they were not alone in those parts. Inside the curious huts they found "great stores of fowls hanging by the neck."[4] These they unashamedly pilfered. It was exhilarating to roam on solid ground amid such plenty, to be free for a spell of their close-quartered ship. The men pleaded with Hudson for an additional day or two "so that we might refresh ourselves with sorrel grass and fowl." But he would have none of that — time was passing rapidly and they were on a mission.

The *Discovery* continued following the treeless, barren coastline, with the drifting ice building up. The coastline began to veer south, which Hudson continued to follow. They had left Frobisher's Straite and were passing along another, narrower channel when suddenly they broke onto "a spacious Sea," a vast expanse of water reaching out well over the horizon, a bay of sorts. This gave every promise of being the long-sought gateway to the East. Could this be it? After years of dreaming and three arduous journeys of exploration, Hudson appeared to have triumphed. Days earlier, there had been disgruntlement and harsh words with some declaring that Hudson was lost and on a fool's mission.

Now, the hardships and discomforts suffered along the way seemed not to have been entirely in vain.

They entered the bay on September 29, and very soon the weather began to change appreciably. It was becoming colder with an unpleasant damp chill, and the days were growing shorter — an unexpectedly rapid shifting of season. During one spell of contrary winds, the *Discovery* was forced to lie at anchor for eight tedious days during which time the restless men grew ever more agitated. How much farther did Hudson plan to sail? Did the master really know what he was doing? What were the chances of becoming icebound and having to winter in these barren wilds? Would they survive to see home again?

Hudson, however, was either oblivious to the state of the crew's morale or he simply chose to disregard it. He order a continued passage south, convinced perhaps that a more temperate climate awaited them once they had cleared the bay and found themselves on open ocean waters on their way to the Indies.

By the end of October the *Discovery* had reached the southern limit of James Bay, a sub-bay, as it were, of Hudson Bay, and by continuing to hug the coastline they found themselves slowly moving north with no sign of a passage. Within days the weather turned dramatically — ice formed all about them and heavy snowfalls blanketed the land. By November 10, the ship was firmly frozen in. Having spent three months travelling "in a Labyrinth without end," the crew realized that they would have to spend winter in the bleakness of where they were. "Our master sent out our boat," writes Pricket, "with myselfe and the carpenter to seeke a place to winter in; and it was time, for the nights were long and cold, and the earth covered in snow."

On board they carried nearly a half-year's worth "of that which was good" by way of food. In addition, there had been promise of hunting and fishing (but these results generally proved disappointing). Seven months were to pass before the ice loosened its grip on the imprisoned vessel, and in that time the crew suffered within cloistered quarters from cold and boredom. Few details are known of the conditions under which they lived out their daily lives — Pricket's account offers only scant glimpses. He does, however, give vivid observations of the tensions and discord that prevailed among the men during those dark, grim months, tensions that eventually burgeoned into the mutiny that sealed Hudson's fate.

"About the middle of this month of November died John Williams, our gunner," Pricket wrote. And then he added a gratuitous comment, "God pardon the master's uncharitable dealing with this man." A pointed remark, indeed. What the nature was of Hudson's "uncharitable" behaviour toward the deceased Williams is not known. It is obvious, however, that some sort of falling out had taken place between the two men, just as had previously happened with Juet. (One harks back to Hudson's 1608 voyage, when he felt compelled to issue certificates to every man, an exoneration from possible accusations of mutinous behaviour.)

The Juet demotion was a serious enough affair that created bitterness among some of the crew, but now a fresh fracas caused further divide, one with lasting consequences. And of all things, it began about the dead man's overcoat. It was customary in those days that when a death occurred at sea the belongings of the deceased were distributed by the captain among the crew members as he saw fit. Travelling with Hudson was a certain Henry Greene, not a member of the crew, but a one-time servant in the Hudson household and now a supernumerary who came on board the *Discovery* at the final moment of departure from England, as if an afterthought. We are informed by Pricket that "the young man [was] born in Kent, of worshipful parents, but by his lewd life and conversation he had lost the goodwill of all his friends, and had spent all he had." An unsavoury character, it might seem. The reason Hudson brought him along was that "he could write well" and being literate, he would serve as a back-up chronicler. When time came to dispose of the dead gunner's warm "gray cloth gown" Hudson awarded it to Greene. The garment was coveted by many and having it fall into the hands of a supernumerary was unwarrantable and deeply resented.

On the following day the carpenter decided on a hunting excursion. Since this was polar bear country, Hudson had issued strict orders that every person venturing out must be armed with a musket or pike and that nobody should go out alone. The carpenter accordingly invited Greene to join him which he did, but the man neglected to take along the required weapon; between the two there was but one musket. When the couple returned to the vessel they were met by a furious Hudson who vented his rage on Greene for having openly disobeyed orders. So overwrought was he that he not only withdrew the promise of a wage at the journey's conclusion, but he demanded the return of the overcoat, which he then presented to Robert Bylot, a senior member of the crew. From that moment on the aggrieved Greene took every opportunity to do "the master every mischief he could in seeking to discredit him." Hudson, who had brought Greene into his household and who for years looked after him, had now become a mortal enemy to the supernumerary. In large measure it was he who had Hudson "thrust out of the ship in the end." Pricket concludes this vignette by saying that it "would be too tedious" to go on with it, given the company's uncertain and terrifying circumstances, and he drops the subject. Conditions on board the *Discovery* at the time were indeed appalling: the ship was being squeezed terrifyingly on all sides by ice floes; gusting snow blanketed everything; cold "lamed most of the men"; restlessness and discord permeated the vessel, and cabin fever set in.

Yet in all the misery surrounding them, "mercifully God dealt with us at this time" for the hunting proved excellent, at first. During the first three months over a thousand partridges and ptarmigans were brought to the table, as well as copious quantities of fish. Once "they went, caught five hundred fish, as big as good herrings and some trout," but birds became scarce. With the passing of time, the fishing and hunting became less rewarding. On one three-day expedition, for example, "the men brought back only four score small fish, a poore reliefe for so many hungry bellies." By early spring the ship's larder had become alarmingly reduced and food had to be rationed. The nearly depleted supply of bread and cheese was particularly strong-felt, both important daily staples. There finally came a point when Hudson ordered all the remaining bread be brought to the upper deck. With the entire crew assembled about him, he distributed equally what there was among the men, a pound per man, "and he wept when he gave it to them."

By early June the warm sun had loosened the *Discovery* appreciably from its prolonged confinement and finally with concerted effort by all on board the vessel was freed. Seven idle months had passed and at long last the ship's sails were unfurled and it "stood out of our wintering place." They found themselves once more "in the sea," re-entering Hudson Bay from James Bay. "Our bread being gone," Pricket wrote, "the store of cheese was to stop a gap." The divided bread of a few days earlier had been rapidly consumed — the boatswain eagerly consumed his entire ration within the day, becoming violently ill as a result. Faced with a crew of starving men, Hudson ordered the remaining cheeses be brought up. To the dismay of the men, only five cheeses were produced when they had reckoned nine remained in stock. Hudson carved the five rounds into portions, judiciously presenting each man with equal parts of the best-preserved sections and of the moldy parts, three and a half pounds per man, the equivalent of a seven-day ration under normal circumstance.

Four days later the drama of the mutiny began to unfold. On the night of the 21st, Pricket was awoken in his cabin by Henry Greene and Boatswain Wilson who came to inform him that they, with others, planned to get rid of Hudson, together with those who were sick. They intended to place them aboard the shallop and "let them shift for themselves."[5] Even under strictest rationing, they argued, there remained but fourteen days of food for the entire complement. The sick ones wouldn't survive in any case. As for the master, they understood that he intended to resume the search for the passage, and had no plans of an early return home. Here they were in these ice-filled waters, with him "not caring to go one way or other," and threatened with having to pass another winter in this godforsaken land. It was beyond the pale and enough was enough. They had "not eaten anything these three days, and were resolute … what they had begun they would go through with or die."

The shocked Pricket tried to persuade the two that what they were planning was sheer madness. By committing "so foul a thing in the sight of God and man as this would be," they were embracing the hangman, to which Greene retorted "he would rather be hanged at home than starve abroad." Greene tried unsuccessfully to convince Pricket to join their group, but he would have none of that. "I came into the ship not to forsake her," he rejoined, "nor yet to hurt myself and others by any such deed." Greene then, having threatened Pricket that he might well find himself sharing Hudson's fate, went off in "a rage, swearing to cut the throat of any who tried to thwart him." Wilson remained behind and Pricket tried in vain to persuade him in abandoning the outrageous scheme, but the sailor was determined "to go on with the action while it was hot."

Juet then came to Pricket, but he too could not be dissuaded — "he was worse than Henry Greene for he swore plainly that he would justifie this deed when he came home." Four others, "birds of a feather," also visited with Pricket, who in the course of discussion finally demanded whether they were truly "well advised what they had taken in hand. They answered, they were, and therefore came to take their oath."

What unfolded next is told simply, without flourish or editorial comment. Close to daybreak, Pricket went below to fill a teakettle and as he did so someone slammed shut the hatch behind him. On the deck above Henry Greene, the carpenter Staffe, and one other chatted idly in anticipation of Hudson appearing on deck. When Hudson exited his cabin, Wilson jumped him from behind, pinioned him, and bound his arms with rope. Hudson demanded what this was all about, and was informed that "he should know when he was in the shallop."

The smaller vessel was brought to the ship's side and "sicke and lame were hauled" from their quarters, gathered together and placed within it. Staffe at this point demurred and challenged the mutineers by demanding whether they realized that they might be hanged on returning home. He then declared that he would have no part of the appalling affair, to which he was invited to take a place in the shallop. The carpenter agreed on the condition that his chest of instruments be placed with him, and this being done he boarded the little boat. As the sick were being brought from their cabins, a squabble broke out among the rebels, two of whom suddenly realized that each had a close friend among those appearing on deck. They objected to the selections, insisting that their pals be spared. Greene overruled the protest, heated words were exchanged, but finally the two men had their way and their friends were spared.

Henry Hudson, one-time commander of the *Hopewell*, the *Half Moon*, and the *Discovery*, now found himself in command of his ship's tiny open boat of not more than twenty-six feet, accompanied by his young son, the carpenter, and six semi-invalids. In addition to his carpentry tools, Staffe was successful in persuading the mutineers to provide a musket with powder and shot, some pikes, an iron pot, a quantity of meal, and a few other items. With the shallop in tow, the *Discovery* stood out of the ice and when it came to clear waters the towline was severed and course set for the East.

With the shallop adrift and fading farther and farther away, those remaining set about searching and ransacking the *Discovery* — "they acted as though the Ship had been entered by force, and they had free leave to pillage it." In the course of the looting they uncovered in the main hold a surprising store of secreted food: a container of meal, two casks of butter, twenty-seven pieces of pork, and a half bushel of peas. In Hudson's cabin they discovered two hundred biscuit cakes, a goodly quantity of meal, and "beere to the quantitie of a butt [approx. 110 gallons]."

While this frenzy was unfolding, Hudson's shallop, under a jerry-rigged sail, had steadily closed in on the mother ship. As soon as the lookout spotted this, they "let fall the main sail and broke out the topsails, and then let fly as from an enemy." It wasn't long that the little vessel was once more falling back, eventually becoming a speck on the horizon. It then disappeared from sight, and with that Hudson and his companions vanished from the pages of history.

What fate these individuals met is a matter of conjecture; nothing was heard of them again. Some have it that their boat may have reached one of the islands of lower James Bay or perhaps even the mainland, but there is no hard evidence of such. The suffering these men endured can only be imagined — their physical deprivations and hardships and equally their mental agonies. Perched on a thwart with young John at his feet, Hudson coped as well as he could with the inadequate sails, all the while observing the *Discovery* drawing farther and farther away and finally dipping beneath the horizon. What might have gone through his mind? Anger at the turn of events, particularly at the traitorous Greene? Despair at their impossible situation? Or visions perhaps of his family back home, of his younger sons, Richard and Oliver? Possibly regrets over his obsession regarding a quick route to the East?

It had all come to naught. Four arduous years had been given over to the quest and Hudson had failed, succumbing, if you will, to his own ego. Through his carelessness he and the rest found themselves in the fatal embrace of the Arctic. One wonders how it was that Greene, the supernumerary unlisted in the roster of crew, commanded such a leading role in the developing event. The authenticity of Pricket's account is also open to question. He was the "star witness" to the drama and it is entirely possible that embellishments crept into his narrative in order to exculpate himself. On the return of the *Discovery* to Britain, the survivors were questioned by the authorities, but only one mutineer's disposition taken. The Admiralty, it seemed, was in no hurry to deal with the matter, and five years passed before the recording of other dispositions, by which time some of those involved had died and memories of others had become clouded. In 1618. the surviving mutineers were brought before the High Court of the Admiralty on the charge of murder — all were acquitted. Had the charge of mutiny been laid, most certainly the accused would have been convicted and hanged. Closure was thus clumsily brought to one of the Arctic's most poignant chapters in her history.

5

A Dane at Hudson Bay

HENRY HUDSON'S APPALLING end brought a premature close to his career and one wonders where the winds might have carried this venturesome, single-minded sailor had he survived the mutiny. The crowning pieces of his legacy are the exploration of the lower reaches of New York and the claiming of "*Manna-hata*" for the Dutch, who in short order established a colony at the island's southern tip. The other noteworthy achievement, of course, was the penetration of Hudson Strait and the discovery and exploration of the vast bay that bears his name.

Hudson Bay is considered part of the Arctic Ocean and its shores, in terms of climate and vegetation, are sub-Arctic. It is the world's second-largest bay (Bengal is the first), stretching north–south over eight hundred miles and over six hundred miles east–west. In reality it is an inland sea, one that penetrates deeply into Canada and provides the country with its east–west divide. Sixty major rivers flow into it, emptying an astonishing mean average of 8,163,000 U.S. gallons of fresh water *every second*. The labyrinth of rivers and streams defining the bay's watershed spreads not only over four Canadian provinces and one territory, but stretches far into the American mid-west — Montana, Minnesota, and the Dakotas.

The voyage of the *Discovery* took it along the bay's east coast and into the southern reaches of James Bay. It was left to an extraordinary sailor, Norwegian by birth, but sailing for the Danish, Jens Eriksen Munk, to reach the west side. His personal story is one of the more compelling ones of early Arctic exploration and his escapades and exploits in that part of the globe and elsewhere are epic. By the time he reached twenty-five years of age it might seem that he had already lived the full lives of two men. Insofar as the Arctic is concerned the crux of Munk's adventures took place in the dreadful winter of 1619–20, which he spent at what is now Churchill, Manitoba, nine years after Hudson's foray. He arrived there on two fine ships and with sixty-five men, but returned home on one crippled vessel with four men.

Munk's childhood was a fatherless one, for his father languished in a Danish jail having fallen out of the king's favour. Jens left home at age twelve and somehow made his way to Oporto, Portugal, where he secured a position in a prosperous shipping firm. By the end of that year he took to the ocean waves from which he never parted, continuing to sail until his death at age forty-eight. He put out to sea as a cabin boy on board a Dutch vessel in a small convoy bound for South America. French pirates ruthlessly assailed the ships off the coast of Brazil, and as the vessels were being ransacked Jens and the survivors clung to wreckage in shark-infested waters. A French warship happened by and hauled on board what few men remained alive. But it did them no further favours; they were deposited on an untamed coastline where most perished from starvation, disease, or Indian attack. Jens somehow managed to reach civilization and safety — one of the seven survivors of that convoy. The boy remained in Brazil for six years and then under dramatic circumstances made his way home to Copenhagen where he embarked on a career of a seafaring tradesman. (One incident of that chapter of his life saw him brazenly swimming across a Brazilian harbour to warn his Dutch compatriots of an impending attack by Spaniards).

By age twenty-four, Munk was in command of his own ship and busying himself in a number of diverse endeavours — establishing the first Danish whaling station at Spitzbergen; trading with the natives of the Barents Sea; successfully attacking a Swedish fortress near Göteborg; and capturing the notorious Spanish pirate Jose Mendoza off the mouth of the White Sea.

Denmark at the time was ruled by the mercantilist King Christian IV, who early in his reign initiated a policy of overseas expansion. The Northwest Passage was of particular interest to him. In 1619 he commissioned Munk to continue the search and two ships, the frigate *Enhiörningen* (*Unicorn*) and the sloop *Lamprenen* (*Lamprey*), were placed under his command. They sailed out on May 9 under inauspicious circumstances for within a couple of days one of the crew committed suicide by throwing himself overboard and drowning — an ill omen indeed. By late June they had passed the Shetlands and Greenland and were encountering "such fog and great cold that icicles a quarter's length [eighteen inches] hung in the rigging so that none of the men could protect themselves from the cold."[1] Their progress was retarded by a series of storms and by a costly miscalculation of the chief navigator who at one point brought the vessels deep into Frobisher Bay in the mistaken belief that it was Hudson Bay. The navigator finally got it right and the correct entrance was eventually reached. Over three months had passed since the ships quit Copenhagen with time being lost in battling adverse weather and dealing with the navigational error.

Hudson Bay was reached at the end of August, "so great and hallow a sea, as neither I nor any other being on board had ever seen." Munk renamed it *Novum Marum* and then proceeded to sail directly across to the west side according to the king's precise instructions to seek out the illusive entrance to the passage. On his eventual return home, Munk published a memoir of his astonishing experience entitled *Navigo Septenfrrionalis: that is Relation or Description of a Voyage in Search of the North-West Passage* (the full title runs 166 words), in which he offers striking snapshots of the manner in which the year was spent in North America.

The first days on the western side were spent in comparative comfort despite the cold, but the remainder of the stay is a horrific tale of endurance. On the night of September 10, Munk wrote, "there was such a terrible snowstorm and gale that nothing could be done." It was clear that winter was fast approaching and that further sailing would be overwhelmingly difficult if not impossible. The decision was taken to suspend further exploration and to seek refuge along the least exposed bit of shoreline. On the 13th the ship's boat was sent out "to examine what

A contemporary drawing from Munk's narrative, published in 1624, showing the Dane's two ships at the mouth of the Churchill River, Hudson Bay. After spending a disastrous winter at the spot, Munk and two others eventually returned home, the sole survivors of the sixty-five-person expedition.

accommodation the land afforded and whether there were any better harbors there than the one we were in," but since none was found, Munk decided to sail no farther. They would remain where they were to wait out the winter. Orders were given to beach the *Lamprenen*, and the sloop was brought ashore, "By means of high tide, I caused the ship's keel to be dug down into the ground, and [to anchor it firmly] branches of trees to be spread under the bilge, packed together with clay and sand." The docking was subsequently reinforced and protective breakwaters erected against intruding ice. The heavy *Enhiörningen*, however, remained afloat just off shore and soon became firmly ice-locked. Thus they settled in.

Munk ordered "a part of [the *Lamprenen's*] goods to be brought ashore in order that the deck might be clear and the men have more space to move about." In the interest of fuel economy, the crew of one ship was ordered to take meals on board the other. "Clothes, shirts, shoes, and boots and whatever else could be of use as a protection against the cold" were distributed among the crew, and "two large fireplaces, round each of which 20 men might easily sit" were arranged on the deck. Rations of wine were distributed daily, "but beer they were allowed to drink according to their want, as much as every man himself liked." A routine was put into place "for keeping a watch, the fetching of wood, and burning of charcoal, as well as with regard to whose duty it was to be during the day to melt snow into water; so that everybody knew what he was to do, and how to conduct himself."

In addition to trapping wild game, parties went out in early days to "the open country for shooting, because there was plenty of ptarmigan and hares, as well as all kinds of birds, as long as the snow was not too deep … and [in fine weather] they never went ashore but they carried home something good." On one exploration of the neighbouring countryside evidence was found of "where people had been and had their summer abodes … in many places, great heaps of chips, where they have cut wood or timber, and the chips looked like they had been cut off with curved iron tools." A peculiar construction of four flat stones was discovered with pieces of charcoal scattered about, which lead to the conclusion that it must have been a small altar of sorts which "had been used for idolatrous worship; and, if that is so, it is to be wished that these poor blinded pagans might come to the profession of the true Christian Faith."

Weeks passed and living conditions began to deteriorate. On November 27 "there was a very sharp frost by which all the glass bottles we had (which contained all kinds of precious materials) were broken to pieces." On the previous evening, Munk records in passing, "a sailor who had been long been ill was buried" — the expedition's first death. November 30 was St. Martin's Eve and "the men shot some ptarmigan, with which we had to content ourselves instead of St. Martin's goose; and I ordered a pint of Spanish wine for each bowl to be given to the men, besides their daily allowance; wherewith the whole crew were well satisfied, even merry and joyful. Of the ship's beer there was given them as much as they liked." Munk offers a telling explanation of why he permitted such a liberal distribution of alcohol. "Because the common people, after all, are so disposed that whatever is most strongly forbidden them, they, notwithstanding, are most apt to do on the sly, without considering whether it be beneficial or harmful to them."

By this time the waters surrounding the *Enhiörningen* were frozen solid, many feet thick. Farther out, drift-ice from the many surrounding streams and rivers floated about, buffeted about by strong winds, creating "large masses rising quite twenty fathoms above water [sixty feet]; and some such masses of ice which I myself have had examined, stood firm on the sea-bottom in more than 40 fathoms [120 feet], which perhaps may seem incredible, but nevertheless is so in truth." On December 12 the ship's surgeon from the *Lamprenen* died and "his corpse had to remain on deck for two days because the frost was so very severe that nobody could get out to bury it."

Christmas was "celebrated and observed solemnly, as a Christian's duty is. We had a sermon and Mass; and after the sermon, we gave the priest an offertory, according to ancient custom, each in proportion to his means. There was not much money among us, but they gave what they had. Some of them gave white fox-skins so that the priest got enough wherewith to line a coat. However, sufficiently long life to wear it was not granted to him."

New Year's Day 1620 was had in good form. "The weather was mild ... the men practiced all sorts of games ... the crew, most of whom were at that time in good health, consequently had all sorts of larks and pastimes, and thus we spent the Holy Days with merriment ..." Within a fortnight, however, the lives of the stranded men took a sharp turn. First, the priest and *Enhiörningen*'s surgeon "took to their beds ... and after that, violent sickness commenced amongst the men." Soon those two died along with the cook, as a result of dysentery. Before the surgeon's death, Munk asked for whatever remedies he~~may~~ *might* have, to which the dying man replied that he had tried everything "to the best of his ability and as seemed to him advisable, and that if God would not help, he could not employ any further remedy at all that would be useful for recovery."

Winter firmly enveloped the party, bringing blinding snowstorms and severe cold. Game had become scarce — the pathetic notation for February 12 read: "We caught two ptarmigan, which was very useful for the use of the sick." In the days that followed, "there was nothing but sickness and weakness, and every day the number of sick was continually increased, so that on this day there were only seven persons in health that could fetch wood and water." A seaman died "who had been ill the whole voyage, and one may truly say he was so dirty in his habits as an untrained beast" — the poor fellow's inability to control bloody bowel discharge. On the 17th, two more died "and, of the crew, there had then already died twenty persons. On that day, we got a hare, which was very welcome."

As weeks passed, days grew longer and with the increased sunshine, the weather seemed slowly to change for the better, although "the frost continued very hard." The numbers of sick continued to grow, as did the death rate. In one hunting foray, "we caught five ptarmigan in the open country, which were very welcome to us. I ordered broth to be made of them, and had that distributed among the men; but, of the meat, they could eat nothing, because their mouths being badly affected by scurvy." This dread disease was the grim bane of sailors at sea, a sickness that developed through a dietary deficiency of Vitamin C. The remedy for its prevention was uncovered a century after Munk's voyages — a daily consumption of citrus fruit. Samuel de Champlain offered a horrific description of scurvy in a 1613 writing:

> There developed in the mouths of those who had it, large pieces of excess fungus which caused great rot. This increased to such a degree that they could hardly eat anything except in very liquid form. Their teeth barely held in place, and could be removed with the fingers without causing pain. This excess flesh was often cut away, which caused them to bleed extensively from the mouth. Afterwards, severe pain developed in the arms and legs. They could not walk due to the tightness of the nerves. Consequently, they had no strength and suffered unbearable pain. They also had severe cramps of the loins, stomach and bowels, together with a very bad cough and shortness of breath. Unfortunately, we could find no remedy with which to cure these symptoms.[3]

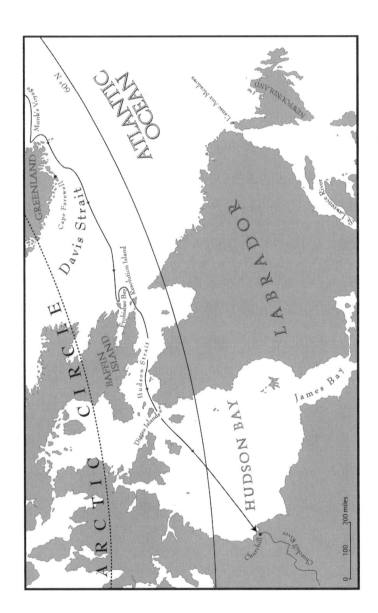

Following up on Henry Hudson's expedition, Danish naval officer Jens Munk continued the search for the gateway to the Northwest Passage. Taking much the same route as the earlier explorer, he wintered on the bay's west side at the mouth of the Churchill River.

Map by Cameron McLeod Jones

Munk's entries for the ensuing weeks dwelled almost entirely on the spread of sickness and incidences of death — "now and afterwards, the sickness raged more violently every day, so that we who were still left suffered great trouble before we could get the dead buried." On March 24, the first open water was spotted in what before had been a solidly frozen inlet. Berries began to appear on the bushes — "they were very welcome, and did not disagree with [the men]." In desperation, Munk searched the deceased surgeon's medicine chest for "I had now to do the best I could myself." He found a disordered array of bottles with no indication which was for what use. "I am certain and would venture my life," he wrote, "that there were many kinds of medicaments in the surgeon's chest which … he did not know for what purpose, and in what way they were to be employed; because their names were in Latin … and whenever he was going to examine an bottle or box, the priest had to read the description out for him."

April 3: "It was a fearfully sharp frost, so that none of us could uncover himself for cold. Nor had I not anybody to command, for they were lying under the hand of God, so that there was great misery and sorrow." Those who remained on their feet were now insufficiently "strong enough to go into the forest to fetch wood and fuel. We were obliged during those days to collect everything that was in the ship and would serve for fuel; when that was consumed, we were obliged to take our shallop for fuel." On Easter Day, Munk made his first indication of personal despair: "I was then quite miserable and abandoned by all the world, as everybody may imagine." And, some days later: "not a man left his berth save myself and the under-cook who could still do a little." By May 10, only eleven of the *Lamprenen*'s crew remained alive, and within the fortnight there were only "seven miserable persons who were still lying there alive, looked mournfully at each other, hoping every day that the snow would thaw and the ice drift away."

June 4 found Munk giving up all hope:

> There remained alive only three beside myself, all lying down unable to help one another. The stomach was ready enough and had appetite for food, but the teeth would not allow it. Not one of us had the requisite

strength for going into the hold to fetch us a drink of wine. The cook's boy lay dead by my berth, and three men on the steerage. Two men were on shore and would gladly have been back on the ship, but it was impossible for them to get there as they had not sufficient strength in their limbs to help themselves on board, so that both they and I were lying quite exhausted, as we had now for four entire days eaten nothing for the sustenance of body. Accordingly, I did now hope for anything but that God would put an end to this misery and take me for Himself and His Kingdom.

He prepared for death by writing the following poignant letter:

Inasmuch as I have no more hope of life in this world, I request for the sake of God, if any Christian men should happen to come by here, that they will bury in the earth my poor body together with the others are found here, expecting their rewards from God in Heaven; and, furthermore that this my journal may be forwarded to my most gracious Lord and King (for every word that is found therein is altogether truthful) in order that my poor wife and children may obtain some benefit from my great distress and miserable death. Herewith, good-night to all the world; and my soul into the hands of God, etc

Jens Munk

Four days later the overpowering "smell and stench of the dead bodies" permeated Munk's cabin so badly that he "managed to get out of the berth as best I could" and force himself out of the cabin — "I spent that night on the deck, using the clothes of the dead." On the next morning "when the two men who were ashore saw me and perceived that I was still alive — I, on my part, had thought that they were dead long ago

— they came out on the ice to the ship and assisted me in getting down from the ship to the land, together with the clothes I threw to them." The *Lamprenen* had been beached some seventy feet from shore, which distance they crawled and found cover under a nearby bush. Fire was made and nearby they discovered some "greens growing out of the ground," which roots they sucked — "as with the warmth now commenced to increase nicely, we began to recover."

More days passed and as the offshore ice began to break up, schools of fish were spotted. A makeshift weir was set and on the first try, "God gave us six large trout which I cooked myself, while the two others went on board the *Lamprenen*, to fetch wine, which we had not tasted for a long time, none of us having an appetite for it." Since scurvy had loosened their teeth, they were unable to chew the flesh, so instead they made a thick broth of the catch. Shortly afterwards they "got a gun on shore and shot birds, from which we obtained much refreshment; so that, day by day, we got stronger and fairly well in health." Three weeks had passed since Munk wrote his last testament and in that brief period he and his few companions made remarkable progress in the recovery of health. So much so that it was decided to prepare for an attempt to return home.

June 26 proved arduous for the men:

> In the name of Jesus, and after prayer and supplication to God for good fortune and counsel, we now set to work to bring the *Lamprenen* alongside *Enhiörningen* and worked as diligently as we could in getting sails ready for us. But therein we encountered a great difficulty and much anxiety, because the *Lamprenen* stood high on the shore, having been carried up by the winter flood. We were consequently obliged first to unload all that was in her, and then look out for a high spring tide in order to haul her out. In this we succeeded, and brought her alongside the *Enhiörningen*. When we got on board the *Enhiömingen*, we were obliged first to throw overboard the dead bodies, which were then quite decomposed, as we could not move about or do anything there for had

smell and stench, and yet were under the necessity of taking the *Enhiörningen* and placing on board *Lamprenen*
victuals and other necessities for our use in crossing the
sea, as far as we three persons could manage.

For three weeks the small group toiled in the preparations for sailing.
On the afternoon of Sunday, July 16, after prayers in the morning, sails
were set and the *Lamprenen* moved out slowly from its winter imprisonment into the bay's relatively open waters. Initial progress was slow
because of the incessant ice floes. In addition, gales were encountered
and then fogs, and the rudder was once broken by jagged ice and had
to be repaired. A month later they found themselves hugging the north
coast of Hudson Strait, making their way east under favourable winds
at a rate of twenty-five to thirty miles a day. On September 11, "towards
night a gale sprang up and our foresail was torn from the bolt-line, so
that we three men had plenty to do to get it in, and then the ship was
half full of water." Three days later they passed the Orkneys and on the
20th Norway was sighted. Five days later the sloop sailed into Bergen; it
"had returned into a Christian country. We poor men could not hold our
tears for great joy, and thanked God that He had graciously granted us
this happiness."

Munk closed his journal by thanking God for his safe delivery home:
"… Thou hast saved me from icebergs in dreadful storms.… Thou has led
me out of anxiety, disease and sickness.… Thou wast my highest pilot,
counselor, guide and compass …" And then he quotes Isaiah 43: 2–3:

> *Fear not, for I have redeemed thee … When thou passest*
> *through*
> *the waters, I will be with thee, that the rivers shall not*
> *drown thee.*

A hundred years later James Knight, an official of the Hudson's Bay
Company, arrived to the area of Munk's wintering to establish a trading post. He selected for the site the same "high ground" at the mouth

of the Churchill River used by the earlier explorer to bury many of his dead. Traces of the tragic Danish expedition remained, but nothing was left of the *Enhiörningen*. Prior to sailing for home, Munk had effectively scuttled the vessel by walking out to it at low tide and drilling three major holes into the hull. He had hoped that high-tide water pouring through the cavities would anchor the vessel firmly to the ground sufficiently to prevent winter ice from moving it. The result of his efforts was quite the opposite — the water in the hold froze solidly and the ship splintered apart, with pieces being carried out to sea. Knight reported that:

> [I]t is a poor and miserable spot ... for here is neither fish, fowl, nor game. Given time it will, I believe, prove advantageous for the Company, but it will never be good for those of its servants who must live here. We are compelled to build in a place where we cannot keep ourselves warm, for there is only lee on a sixth of the compass. Yet can I find no better place. The many graves and bones from the folk who lie buried here are a revelation of that which awaits us if we do not lay in supplies before the winter sets in. For although they were Danes and very hardy people, almost 130 [*sic*] of them lie buried here, and a great part of their graves lie under our building. I pray that the Lord may protect and preserve us.

King Christian, disappointed as he no doubt was with the inconclusive results of Munk's expedition, determined to give it another try, and the spirited explorer was ordered in 1621 to prepare for a fresh expedition. Work began on the outfitting of new vessels, but the effort was soon aborted for an inability to gather a willing crew. Tales of the initial expedition had been sensationally circulated, and sailors were simply scared off — no way would anyone hazard a repeat of such misadventure.

A grim misadventure it certainly had been and the unparalleled tale of death is unlike any other in the history of Arctic exploration. Munk may rightly be accused of having given insufficient care to the provisioning and supply of his expedition. It must be noted, however, that the intelligence available to him on the western Arctic was scant and often fanciful. As for scurvy, virtually nothing at the time was known of the dread disease. Munk cannot be faulted for ineptitude or incompetence of the sort displayed by Willoughby or Hudson. Although his journey of exploration to Hudson Bay was void of tangible results, it is a notable story of endurance, fortitude, and skill.

That Munk failed to enlist sailors for a fresh expedition for reasons of fear is one thing, but there was more to it than that. Europe at the time had just plunged itself into the Thirty Years' War, one of the most destructive conflicts in its history. The war raged from France to Hungary, from Sweden to Transylvania. Denmark became enmeshed and Munk found himself putting out to sea on an altogether different mission. Protestant King Christian ordered him into battle against the Catholic navies of the Holy Roman Empire. Among his more notable achievements in that struggle was a successful blockade of the Weser River in the North Sea and attacks on German troops in the Baltic. In 1625 he was promoted to admiral and three years later he died, in all probability from a battle wound. (One alternative account has it that his death was caused by a blow allegedly suffered at the hands of the king, who in the course of a dispute furiously lashed out at him with a stick.)

At about the time that Munk was suffering through his winter at Churchill, William Baffin was leading an expedition into more northerly reaches of the Canadian Arctic. The celebrated navigator had once been in the employ of the Muscovy Company, serving on expeditions to Greenland and Spitzbergen. He possessed an uncanny skill in calculating latitude, and it was he who first recorded longitude by using lunar observations. The North West Company had made three unsuccessful attempts at uncovering the fabled passage west, but despite its failures it was prepared to launch yet another try. Henry Hudson's *Discovery* was refitted and Baffin was engaged to lead the fresh expedition jointly with Hudson's former shipmate, Robert Bylot, as the ship's captain. A small crew of sixteen men and two boys was gathered and the little vessel set off from London on April 16, 1615. A month later the *Discovery* found itself off Resolution Island at the entrance to Hudson Strait. Along the way Baffin recorded, "We sayled through many great islands of ice,"[4] which he described as being over two hundred feet high with one at 240 feet. He then calculated that the visible part of the iceberg was only one-eighth of the whole with the bulk spreading beneath the waters.

At this juncture, disagreement was had regarding which direction to proceed. Bylot wished to advance up the strait to explore the regions north of Hudson Bay, while Baffin urged a sail directly north, up Davis Strait past Frobisher Bay, and onward. Bylot prevailed and the *Discovery* began its journey west, retracing Hudson's earlier path. It was slow going, what with the ice packs, storms, and vicious currents; it took three weeks to cover a distance of sixty miles.

Anchoring off one of the Savage Islands, they heard the barking of dogs. Baffin went ashore with some men and found a small cluster of primitive tent-like shelters outside of which were tethered over thirty dogs "about the bigness of our mongrel mastiffs looking most like wolves." The camp had obviously been abandoned in haste. Baffin continued:

> When finding no people, we went to the top of the hill where we saw one great cannoo, or boat, having about fourteen persons in it ... being from us somewhat above a musket shott away. I called them (using some words of Greenlandish speech) making signes of friendship. They did the like to us, but seeing them to be fearfull of us, and we did not willing to trust them, I made another signe to them, showing a knife and other small things which I left at the top of the hill, and returned down to their tents agayne.

The five tents were made of sealskins and in searching through them they found, among other things, fourteen whale fins which they took, leaving in return some knives and beads. They also discovered in "a small leather bag a company of little images of men and one the image of a woman with a child on her back all of which I brought along" — the first recorded reference to Inuit art. The encounter — rather the non-encounter — with natives clearly showed that the Inuit had learned to exercise caution in any potential exchange with Europeans.

On the following day, the *Discovery* weighed anchor and continued on its sail west. By July 8, it had come to Foxe Basin, the large, shallow body of water north of Hudson Bay, which is rarely free of ice. The hollowing winds and severe currents of the area discouraged further exploration in those parts, and having decided that they were not on the track of the passage, they turned about and headed for home, reaching Plymouth on September 8.

Baffin completed his account of this, his first voyage into the Canadian Arctic by stating, "And now it may be that some expect I should give my opynion concerning the passage. To these my answer must be, that doubtless there is a passage. But within this strayte, called Hundson's Straytes, I am doubtfull … but whether there be or no, I will not affirm."

It was an inconclusive expedition, and no doubt as disappointing to those who financed it as it was to Baffin and Bylot. Whatever the regret, the principles of the North West Company remained resolute and the following year they sent off the same two men once more, but this time their path was pre-determined. According to specific written instructions, they were to follow Greenland's west coast and try to reach 80°N, at which point they were to turn west and move "so far southerly that you may touch the north part of Japan." On March 26, 1616, the *Discovery* put out from London on its mission.

They arrived off Greenland in late May and began to follow the coastline. At 75°45' N they came upon a small Inuit enclave inhabiting a group of islands at a distance from shore. As soon as the natives spotted the ship, they fled, but with the Englishmen making every sort of friendly sign they soon returned. Very quickly, gifts were being exchanged — objects of iron "which they highly esteeme" for sealskins, seal meat, and blubber. Baffin took pains in describing the people, their tents, clothing, and hunting equipment. Some vignettes: the women "are marked in their face with diverse black strokes or lines, the skin being raised with some sharpe instrument when they were young, and black color put therein." Regarding Inuit religion, "I can little say, only they have a kind of worship or adoration of the sunne, which continually they will point onto and strike their hand on their breast, crying 'Ilyout." On their funerary custom: "Their dead they burie on the side of hills where they live making a pile of stones over them, yet not so close but that wee might see the dead body, the aire being so piercing that it keepeth them from stinking savour."

The *Discovery* moved on after a few days at the islands. Battling the inevitable ice floes, currents, and storms, it arrived on July 5 at the head of Baffin Bay to a narrow body of water, the mouth of Smith Sound. Here they not only encountered massive blocks of ice, but they were whipped by a storm "so vehement that it blew away our fourcourse [foresail], and ... wee lay adrift till about eight a clock." Refuge was attempted in a cove, but the force of the wind broke the cable and the anchor was lost. A dead end had been reached and nothing remained but to return back, this time following the coastline of adjacent Ellesmere Island. Disappointed as Baffin may have been in not reaching the targeted 80°N, he had come marginally close to it: 77°45' N, further north by 300 miles than Davis had thirty years earlier — a new record that was to remain unbroken for over two hundred years.

As the *Discovery* progressed south, it prodded — as well as conditions permitted — every sound along the way, the most promising of which was the ice-clogged Lancaster Sound. It was at that point that Baffin first expressed a doubt on the existence of the fabled Northwest Passage. "Here our hope of passage began to be less," he wrote. (Poor Baffin: nearly three centuries later Roald Amundsen the Norwegian explorer, completed the first successful navigation of the long-sought waterway, which he entered through Lancaster Sound). Baffin's expedition returned home empty-handed once more. He was, however, able to inform his principals of the existence of vast herds of whales in the upper reaches of Baffin Bay, but, he warned, accessibility to those parts was possible only in the month of July.

In those early forays into the eastern Arctic, it was the London merchants who were the principals and their motive, pure and simple, was profit. The captains and crews who carried them out were opportunists cum visionaries eager to make a name for themselves, to find favour with their monarchs and, of course, to receive suitable rewards. By 1630, English interest in providing further venture capital into continued exploration had all but died, particularly after Baffin's opinion that the passage did not exist — "when we coasted the land so far to the southward, hope of passage was none." At the time, the continent was well enmeshed in the Thirty Years' War and monarchs had no time for overseas exploration. Nevertheless, two Englishmen independent of each another did meet success persuading investors for a final try. The Bristol Society of Merchant Adventurers agreed to outfit a ship for Thomas James, while a second consortium of merchants sponsored Luke Foxe. Neither was aware of the other, and in Spring 1631, they set out from different ports within five days of one another in similarly sized ships each carrying crews of twenty men and two boys.

Both captains entered Hudson Bay and explored various west coast coves and straits, but, as with the earlier expeditions, no trace was found of a route to Cathay. Imagine, however, their utter astonishment when in mid-July, near the top of James Bay, the two ships spotted each other at a distance, sails billowing, and fast approaching one another. Amid much excitement, enthusiastic greetings were exchanged by the crews and James invited Foxe to dine on board his vessel. "I was well entertained and feasted by Captaine James with varieties of such cheer his sea provisions could afford,"[5] writes Foxe in his memoir. But he quickly moved to find fault with his host's seamanship, stating, "That Gentleman could discourse of Arte, as observations, calculations and the like, and showed me many instruments, but when I found that he was no Seaman, I did blame those very much who counseled him to make choice of that ship for a voyage of such importance." During the meeting, James informed his guest that "he was going to the Emperor of Japan with letters from his

Majestie." Since no such munificence had fallen to Foxe, possibly it was a touch of jealousy that prompted the unflattering comments regarding the other's seamanship.

After wintering in the Arctic the men returned home, each met by disenchanted investors. James had essentially sailed charted ground, while Foxe managed only to penetrate Foxe Basin; nothing substantial had been achieved. Both men left behind rich accounts of their travels and each confirmed Baffin's contention that the Northwest Passage through the eastern Arctic simply did not exist.

6

Russians in the Arctic

IN THE LATE SEVENTEENTH century, Peter the Great burst onto the Russian stage, all six-foot-eight of him, a man of boundless energy, burning intellectual curiosity, and unfettered ambition. His first order of business was to open a "window to the west" in order to drag his parochial and unwilling people into the world outside their country. But he was equally set on expanding and consolidating his empire; a push into Siberia and the Pacific was of no less importance than looking to Western Europe. Like the double-headed eagle of the Russian coat of arms, Peter gazed east and west simultaneously. The prospect of a Northeast Passage particularly intrigued him, a sea lane that would connect his Russia with China. What a splendid avenue it would be for the expansion and consolidation of the empire and for further developing the lucrative fur trade.

Early in his forty-three-year reign, the young tsar travelled to Western Europe, and when in England, in 1698, he met and took a liking to William Penn, an eccentric Quaker who some years earlier had received the proprietary rights to the colony of Pennsylvania. The two men, communicating in the Dutch language, met on several occasions and got along famously. As discussions one evening turned to geography, Penn challenged Peter to determine once and for all whether Eurasia was connected to North America, a tantalizing, unresolved question that continued to challenge the scientific world.

A quarter century later, after years of warfare and frenetic empire-building and transformation, Peter set out to meet that challenge. If the landmasses were unconnected, a way might be found to the Northern Sea Route from the Pacific end. On the recommendation of the relatively new Ministry of Marine, he found the person who might lead such an exploration, the forty-four-year old Vitus Bering, a trusted Danish officer serving as a captain in the Russian Navy. Bering had at one time sailed for the Dutch East India Company and was reputed to be an excellent seaman. A stern, plodding individual, he did not shirk responsibility; he did what he was ordered, but rarely ventured beyond those bounds. The Dane, as Professor Neatby puts it in *Discovery in Russian and Siberian Waters*, "was a brave and experienced mariner who executed his orders with all the thoroughness and exactness which conditions permitted but without any imaginative overtones."[1] Inquisitiveness seems not to have been his forte, and he is judged as having lacked the sort of zealousness that impelled committed explorers to push limits.

In February 1725, Peter commissioned the Dane to proceed to Kamchatka, the huge Siberian peninsula lying northeast of Japan, there to build a vessel and thence to sail north into the Arctic. If anyone could ascertain whether a physical connection existed between Siberia and North America, he had been assured, it would be the likes of Bering. The tsar, however, did not live to savour the fruit of this initiative, for within six months he lay dead at age fifty-three. His widow and successor, Catherine I, however, was quick to endorse the Dane's appointment and she urged him to press forward in accordance with the directive dictated earlier by Peter – a commission that sparkles with naïveté:

I   You shall cause one or two convenient vessels to be built at Kamchatka or elsewhere.

II   You shall endeavor to discover, by coasting with these vessels, whether the country towards the north, of which at present we have no knowledge, is a part of America, or not.

III If it joins to the continent of America, you shall endeavor, if possible, to reach some colony belonging to some European power. In case you meet with any European ship, you shall diligently inquire the

name of the coasts, and such other circumstances as
it is in your power to learn. These you will commit
to writing, so that we may have some certain mem-
oirs by which a chart may be constructed.

On February 5, 1725, eight days after the tsar's death, twenty-five
sleighs pulled away from the Admiralty in St. Petersburg, in the tracks of
an advance party that had quit the capital a fortnight earlier under the
command of another Dane, Martin Spanberg. Bering, accompanied by
an entourage of thirty-three carpenters, blacksmiths, sailors, and support staff, was at the start of an arduous twenty-one-month journey to
the Pacific across seemingly endless Siberian stretches. Roads, for the
most part, were non-existent and those available were primitive; numerous rivers had to be forded, many requiring the construction of rafts;
settlements were few and far between. Freezing temperatures and deep
snows brought misery in winter; unbearable heat and clouds of mosquitoes in summer. The first winter was especially harsh and one diarist
noted that "the local people who have lived here more than twenty years
say that it is the worst winter in memory." The passage of the valiant travellers was made all the more laborious by the immense quantity of food
and equipment they hauled.

Bering met upwith Spanberg's advance party only after the two had
arrived at the Pacific coast. The Siberian trek of the former was difficult enough, but his colleague's journey was considerably more gruelling. The excessive cold suffered by Spanberg's group was compounded
by hunger, and a number of his men had perished en route. Bering gives
us a sense of that passage:

He [Spanberg] arrived with his companions almost the
first part of January, 1727, without, however, in any of
the material, which he had left in four different places
along the uninhabited trail. They had been on the road
since November 4 and during that time had suffered
greatly from hunger, having been compelled to eat the

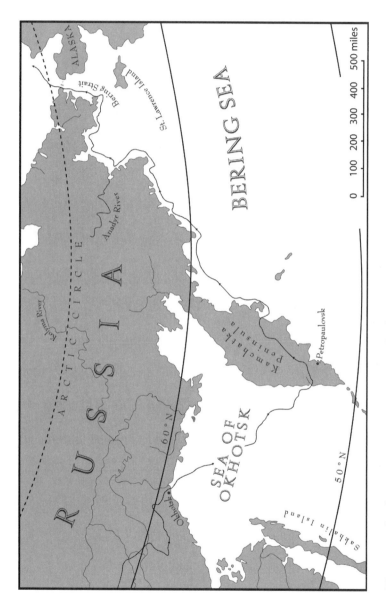

The route taken by Vitus Bering in 1727–29 on his first journey of exploration into far northern Pacific in search of a gateway to the Northeast Passage.

Map by Cameron McLeod Jones.

dead horses that had dropped by the wayside, the harnesses, their leather clothing, and boots. Fortunately
they found at Yukoma Cross the 150 poods [1650
pounds] of flour which we had left behind when some
of our horses gave out.[2]

By early January 1727, the reunited party was installed on the
shores of the Okhotsk Sea, where it found a miserable collection of
native huts and houses belonging to a handful of Russian colonists.
Since leaving St. Petersburg, the expedition had travelled nearly five
thousand miles, but another one thousand miles lay ahead before the
final destination would be reached on Kamtchatka's east coast. Despite
exhaustion from taxing months of travel, work got underway in the
construction of a vessel suitable for crossing the Sea of Okhotsk, that
large body of water lying between the Kamchatka Peninsula and the
Siberian mainland. Local boat-builders carrying out the work naturally
favoured the design of their native boat, the *shitik* (from the word "to
sew"). A rough-hewn tree trunk served as the base of this flat-bottomed
vessel, to which wooden planks were "sewn" together by leather belts
and fir rods, a primitive construction to say the least, but one that was
effective in local river and coastal navigation. The single-mast, shallow
draught *Fortuna* was soon launched, a vessel approximately forty-five
feet long and twelve feet broad.

The boat made two crossings to the peninsula's southwest coast. The
first transported tons of equipment and supplies, and the second carried
Bering and the bulk of his party. The passages were completed by late
August and now men and baggage had to be conveyed overland to the
peninsula's east side, a three-hundred-mile trek through volcanic mountain ranges.[3] Native Kamchadales and their dogs were mobilized and the
traverse began. The initial passage through swampy valleys was difficult
enough, but with the onslaught of winter's freeze, conditions became
even more acute. The expedition was hampered by gales, blizzards, and
temperatures that fell as low as -50°F. "The wind began to blow with
great violence, and drifting snow in great quantities, thickened the atmosphere so that we could not see a yard before us," reads one account.[4]

At this point the legitimate question arises: why did Bering elect to undertake this arduous and time-consuming winter trek rather than simply circumnavigating the peninsula on board the *Fortuna* and continuing north on with his mission entirely by sea? The answer most probably lies in the vessel's construction. Having put out to sea, Bering likely realized the vessel's inadequacy for a circumnavigation of the Kamchatka Peninsula, much less a sail of the rough, stormy, and ice-strewn Arctic waters. Bering's apparent lack of management in the construction of the vessel has raised questions about his feelings toward the entire Siberian venture. Was his heart truly in it? Soviet scholar Yuri Semyonov offers an intriguing observation in *Siberia: Its Conquest and Development*, albeit one in reference to Bering's second expedition to the Pacific at age fifty-seven (and one that smacks of nationalistic fervour):

> He did not trust his first vessel and one can imagine that he did not feel more comfortable on the second one, which was built in Kamchatka. He lacked that organic "Siberian" sympathy with nature, that capacity for adapting oneself to one's surrounding, which the Russians possessed in such large measure. Very significant in this connection is a remark in the diary of his companion, Steller. Steller says that Bering wished that the whole affair could be entrusted to "a young and impetuous man from the country" [i.e., a Russian] ...[5]

After a series of trials and mishaps, the party at last reached its destination at the lower part of Kamchatka. Here a new vessel was constructed, one larger and more substantially built than the *Fortuna*. The hull of the *Saint Gabriel* was reinforced with iron that had been brought in from Tobolsk and it was equipped with canvas and cordage delivered from St. Petersburg. On July 13, 1728, Bering put out to sea with a forty-man crew and headed north. The tsar's commission would now be fulfilled: if Russia was connected to America, he would soon know, and if an entrance to the Northeast Passage existed, it was his to realize.

In the weeks that followed, the *Gabriel* steadily followed the coastline, fighting fogs and drenching rains and enduring the depressing omnipresent dampness. A month after setting out, they passed an island to their starboard which Bering named St. Lawrence Island in honour of the day. They were less than a hundred miles from Cape Chukhotski, Eurasia's eastern tip; the Bering Strait lay dead ahead and Alaska was less than three days away. But they did not realize this and with the coastline unfailingly veering west, Bering became certain that they had passed along the waters separating Russia from America and that they were at the start of the Northern Sea Route. Winter comes early to those parts and that year the weather turned foul in late summer — they had either to prepare to spend the winter there or to return to Kamchatka. The men had been at sea steadily for over a month, beset by a particularly thick and depressing fog and conditions on board had grown grim and unhealthy. Enough was enough — the explorer ordered a return home "because the coast did not extend farther north and no land was near ... and therefore it seemed to me that the instructions of His Imperial Majesty of illustrious and immortal memory had been carried out." He was returning home satisfied that the two continents were unconnected ... had fog not enveloped his ship he would have had a good view of close-by Alaska.

By March 1730, the exhausted Dane was back in St. Petersburg and had submitted his report to the fledgling Academy of Science, to the Admiralty, and to the Senate. He had crossed Siberia, he had overseen in the wilderness the construction of two ships and, per the tsar's instructions, he had determined that "the country through the north ... is [not] a part of America." In the process he had given the state five years of his life — surely a heroic achievement worthy of high recognition. Alas, this was not to be. The authorities received the report with skepticism and dissatisfaction, the consensus being that no concrete proof was offered of the continents' separation. Had Bering continued to follow the coastline after it veered west a further seven hundred miles or so to the Kolyma River there would be no denying that the White Sea and the Pacific are connected by a continuous coastline and that America was indeed a separate continent. The anticipated reward of 1,000 rubles was denied Peter's appointed man. Adding salt to the wound, Bering's salary was left unpaid for over a year and he was refused a request for promotion to rear admiral. Poor man: the injustice of it all.

One by-product, if you will, of the Dane's ventures into the Siberian Arctic was a surge of awareness in the country's Pacific holdings. A series of explorers followed Bering's footsteps, with Ivan Feodorov and Michael Gvosdyov being among the most notable. In 1732 they sailed on board Bering's *Gabriel* to become the first Russians to set foot in Alaska. The more St. Petersburg learned of its far distant holdings and of America, the greater its enthusiasm for continued exploration of Pacific and Arctic Ocean. The focus, however, soon shifted from furs and scientific inquiry to geopolitical considerations. In 1733, for example, one St. Petersburg study spoke for the first time of Korea as part of a Far Eastern political complex. Japan came onto the horizon — European commercial relations with that country were in nascent days, and Russia was not going to find itself excluded. Interest grew in intensity, and despite the indifference that greeted Bering at the conclusion of his first expedition, he was given a mandate for a fresh expedition east, one that would "benefit of her Imperial Majesty and to the glory of the Russian Empire." The newly throned Empress Anna endorsed the enterprise.

In spring 1733, the fifty-three-year-old persevering Dane set out once more from St. Petersburg to travel across Siberia. By the time his first expedition had been completed, a hundred or so men had become involved; by the time his second one was terminated, three thousand men would be drawn into the work. The initial budget for the new expedition was 10,000 rubles; ultimately, over 300,000 rubles were spent. It took the vast party seven years to complete the traverse, to establish a base of operations, and to construct two vessels. The lengthy duration of the passage was due in large measure to time-consumptive ancillary explorations and to scientific studies of flora and fauna — all part of the program. What began as a fresh attempt to chart Siberian Arctic shores and the northwest coast of America had developed, as Professor Golder notes in *Bering's Voyages*, into "one of the most elaborate, thorough, and expensive expeditions ever sent by any government at any time."[6]

Once established on the Sea of Okhotsk, work got started on the construction of two substantial ships, the *Saint Peter* and the *Saint Paul*, vessels significantly better suited for their tasks than those of the previous expedition — eighty feet in length with twin masts, the hulls were strongly reinforced with iron strapping. Bering commanded the *Saint Peter* and its sister ship was under Captain Alexsei Chirikov, a veteran of the first expedition. Chirikov was considerably younger than the Dane, but he was well-educated, with a strong sense of curiosity, and had some scientific training. By autumn 1740, the expedition had crossed the Okhotsk, rounded the tip of Kamchatka and established itself on the east coast at what was to become Petropavlovsk, the peninsula's capital.

In the following spring, the two ships put out to sea and headed southeast to America, where it was planned to explore the coastline south; the further investigation of the Northeast Passage would come later. But best of plans can go astray and these certainly did — shortly after moving out, the ships became enveloped for days by impenetrable fog within which they simply lost one another. Extensive circling about in search of the other came to naught and the two captains, each in his own time, gave up the hunt and moved out on his own.

A couple of weeks later, Chirikov found himself at latitude 55°21', halfway down the Alaskan panhandle, south of Sitka, today's fourth-largest Alaskan city, where he made the first Russian contact with American natives. After a series of adventures the *Saint Paul* returned to Kamchatka on October 19. Along the way, Chirikov took to his bunk, physically incapacitated, his lungs permeated with tuberculosis. Before reaching home, he expired.

In the meantime, Bering had altered course for the North. At first he was beset by continued fog, but on July 6 that changed when the fog suddenly cleared and the skies opened up into dazzling blue, revealing a brilliant congregation of snow-covered peaks soaring almost vertically to heights of over seventeen thousand feet. He was at 60° where today the boundary line dividing Alaska and Canada reaches the coastline. The Dane named the tallest mountain of the range Mount Saint Elias, a sight which is as inspiring to modern-day travellers as the one that greeted the weary explorers over 250 years ago. For them, however, it was not simply glittering nature; it was a reward for the years of gruelling toil and a justification for the explorations. And then, as suddenly as it had cleared, the fog redeveloped and once more shrouded all. Bering was confident that he had discovered Alaska, but he was even more pleased that now, having executed his commission, he could return home. He couldn't wait; he had enough of rain and fog, of the restless and fickle sea, and of unpredictable winds.

The crew of the *Saint Peter*, on the other hand, after thirty-two days of steady sailing, was desperately anxious to set foot ashore, particularly the scientists on board who itched to explore the new land. In his anxiety to quit the place, Bering would have none of that and he ordered a sail for home. Only after strongest protest of his fellow officers and scientists did he acquiesce and grudgingly permit a brief ten-hour shore leave. Bering, himself did not go ashore; "the discoverer of Alaska" never set foot on it — nor did he know that Chirikov already had weeks earlier.

With shore leave expired and his unfulfilled mates back on board, the impatient Dane turned the *Saint Peter* about and made for Kamchatka. The return passage was anything but happy. Shortly after quitting Alaska's mainland, dreaded scurvy struck the unfortunate crew with a vengeance, killing twelve and affecting most of the rest. Then, when they were beyond the farthest point of the Aleutian archipelago, a violent gale struck with overwhelming force. The weakened crew was unable to cope with the frightful situation and Bering decided that their only salvation was to beach the ship on one of the nearby islands. The *Saint Peter* was driven ashore and in the process it broke upon the rocks. And there, through long, dark, and frigid weeks, the stranded men wintered in appalling conditions. The island teemed with fox and since the animals had never encountered humans, their natural curiosity made them increasingly bold and vicious. Quite fearless, they approached so close that the men were forced to beat them off with clubs. Scores of these animals were killed and so plentiful were they that the pelts not only provided the crew with winter protection, but the stuff was used as caulking for the huts they had constructed, expensive building material, indeed. As one man after another died off from the ravages of scurvy, the solidly frozen ground made burial impossible and the bodies were simply dragged away some distance. Survivors were long haunted by the terrible spectacle of foxes fighting over and playing with the corpses.

The island's abundant animal life sustained the men, most of whom survived to tell the tale of their ordeal. In late spring, after months of creative toil, they managed to construct from the wreckage of the *Saint Peter* a small, rudimentary vessel in which they sailed off and eventually reached their starting point at Petropavlovsk. As the bedraggled, fur-clad sailors stepped ashore they were greeted by their surviving colleagues from the *Saint Paul*. Bering was not among them. The old man had succumbed to scurvy months earlier, unaware that he was not the discoverer of the strait that bears his name — a simple Siberian trader had traversed it some eighty years earlier.

Argue as one might over Bering's successes or failures, there is no denying that his two expeditions left Russia not only with a greater appreciation of Siberia, the Arctic, and the Pacific shores, but now the country's gaze had been turned east; Peter the Great's east–west strategic vision was on its way to realization. China, Korea, and Japan would soon be feeling the hot breath of the lumbering Russian bear awakening at their side.

The mid-seventeenth century was universally a boom-time for the fur trade, no more evident than in Peter's Russia. Hunters, traders, and Cossacks pushed eastward along Siberian waterways in search of fresh hunting grounds. In encouraging this movement, the ever-inquisitive tsar ordered that records and maps be carefully detailed of new geographic finds and it is from these sources that we learn of the earliest Russian penetration of Arctic Siberia, the land of the Chukchi and Koryaks.

Among those travellers, one audacious son of Siberia stands foremost, an illiterate Cossack named Semyon Dezhnev. Little known outside Russia, he sits high on the pedestal of Arctic explorers and takes no back seat to the likes of Frobisher or Hudson. It was he who in 1648 became the first European to sail around the easternmost promontory of the Eurasian continent through the Bering Strait. Oddly enough, the documentation related to the journey, including Dezhnev's reports to the tsar, languished in the archives at Yakutsk until 1736, long after the momentous voyage — as one historian put it, "the discovery itself had to be discovered."[7]

Details of Dezhnev's early life are sketchy. We do know that he came from the Pomors, an enclave of Russians who had settled in the Arctic coastal regions of the White Sea in the fifteenth century. Accomplished hunters and trappers, these people were also tough and resourceful sailors. At an early age, Dezhnev was determined to migrate to frontier Siberia, where he planned to seek his fortune, perhaps by finding employment with the government. The young man's spirit of adventure no doubt helped to propel him, as did his innate restlessness — a characteristic seemingly shared by hundreds of others — compel him to move to Siberia. The times were reminiscent of nineteenth-century America when Horace Greeley urged, "Go west, young man, and grow up with the country".

In his early twenties, Dezhnev joined a group of migrants from the White Sea on a path that would lead him, in the words of the Canadian scholar Robert McGhee, to "one of the most remarkable and least recognized feats in the history of Arctic exploration." Together these émigrés completed the long trek to Tobolsk in western Siberia. In 1638, Dezhnev, now a government employee, moved to Yakutsk, the administrative centre of eastern Siberia, laying 280 miles south of the Arctic Circle. Assigned to the governor's office, he proved to be an adroit administrator and handled a diversity of assignments with aplomb. Shortly after arriving, he was given the task of pacifying two feuding tribes of the region, a peacemaker's task that normally would have fallen to an experienced mediator. Dezhnev executed the commission within a fortnight. Next he was sent to collect "the sovereign's tribute" from a recalcitrant tribal chief, a certain Sakhey Otnakov. Three earlier attempts to bring the chief to heel resulted in disaster; each of the collectors had been killed. Dezhnev, however, succeeded. We know not how; his report merely states "... I took 140 sables from chief Sakhey, his children and kinsmen and from other ... Yakuts."[8] On another assignment he was charged with transporting back to Yakutsk a tribute of 340 sable furs that had been collected in a remote corner of the administrative district. During the passage home, Dezhnev and his three companions were ambushed by a party of forty bandits. In the ensuing melee, the record tells, the foursome prevailed and the vanquished attackers retreated. After attending to a leg wound, Dezhnev led his small party home and delivered the "sable treasury" to the governor without further incident.

For decades, the richest source of furs in those parts had been a broad belt of territory stretching south from the shores of the Arctic Ocean, from the Lena River in an easterly direction to the Kolyma River. The "sable treasury" and the search for furs was not centred exclusively on sables — of equal interest were the hides of martens, ermines, wolves, arctic fox, and particularly the rare black fox. The sea coast, furthermore, abounded with walrus and the harvest of precious ivory tusk was an important secondary commerce. By the time Dezhnev came into his own, the region was well on its way to being hunted out, and tentative thrusts were being made into the unknown area east of the Kolyma. Dezhnev readily volunteered to help lead an exploration of those distant parts.

Thus it was that in June 1648, seven small vessels put out from the mouth of the Kolyma under the direction of Dezhnev and two others, a Cossack called Gerasim Ankudinov and a trader, Fedot Alexseyev. For a more complete understanding of the conditions under which these self-assured men sailed, it is well to appreciate the appallingly primitive construction of their boats. Professor Golder describes the *kotcha*, as it was called. It was a flat-bottomed decked vessel, about twelve fathoms long (seventy-two feet), put together generally without nail or scrap of iron of any kind, and probably kept together by wooden pegs and leather straps.[9] Buldakof, one of the Siberians, speaks of the ice cutting the twigs of his kotcha. From this statement and hints elsewhere, it would seem that the kotcha was tied together and probably protected on the outsides by twigs. A kotcha had a wooden mast and sails of deer skin, which were of little use in damp weather. The chief motive power, therefore, was the paddle. Anchors were made of wood and stone, and cables of leather. This description gives an idea of the fitness of a kotcha to battle with sea and ice:

> It was in such a vessel, with a crew of fifteen or so, that Dezhnev navigated the hazards of the East Siberian Sea. By the time he had completed his 102 day journey an estimated 2160 miles had been traveled, a remarkable feat indeed. It must be remembered that Dezhnev was

not primarily "a salt"; he was a landsman, at home in forest and taiga albeit skilled in river navigation.

We know little of the ice and weather conditions encountered by the explorer in the weeks that ensued. It is accepted, however, that those waters present much the same challenges as found in the Canadian Arctic, less the extent and size of icebergs. In *Voyage of the Vega*, Adolf Nordenskjöld, the 19th century Swedish explorer gives a sense of the East Siberian Sea:

The ice was heavy and close although at first so distributed that it was navigable. But with the north wind which began to blow on the night before the first [of] September ... it becomes impossible to continue the course which we had taken ... A further loss of time was caused by the dense fog which prevailed all day.[10]

Details of the lengthy journey are scarce, bathed in uncertainty — but one mishap seems to have followed another. Early on, four of the boats simply went missing — probably through storms — and were not heard from again. The expedition's first contact with the Chukchi proved unhappy — the two parties fought and Alexseyev suffered a leg wound during the fray. Ankudinov's *kotcha* was wrecked and the survivors were transferred to the remaining two vessels. Soon afterward Alexseyev's boat was "carried out to sea" to a fate unknown, leaving Dezhnev by himself. Dezhnev eventually arrived at the East Cape (today called *Mys Dezhneva*), the tip of the Eurasian continent, where the coast veers sharply south-southwest. In his own measured words dictated seven years later, he provided the following fragmentary account:

In the year 1648, June 20, I Semyon, was sent from the Kolyma River to the new river to the Andyr to find new, non-tribute paying people. And in the year 1648, September 20, in going from the Kolyma River to sea, at a place where we stopped, the Chukchi in a fight wounded the trader Fedot Alexeyev, and that Fedot was carried out with me to sea, and I do not know where he is, and I was carried about here and there …[11]

Wind and storms bore Dezhnev's *kotcha* steadily south, past the mouth of the Anadyr, one of the major waterways emptying into the Pacific. On October 1 the vessel was driven ashore by an especially fierce storm and wrecked. Little was left for the twenty-four survivors to do, but to abandon the sea and set out on foot inland. "We all took to the hills," writes Dezhnev, "not knowing which way to go … we were cold and hungry … and I, poor Semyon, and my companions went to the Anadyr in exactly ten weeks …" Hunger was such that it was decided to split up, perhaps thereby bettering their chances of survival, with one party of twelve moving out on its own. It was never heard from again — "disappeared without our knowing what became of them." Dezhnev's party remained where it was on the endless taiga and spent the winter at the spot. Difficult to imagine the suffering of those unfortunates during the long dark months in an inhospitable territory with nothing but the clothes on their backs and what little they had carried away from their wrecked *kotcha*. What followed after that dreadful first winter is anyone's guess, suffice to say that Dezhnev did not reappear in the outside world until 1655, nearly seven years after the start of the expedition. His terse accounts are agonizingly brief on fundamental information. One report, however, does tell us of his two colleagues who were lost early on:

> In the year 1654 in a fight I captured from the Koryaks a Yakut woman belonging to Feodot Alexseyev, and she said that Fedot and Gerasim died of scurvy, some of their companions were killed and the few who remained escaped in boats with their lives, and she did not know what became of them.

Dezhnev's mission was all about tribute — to scout fresh sources of furs through taxation of native populations. Unlike Barents, Hudson, or others,

Dezhnev did not set out to make a notable discovery, but, having passed through the Bering Strait, he quite likely took satisfaction in his significant achievement. A pity only that we know so little of this man or of the full story he might have told of his extraordinary journey. But here a word of caution: differences of opinion exist among scholars as to Dezhnev's claim, with question being raised by some on the genuineness of the documentation related to the exploit. The various reports and attestations that tell of this singular Cossack, it has been suggested, were authored by one and the same person long after Dezhnev's death and are therefore unauthentic; majority opinion, however, favours their authenticity. Whatever the case, the discovery or non-discovery by Dezhnev or by Bering of the channel separating Eurasia and America not only provided new avenues for trade and commerce, but showed the way for the extension of the Russian Empire into America. The strait also opened a fresh gateway to the high Arctic and the pole, over which many would travel in the years to come.

Dezhnev came from the White Sea, from among the Pomors (literally "seacoast dwellers"). These were resilient and resourceful individuals who ventured far and wide in search of fresh hunting grounds, not only for fur-bearing animals and walrus, but also for whales. The Barents Sea and the Kara were familiar waters, as were Novaya Zemlya and the Svalbard Archipelago in the North Sea.

Survival in the Arctic is an art form, and in its literature an assortment of superlatives is used to describe any given such story or the men involved. One gripping tale, however, comes to us of four Pomori hunters for whom all adjectives seem inadequate. In 1743, the four found themselves accidentally marooned on Edgeøya Island of the Svalbard Archipelago (77°40′ N). For *six years* of deprivation and Arctic isolation they survived the unrelenting weather and constant threat of polar bears with what few items they had carried at the very start. The resolute mindset of these men confounds explanation.

In 1749, word of the feat reached the ears of Count Pyotr Shuvalov, a favourite of Empress Elizabeth. So outlandish and improbable did it all seem that he invited two of the survivors, Alexsei Inkov and his cousin Khrisani Inkov, to St. Petersburg to hear their story first-hand. Their account was so improbable that initially the men was viewed as hoaxers. But with continued examination and cross-examination, the credibility of their account gradually came to be accepted and the chief interrogator, a certain Pierre Le Roy, was asked to record it. The Frenchman was the tutor to Shuvalov's three sons, and his seventy-six-page report forms the crux of what is known of the four men who unflinchingly stood up to the Arctic Siren.

In 1743, fourteen Pomori hunters sailed from the village of Mezen on the White Sea coast aboard a small vessel and headed west for the North Sea. They were out to hunt walrus in the waters of the Svalbard Archipelago. The first eight days of the passage were had in favourable weather, but on the ninth the wind changed direction and grew so intense that they found themselves rapidly being driven off course toward Edgeøya Island at the archipelago's southeastern corner. The whaling grounds were on the opposite side of the island cluster, and whalers rarely passed there, not only for lack of the animals, but for the prevalence of ice packs. The ice buildup that year was exceptionally great and before long their little vessel found itself precariously ice-bound within sight of land.

The situation deteriorated in the passing days, and it became apparent that the ship might be crushed. Therefore, the decision was made to send a four-man party to the island to reconnoitre possibilities of sheltering ashore. It was known that years earlier a group of Russian sailors had wintered there in a hut that they had constructed with material especially carried from home. The two Inkovs volunteered to cross by foot over the hazardous ice in the hope of locating that cabin, and they were joined by two others: Stephan Sharapov, Alexis Inkov's godson, and Feodor Verigin. They did not plan to be absent for a long time, and since they knew that the hunting would be excellent only the barest essentials were carried. Le Roy lists the articles: "a musket, a powder horn containing twelve charges of powder, with as many balls, an axe, a small kettle, a bag with about twenty pounds of flour, a knife, a tinder-box and tinder, a bladder filled with tobacco, and every man his wooden pipe."[12]

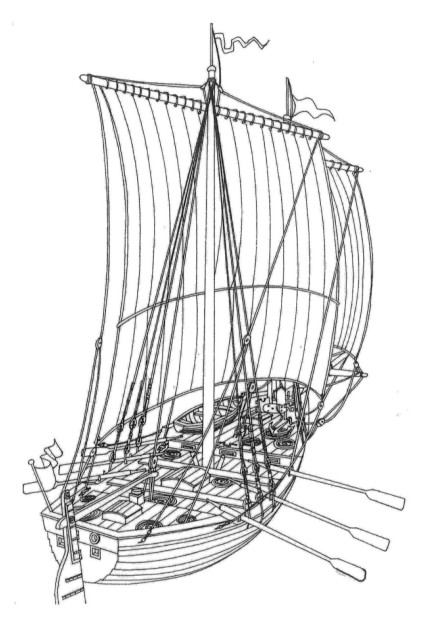

An eighteenth-century kotcha, *the sort of vessel the Pomori sailed from the White Sea to Svalbard in 1743 when they became shipwrecked and were stranded for six years.*

On making landfall, he writes, "their first attention was employed, as may easily be imagined, in devising means of providing subsistence … The twelve charges of powder which they had brought with them, soon procured them with as many reindeer, the island, fortunately for them, abounding in these animals." At first glance, an astonishing achievement — twelve shots and twelve dead animals. It must be noted, however, that the island's reindeer were unused to humans and being naturally curious they made easy targets.

The prize they sought was had in short order: they found the hut less than a mile from shore. It was constructed with pre-cut logs from Russia and measured thirty-six feet by eighteen, with an inordinately high ceiling also of eighteen feet. A small vestibule complete with door separated the inner room from the main entrance for the preservation of heat. In one corner stood an intact traditional clay stove, "a kind of oven without a chimney, which serves occasionally for baking, for heating the room, or as is customary amongst the Russian peasants, in very cold weather, for a place to sleep upon." Since it was built "some time before" the building was not in top shape but readily repairable.

The men overnighted in the cabin while a heavy gale blew outside, and on the following day they made their way back to the ship to share the happy news of their find with their comrades. Imagine their utter stupefaction when on reaching the shore they discovered that the farthest portion of the ice pack was gone and with it, their vessel — gale winds had presumably carried all away. "This melancholy event depriving the unhappy wretches of all hope of ever being able to quit the island, they returned to the hut whence they had come, full of horror and despair." A continuous watch was kept in the ensuing days for sign of sail, but none was had; their ship had no doubt foundered and their fate was sealed. (Since the vessel never returned to home port, their assumption was undoubtedly correct.)

However bleak their prospect, the men resolved to make a go of it. They first set about patching up the hut, principally by trimming some of the logs and caulking openings between them using moss that grew abundantly throughout the island. "Repairs of this kind," Le Roy editorialized, "cost the unhappy men the less trouble, as they were Russians, for all Russian peasants are known to be good carpenters: they build their own houses, and are very expert in handing the axe." With repairs completed and twelve deer carcasses lying outside, some sense of achievement was had, despite two unsolved problems of profound magnitude. First, all their ammunition had been expended. How then to provide food in the long-term, and equally, how were they to fend off polar bears? Spitzbergen in those days was home to huge concentrations of the animals, and Edgeøyen was a favourite breeding ground. Not for a moment could they ease their vigilance against attack by this stealthy, oft-time imperceptible carnivore that was prepared to attack most anything that moved be it a seal, walrus, or human.

And then, how were they to keep themselves from freezing? Edgeøya is a barren island, void of trees or shrubbery — what therefore to burn? Indeed, how were they to cook? The tinderbox they had carried would soon be empty — how to start fires? In the absence of weapons and fuel, starvation was inevitable; prospects of survival appeared negligible.

On further exploration of the island they discovered abundant quantities of driftwood littering parts of the coast. Periodic floods of the great rivers emptying into the White Sea bear large amounts of uprooted trees, which ocean currents carry west and after months of drift and salt-water wash quantities are beached on Svalbard. A treasure trove this was; the concern over fuel was allayed, and the foursome set about hauling huge amounts of the stuff to their cabin.

Weeks passed and the supply of reindeer meat had become nearly depleted. Although seen in places, bears thus far had been few and far between, but the change of season migratory paths would bring them to the island in numbers. Lacking ammunition for further hunting or to ward off the marauders, the situation must have appeared hopeless. But then, all changed; fortune favoured the brave. One day, as the men gathered driftwood along the shore, they came across a couple of weather-beaten planks, "the melancholy relicks of some vessel cast away in these remote parts." One of these had a long iron hook attached and the other, five or six nails "and other bits of iron." This innocuous debris became a lifeline.

Using reindeer antlers as tongs, the hook was heated red-hot and placed on a makeshift anvil of smooth stone. One blow of the axe made two pieces of it. The thicker section had a hole, and with the primitive forge it was sufficiently enlarged to allow a nail be driven through it. The hole was then made even bigger by working the nail to and fro. After the piece had cooled, a firm piece of driftwood was driven through the hole, and thus a hammer came to be. The curved part of the hook was reworked with the hammer and cut in two, with the halves then being fashioned into straight points. The edges of these pieces were sharpened by stone and attached to straight driftwood poles "about the thickness of a man's arm." This was done by using strips of well-soaked deerskin, which, in the process of drying, contracted so tightly that a ridged bond was achieved. In addition to a hammer, our Pomori now possessed two spears.

Until then, the men had deliberately avoided having anything to do with bears, but now that they were armed they set out to hunt one down. And this they did successfully, as the Frenchman explained without mincing words, "after a most dangerous encounter, they killed the formidable creature, and thereby made a new supply of provisions." David Roberts in *Four Against the Arctic* imagines the scene:

> To thrust their spears home, the sailors must have danced within a foot or two of the beast's ferocious paw swipes. And if the spears failed, breaking on impact, at least one of the sailors would have paid with his life. I tried to hear the bear's outraged roaring, I saw torrents of blood matting its white fur, I envisioned the Pomori feinting and retreating, the two men without the weapons trying to distract the animal from the two who hoped to slay it.[13]

The larder, as it were, had been replenished and "the flesh of the animal they relished exceedingly, as they thought it much resembled beef in taste and flavour." The skin was scraped and later fashioned into clothing. But of equal interest to the hide were the animal's sinews and tendons. In an earlier foray to the shoreline, they had come upon a relatively fresh "root of a fir tree, which nearly approached to the figure of a bow." By dividing the tendons into several thick twinelike filaments, they were able to fashion a string for the bow. Nails were shaped on the anvil into darts, which then were attached to with bear sinew to shoots of fir tree. By securing "feathers of sea-fowl" at the appropriate place, credible arrows were formed.

First a hammer, then a couple of spears, and now a bow and arrows. Little wonder that when the Pomori's amazing tale surfaced in Russia it was initially received with skepticism. The resourcefulness and skills the four men demonstrated in beating all the odds were astounding. Le Roy wrote:

> Their ingenuity, in this respect, was crowned with success far beyond their expectations; for, during their time of their continuance upon the island, with these arrows they killed no less than two hundred and fifty reindeer, besides a great number of blue and white foxes.. The flesh of these animals served them also for food, and their skins for clothing, and other necessary preservatives against the intense coldness of a climate so near the Pole.

As the days shortened and temperatures fell, concern focused on maintaining the cabin's heat. Supply of accessible driftwood had diminished rapidly and there was no telling whether sea storms would throw up fresh quantities sufficient to last the winter. Fuel economy therefore became the order of the day. Fundamental to all was the question of fire, "if it should unfortunately go out, they had no means of lighting it again; for though they had steel and flints, yet they wanted match and tinder." Flint would do little without having the sparks fall on dry, combustible material such as birch bark, but such was unavailable on Edgeøya. The bow-and-drill method used by the natives of Kamtchatka and North America would undoubtedly have served them well, but this depended on dry wood, and fresh driftwood was never fully free of waterlog.

The Pomori were well aware of what Arctic winter brings — its freeze and darkness, its isolation, deprivation, and dangers. A loss of heat is a death sentence. Whatever the cost, whatever the means, under no

Remains of a hut on Spitzbergen from an 1871 illustration by a British yachtsman. Such eight-point Orthodox crosses were frequently erected by the Pomori in the Arctic in thanks for a safe arrival and escape from dangers at sea. The crosses also served as navigational points for ships at sea.

circumstance could they permit the fire to extinguish, and there should always be another by way of backup. On one of their explorations inland "they had met with a slimy loam, or a kind of clay in the middle of it." They gathered a mass of this material and worked it into a lamp-like vessel. Reindeer fat was placed into it and a narrow strip of twisted linen served as a wick. For a brief period, flames flickered brightly, but when the fat melted, it permeated the clay and their handicraft collapsed. A second try was had at lamp-making, but this time they allowed the moulded piece to dry in the outside air. After it had hardened, they cooked it in boiling water together with a quantity of flour, following which the exterior was coated with a flour paste. Thus came to be a lamp, which held melted fat and one that worked well enough to serve as a model for fabricating others. Such was their success that the men resolved to save the remaining flour exclusively for lamp-making and to be sparing in the use of shirts, trousers, and drawers, essential for future wicks.

They fashioned clothing from animal hides. For undergarments, certain skins were left to soak for several days in fresh water until the hair loosened sufficiently to be plucked out. The hide was then rubbed thoroughly by hand and allowed to dry, and then reindeer fat was rubbed into it to give softness and pliability. The hair on hides destined for outerwear and boots was retained for maximum warmth and waterproofing. "Though there was neither tailor nor shoemaker among them, they contrived to cut out their leather and furs well enough for their purpose." All was sewn with thread made of filaments of bear sinew and with ingeniously fabricated needles forged from odd bits of iron. Le Roy noted:

> [T]he eyes gave them indeed no little trouble; but this they also performed with the assistance of their knife; for having ground it to a very sharp point, and heated red hot a kind of wire forged for that purpose, they pierced a hole through one end, and by whetting and smoothing it on stones, brought the other to a point, and this gave the whole needle a tolerable form.

Other than moss, lichen, and certain grasses, virtually no vegetation is had on Edgeøya, and so for the six years of their forced captivity, the men became involuntary carnivores, with reindeer, fox, and bear forming the diet. Apart from their first bear kill the others, ten in all, were taken in self-defence in warding off attacks on their hut. "Some of these creatures even ventured to enter the outer room of the hut, in order to devour them." Since their kettle served as a repository for fresh water drawn either from nearby springs or made by melting snow or ice, meat had to be cooked over the open fire. Morning, noon, and night: the same diet — "reindeer, and blue and white foxes, and the white bears were their only food these wretched mariners tasted during their continuance in this dreary abode." To break the dietary monotony, they suspended certain cuts from the high ceiling for exposure to the ever-present smoke within the hut. The smoked pieces were then taken outdoors and placed on the roof to allow them to dry hard, and then slices of the stuff were chewed as "bread," no doubt a wel-comed garnish to roasted meat.

Krisanf was well aware of the dangers of scurvy and he urged his companions to drink warm reindeer blood "as it flowed from the veins immediately after [the kill]." In addition he instructed them to consume raw scurvy-grass, which grew in parts of the island, and lastly he rec-ommended "to use as much exercise as possible," whatever the weather. Three of the four lived by these recommendations and survived to tell their tale. Peter Verigin, however, "who was naturally indolent and averse to drinking reindeer blood," stubbornly avoided leaving the hut unnecessarily and wanted nothing to do with blood. Within weeks of arrival on the island, he took sick and became bedridden. "He passed almost six years under greatest sufferings," and finally he died. Le Roy tells of the effect this death had on the others:

> Though they were thus freed from the trouble of attend-ing him, and the grief of being witness to his misery, without being able to afford him any relief, yet his death affected them not a little. They saw their numbers less-ened and everyone wished to be the first that should follow him. As he died in winter, they dug a grave in the snow as deep as they could, in which they laid the corpse, and then covered it the best of their power, that the white bears might not get at it.

In such form, Le Roy tells of how the four Pomori lived out the first year on the island, and from this we have an impression of how the ensu-ing five years passed. We hear of their hut and weapons and we learn how food, heat, and clothing were secured. Primitive as all this may have been, it was sufficient for the survival of the stranded — at least three of them. What our chronicler fails to offer us, however, is a sense of the men's psy-chological condition. How did they deal with the monotony of seemingly interminable dark winters with snows so deep that at times it "wholly covered their hut, and left them no way of getting out of it, but through a hole they had made in the upper part of the roof"? What of their mental strength in coping with the cold and primitive condition of their bleak smoke-filled hut, where no doubt cabin fever prevailed? Above all, the loneliness and sense of abandonment and uncertainty— most of this is left to our imaginations. The closest the Frenchman comes to touching on these matters is one paragraph:

> Excepting the uneasiness which generally accompanies an involuntary solitude, these people, having thus by their ingenuity so far overcome their wants, might have had reason to be contented with what Providence had done for them in their dreadful situation. But that melancholy reflection, to which each of these forlorn persons could not help giving way, that perhaps he might survive his companions, and then perish for want of substance, or become a prey to the wild beasts, increasingly disturbed their minds. The mate, Alexsei Inkov, more particularly suffered, who having left his wife and three children behind, sorely repined at his being separated from them; they were, as he told me, constantly in his mind, and the thought of never more seeing them made him very unhappy.

At this point Le Roy concluded his narrative by describing the dramatic rescue of the sailors. On August 15, 1749, "they unexpectedly got sight of a Russian ship," a trading vessel out of Archangel on its way to Novaya Zemlya, which had been blown off course and found itself off Edgeøyn. It is difficult to imagine the excitement of the moment as the men scurried about to collect driftwood for two massive fires on the shoreline heights. A reindeer's hide was fastened to a pole to serve as a flag, which then was energetically waved. Fire, smoke, and the flag served them well and the marooned were spotted. "The people on board seeing these signals," Le Roy wrote sententiously, "concluded that there were men on the island who implored their assistance, and therefore came to an anchor near the shore."

A

NARRATIVE

OF THE SINGULAR

ADVENTURES

OF

Four Ruffian Sailors,

*Who were caft away on the defert
Ifland of* EAST-SPITZBERGEN.

'TOGETHER WITH

Some OBSERVATIONS on the Productions
of that Ifland, &c.

BY Mr. P. L. LE ROY,

Profeffor of Hiftory, and Member of the Imperial
Academy of Sciences at St. Peterfburg.

Tranflated from the GERMAN ORIGINAL,
At the defire of feveral MEMBERS of the
ROYAL SOCIETY.

*The title page of the English edition of Le Roy's book describing "the singular
adventures of the four Russian sailors who were cast adrift."*

On September 28, the three men were at last returned home. Word of their miraculous survival had preceded them and a small welcoming committee had gathered on the shore, and here Le Roy gives us a touching vignette:

> The moment of the landing was nearly proving fatal to the loving and beloved wife of Alexsei Inkov, who, being present when the vessel came into port, immediately knew her husband, and ran with so much eagerness to his embraces, that they flipped into the water, and very narrowly escaped being drowned.

And finally, the author shows himself a son of his country by commenting on the effect bread and wine, two basic staples of a Frenchman's table, had on the returnees:

> All three on their arrival were strong and healthy; but having lived so long without bread, they could not reconcile themselves to the use of it, and complained that it filled them with wind. Nor could they bear any spirituous liquors, and therefore drank nothing but water.

At the meeting the Pomori had with Count Shuvalov, they carried with them some of their artifact mementos — a spear, bow and arrows, the hammer, the axe, and needles and thread.

One can only stand in awe of these singular individuals. What manner of men were they, to have achieved what they did? David Roberts offers an appropriate illation: "What the Pomori had accomplished on Svalbard was not some instructive lesson in the virtues of faith, perseverance, or ingenuity. It was a work of art."[14]

7

The Franklin Tragedy

O F ALL THOSE BEGUILED by the Siren's song, no account continuous to generate greater interest or inflames imaginations more
than that of the ill-fated foray of Sir John Franklin. On May 19, 1845,
he sailed down the Thames in command of the best-equipped, best-
prepared expedition that had ever embarked in order to seek out the
Northwest Passage. The 133 handpicked officers and men on board
the *Erebus* and the *Terror* were groomed to spend up to three years on
their Arctic quest. The ships moved out into the English Channel, into
the North Sea, and sailed to Greenland, where they took on fresh water
and discharged four invalided sailors. On July 26, the two vessels met
the whaling ship *Enterprise* off Baffin Island. Greetings were exchanged
and everyone seemed to be in good health and high spirits, as reported
by the whaler's master. That was the last sight anyone had of Sir John
and his company — they continued their sail into oblivion, never to be
heard from again. The greatest Arctic expedition turned into the greatest
Arctic tragedy.

The significance of Franklin's incursion into the Arctic lies not in his
achievements, but in the subsequent explorations of the multiple search
parties sent to look for the man. In the thirty-year period commencing
in 1848, forty-two major expeditions became involved in the hunt, peak-
ing in 1850 when fourteen ships were simultaneously scouring the area.
Franklin's men and ships were not found, but evidence of their movements was scattered widely about the ice-strewn northern wilderness.

The searches did also substantially expand knowledge of the Canadian Archipelago with islands being charted; hydrographic and meteorological finds recorded; geological and magnetic data accumulated; and a greater overall appreciation gained of the vicissitudes of northern survival. The mystery of Franklin's fate has still to be fully unravelled as the search for the explorer's remains and those of his ships continues.

Franklin's expedition might more rightly be called "Barrow's Expedition," for had it not been for the initiative and advocacy of Sir John Barrow, the enterprise would never have gotten off the ground. Sir John was president of the Admiralty Board and a founding member of the Royal Geographic Society. As a young man he had travelled to Greenland on a whaler and was smitten by the Arctic. As second secretary of the Admiralty, it was he who was responsible for the surge of British Arctic explorations in the thirty years that followed the Napoleonic wars. Now, in the twilight of his career, he was determined to present his country one final laurel: the penetration of the final section of the Northwest Passage, making it complete; whereas the latest western forays of Baffin and James proved inconclusive, his initiative would succeed gloriously.

The expedition Burrow planned would be the largest and best prepared of any up to that time. Technologically it would be state-of-the-art, the space shuttle of its day as it were, and he set about the task with vigour rarely found in a seventy-one-year-old. Within an incredible three months, Barrow had the entire enterprise in shape and ready to go: ships had been procured and refitted, equipment put into place and provisions purchased and delivered. The one vexing problem remaining was to find the right person to take charge of the venture. Sir John's first two choices were Rear Admiral William Parry and Sir James Ross, both seasoned Arctic travellers, but they declined the invitations. Captain Francis Crozier, a five-time veteran of Arctic exploration with a brilliant naval record, was also given consideration, but at age thirty-three, objection was raised over his youth. Beside, he was Irish, and that would not do.

All the while, Franklin continued in his anxiety to return to the Arctic, kicking his heels on the sidelines in expectation of a call from Barrow. Lady Jane Franklin, however, was busy at work lobbying friends in high places — her husband, after all, was a distinguished officer with experience in Arctic exploration. A groundswell of support soon developed and with no alternatives left Barrow reluctantly acquiesced to the urgings of colleagues and friends and made the appointment. He knew Franklin's strengths and weaknesses, having on three previous occasions sent him out on assignments. With the command confirmed and

Sir John Franklin shortly after he was knighted by George IV in 1829, sixteen years before his fatal expedition,

Franklin ensconced in the captain's cabin of the *Erebus*, Burrow backed off from appearing to be taking the lead in the project.

At the time of his appointment, Franklin was unemployed on half pay from the Navy. Two years earlier he had been recalled from Tasmania, where for six years he had been lieutenant governor of Van Diemen's Land, a penal colony of three thousand souls. He and his wife Jane had run afoul of the Colonial Office for having pushed for social and educational reforms deemed inappropriate by the government bureaucracy. A balding and corpulent man, he was a month away from his sixtieth birthday, but, in the opinion of Admiral Perry, "fitter than any I know." Franklin was popular with his seniors at the Admiralty, with colleagues, friends, and the men serving under him. Contemporaries variously described him in positive terms: a religious and gentle person; honest with a sense of justice and compassion; a modest man awkward at social gatherings, not flamboyant or abrasive; a man of duty and a sense of purpose; having a sense of humour and viewing life as a glass half full rather than half empty.

Franklin had gone to sea with the Royal Navy at age fourteen and within six months found himself in the heat of the Battle of Copenhagen. Later, as a midshipman he was on the seventy-four-gun *Bellerophon* at the Battle of Trafalgar, and during the War of 1812 he was lightly wounded at the Battle of New Orleans. After the Napoleonic wars, the young officer was discharged on half pay, but later appointed by Barrow to lead an overland exploration to the mouth of the Coppermine River in the Canadian Arctic. It was here that the young officer made a name for himself.

Lieutenant Franklin quit England with four others: his second-in-command, a physician named John Richardson; two midshipmen, Robert Hood and George Beck; and a servant, Ordinary Seaman John Hepburn. Before it was all over the select group had expanded to twenty, including French Canadian *voyageurs* and local Natives. The expedition set off from York House on the southwest coast of Hudson Bay in September 1819 and returned to the starting point three years later. Its purpose was to reach the mouth of the Coppermine River over land and then move east along the continent's north coast in an exploration of a possible channel to Hudson Bay, an additional step closer to linking the Northwest Passage. Two Christmases later, after exhausting slogging and canoeing through the "endless rugged, scabrous landscape of jagged rock and skinny trees" of the Canadian northwest, they reached the juncture of the Coppermine and salt water. It had been an appallingly difficult passage undertaken by birchbark canoes, dog-sledges, and snowshoes. Franklin wrote:

> The task of beating a track [with snowshoes] through deep snow for the dogs was so very fatiguing that each of the men took the lead in turn ... soon after we encamped the snow fell heavily, which was an advantage by its affording us an additional covering to our blankets ... the suffering [snowshoeing] occasions can be fairly imagined by a person who thinks upon the inconvenience of marching with a weight of two or three pounds constantly attached to galled feet and swelled ankles...[1]

Franklin's life seems to have been plagued by bad luck, and certainly what followed in the months after his passage up the Coppermine was a sequence of one misfortune after another. Barrow had made arrangements with the Hudson's Bay and the North West companies to supply the expedition with food and other necessities, but by the time Franklin entered their territories the two rivals were in a bitter struggle with one another and had little time for the naval visitors. Now, twenty-one months into the journey, Franklin was entirely dependent on the Copper Indians, not only as guides, but for their team's food requirements.

In mid-August, however, the Natives decided to quit the group and return home, leaving the five Englishmen, thirteen French voyageurs, and two Inuit to their own devices. The abandoned party set off eastward in two large canoes, hugging the coastline and carrying a ten-day supply of food, and, in the ensuing four weeks, they managed to cover three hundred miles — but found no trace of Hudson Bay. Discouraged, suffering from fatigue and ill-fed stomachs, and with winter rapidly approaching, Franklin decided to terminate the search and strike out overland back to Fort Enterprise where they had spent the previous winter. There they would find shelter and stores of pemmican that had been purposely left by them.

Thus began a 280-mile trek across uncharted tundra called Barren Lands, a vast steppe extending from Hudson Bay to Great Slave Lake, scattered with scrub trees, grasses, mosses, lichens, and sharp rocks that make any crossing treacherous. "If anyone had broken a limb here," Richardson wrote, "his fate would have been melancholy indeed, as we could neither have remained with him, nor carried him on with us."[2] Within the travelling group was a handful of *voyageurs*, those hardy French-Canadian adventurers who played no small role in the opening of the Canadian West through their skills in navigating heavy canoes along the waterways. Hudson's voyageurs had a particularly difficult time of it, for each carried backpacks averaging ninety pounds. Canoes had long been discarded and when time came to cross rivers and streams, they had to be forded by foot. Early winter made game scarce and the kill of a deer, hare, or partridge was an occasion for jubilation. Provisions had become fully exhausted, and the men were reduced to grubbing for lichens — *tripe de roche* they were called — plus the occasional rotting carcass discarded by wolves. Hunger became so severe that strips of leather from spare boots were boiled and consumed. (Franklin's famous account: "there was no *tripe de roche*, so we drank tea and ate some of our shoes for supper.")

The group finally made it to the Coppermine River at a point forty miles from Fort Enterprise, according to Franklin's calculations. Forty miles might just as well have been a thousand as far as any were concerned. Two of the weakest voyageurs stubbornly refused to proceed farther and were left behind where they collapsed. Shortly thereafter, the party split up. Beck, the strongest of the lot, with three others, pressed forward to their destination in order to return with food. Franklin plus seven followed at a slower pace, while Richardson and Hood begged to remain where they were to await Beck's return. Shortly after Franklin set out, three voyageurs accompanying him pleaded an inability to continue and received permission to retrace their steps to rejoin Richardson and Hood. The food situation seemed critical, but the worst was yet to come. Franklin wrote:

> [One of the party] who had been hunting, brought in the antlers and back bone of a deer which had been killed in the summer. The wolves and birds of prey had picked them clean, but there still remained a quantity of the spinal marrow which they were unable to extract. Although putrid, it was esteemed a valuable prize, and the spine being equally divided into portions was evenly distributed. After eating the marrow, which was so acrid as to excoriate the lips, we rendered the bones friable by burning and ate them also.

A couple of days after the voyageurs dropped back, one of them, named Michel Terohaut, staggered into the camp of the Navy men, explaining that he had become separated from his companions who he thought would soon be following. Much to the Englishmen's relief, Michel carried a welcomed quantity of meat — a hare and a ptarmigan he managed to kill, which the two Englishmen eagerly devoured. A couple of days later, the voyageur returned from an unsuccessful hunt, but with meat from the remains of a wolf that had been killed by the stroke of a caribou's horn, and this too was divided and consumed. Spirits were lifted. In the next few days, however, Terohaut became surly and began to exhibit erratic behaviour. He disappeared for hours, not telling the others where he was going; he refused to search for *tripe de roche* or to carry wood, and when Hood asked him why he no longer went hunting, he responded with a remark that was quickly realized as having a sinister connotation, "There are no more animals, you had better kill and eat me." It then dawned on Richardson and Hood that Terohaut possibly killed his companions and was disappearing to feed off their corpses. The hare, ptarmigan, and scraps of wolf they had so ravenously consumed had in fact been human flesh. Richardson wrote, "We became convinced from circumstances, the details of which may be spared, that it must have been a portion of the body of Belanger or Perrault."[3]

The following day was a Sunday and "the morning service was read." In the afternoon, Richardson heard a gunshot and in seeking to find its source, he came across:

> [P]oor Hood lying lifeless at the fire-side, a ball having apparently entered his forehead. I was at first horrified with the idea, that in a fit of despondency he had hurried himself into the presence of his Almighty Judge, by an act of his own hand; but the conduct of Michel soon gave rise to other thoughts, and excited suspicions which were confirmed, when upon examining the body, I discovered that the shot had entered the back of the head, and passed out the forehead, and that the muzzle of the gun had been applied so close as to set fire to the night-cap behind.

Furthermore, the gun that fired the shot was a long-barrelled rifle. No doubting it: the young midshipman had not committed suicide; he had been murdered. In the next two days, "Michel alarmed us much by his gestures and conduct was constantly muttering to himself … assumed such a tone of superiority as evinced that he considered us to be completely in his power." He became aggressive and threatening and it was clear to Richardson that their lives were in danger from this crazed individual. While the weaker ones eked out nourishment from *tripe de roche*, the voyageur had been secretly consuming meat. "Hepburn and I were not in a condition to resist even an open attack, nor could we by any device escape from him. Our united strength was far inferior to his, and, besides his gun, we was armed with two pistols, an Indian bayonet and a knife…. I determined … to put an end to his life by shooting him through the head with a pistol." On Wednesday Richardson did just that.

That evening around the campfire, "we singed the hair off a part of the buffalo robe that belonged to Hood, and boiled it and ate it." Such was the desperation brought on by unmitigated hunger.

Four more days of continued march in "thick snowy weather," often sinking deep into the stuff, finally brought them to Fort Enterprise, where their happy expectations were rudely shattered by a dismal scene of want and neglect. Only four of the expedition's men remained alive to greet them, and the first to step forward was an atrophied Franklin — "the ghastly countenance, dilated eyeballs and sepulchral voices of Captain Franklin and those with him were more than we could at first bear."

The stores of food left behind by them on the outbound passage were gone, stolen by the Natives; the deerskin parchments covering the windows were no longer there — boiled and eaten by the starving men and the floorboards had been pried up and used for firewood.

For a week they remained in the desolate building, grubbing for *tripe de roche* and boiling rotten deerskin and then, on November 7, the stillness of morning was broken by the noises of arriving Natives. Beck had somehow managed to reach their settlement and had sent them to rescue his mates. The new arrivals carried with them a generous supply of pemmican. In the days that followed, they hunted and fished for the survivors and treated them "with the same tenderness they would have bestowed on their own infants." With strength restored, the entire group set off once more and eventually returned to their starting point on Hudson Bay ... and thence home to "England's pleasant pastures green." Thus came to an end Franklin's first Arctic exploration and a seminal chapter in the explorer's life had drawn to a close.

The expedition had travelled 5,550 miles and in the process, eleven of Franklin's men perished. The payoff by any standard was negligible: only a tiny portion of the Canadian coastline had been charted — a disastrous venture by any definition. Many criticized Franklin for his obstinacy in refusing to deviate from the set plan even when it became obvious that shortage of food and scarcity of game would make a safe journey impossible. He was accused of being inflexible and incapable of adapting to changing situations. Rumours and dark innuendos circulated concerning Hood's murder. The only account of the murder was published by Richardson with Franklin's approbation, and, some asked, what was to prove that Richardson himself had not killed and perhaps eaten Hood?

Despite criticisms, the British public adulated Franklin and his account of the journey in book form became a bestseller going into a number of editions and translations. In the mind of the Victorian majority he was a hero — a hero for the courage displayed in the face of adversity and for stalwart perseverance; "the man who ate his boots," as he affectionately became known.

Such was the man commanding the *Erebus* when on that July day of 1845, off Baffin Island, she and the *Terror* left the whaler's company to continue their journey into oblivion. The two ships were nearly identical, the *Terror* slightly smaller at 325 tons with the other at 370 tons. Since they were originally used as floating batteries for the shelling of shore installations, they were solidly constructed to withstand the weight and powerful recoil of five-ton mortars. Squared oak beams eighteen inches thick reinforced the hull athwartship. The extra spacious holds for the storage of shells and explosives were well suited for the expedition's three-year supply of provisions and equipment.[4] Brought into Her Majesty's Dockyard, the vessels underwent major refits: decks were doubled in thickness; additional oak beams were installed fore and aft, hulls were scraped clean and the planking doubled; bows were covered by inch-thick sheets of iron; keels were covered with an extra heavy sheeting of copper, and the sails of the three masts replaced with triple-thick canvas. To withstand the cold hatches and gangways were double-doored, cork insulation was installed throughout, and an elaborate piping system was put into place to serve a central heating unit. Sturdy lifeboats were at the davits with "sufficient capacity to carry all the crew if the vessel was lost."

Both ships were given locomotive engines to power the screw propellers, an invention which had newly come into use by the Royal Navy (until then steam powered vessels had sidewheels). Not only were the seven-foot propellers novel, but the ones on the *Erebus* and *Terror* were made retractable — in hazardous ice conditions they could be hauled up and stored in special wells. Sails were to be the principal means of propulsion, with the engines serving to navigate through ice floes. To fuel the engines specially built bunkers accommodating ninety tons of coal were installed, allowing the vessels a 2,800-mile range under power. For

Victorian times, the vessels were state of the art and proud achievements of Sir John Barrow.

Starvation and scurvy were two fundamental concerns of any Arctic expedition, as experience clearly demonstrated after Franklin's disastrous foray into the Canadian North. Not only did provisions have to be made for the right quantity of each staple, but the three-year supply had to be judiciously packed to prevent spoilage or infestation by vermin.

In 1845, tin cans had just come into use and Burrow adroitly took advantage of the new process by having many basic foods pre-cooked and delivered in the airtight containers, which seemingly offered indefinite shelf life. The "Deptford Victualling Yard report for HMS *Terror*," dated eight days before sailing, tells us that 4,573 pounds of lemon juice were brought on board "in 5 gallon kegs," as were nearly three tons of pickled cranberries, cucumbers, cabbage, onions, and walnuts — all in the interest of scurvy prevention. (The *Erebus* received approximately the same amounts.)

For a sense of overall magnitude, some other of the thirty-seven officially listed items included: 66,704 pounds of flour and 16,884 pounds of biscuit; 2,288 gallons of West Indian rum and 2,490 gallons of ale; 47,008 pounds of salt beef, salt pork, and tinned meat. Additionally: tea, pemmican, macaroni, tobacco (3,510 pounds), chocolate (4,573 pounds), and "for the sick," 200 gallons of wine and brandy.

Officers of both ships had access to government-provided chicken coops for the supply of fresh eggs. (After the chickens ceased laying, they were dispatched to the stew pot.) The officers also had the privilege of bringing on board, at their own expense, whatever they wished by way of supplementary items — things like Westphalia ham, corned beef, canned soups, South Carolina rice, vermicelli, jams, "vegetable essence," and whisky. Cookman observed that the expedition was:

> [T]he most lavishly provisioned Arctic voyage England had ever assembled. On full allowance, free of scurvy, it could subsist handsomely and with great variety for a minimum of three years — more than ample to force the Passage or outlast any conceivable period they might be trapped in the ice.

These ships were never to return home. The instructions Franklin carried from their Lordships at the Admiralty were straightforward: from Baffin Bay he was to proceed west, "guided by your own observations as to the course most eligible to be taken,"[5] using "the small steam engine and a propeller … only in difficult cases." Passing through Lancaster Sound, the expedition was to continue west "without loss of time," hoping "that the remaining portion of the passage, about 900 miles [in fact, 1,400 miles] to the Bhering's Strait may also be found equally free from [ice] obstruction." At Cape Walker "we desire that every effort be used to endeavour to penetrate to the southward and the westward in a course as direct towards Bhering's Strait as the position and extent of the ice, or the existence of land, as present unknown, may admit." The instructions go on to say that "should you be so fortunate to accomplish a passage through Bhering's Strait, you are then to proceed to the Sandwich Islands [Hawaii], to refit your ships and refresh your crews."

Franklin is also advised that should he "meet either Esquimaux or Indians near the place where you winter, you are to endeavour by every means in your power to cultivate a friendship with them, by making them presents of such articles as you may be supplied with." Should the ships "be detained during a winter" the crews are to carry out magnetical and meteorological observations using the portable observatory supplied for the purpose. Furthermore, having passed 65°N, on a daily basis "throw overboard a bottle or copper cylinder closely sealed and containing a paper stating the date and position at which it was launched … for this purpose we have caused each ship to be supplied with paper, on which is printed, in several languages, a request that whoever may find it should take measures for transmitting it to this office."

From Greenland weeks earlier Franklin had sent his wife a final note, one which brimmed with hope and pride:

> Let me now assure you, my dearest Jane, that I am amply provided for with every requisite for my passage, and that I am entering on my voyage comforted with every hope of God's merciful guidance and protection, and that He will bless, comfort and protect you, my dearest …

and all my other relatives. Oh, how much I wish I could write to each of them to assure them of my happiness I feel in my officers, my crew, and my ship![6]

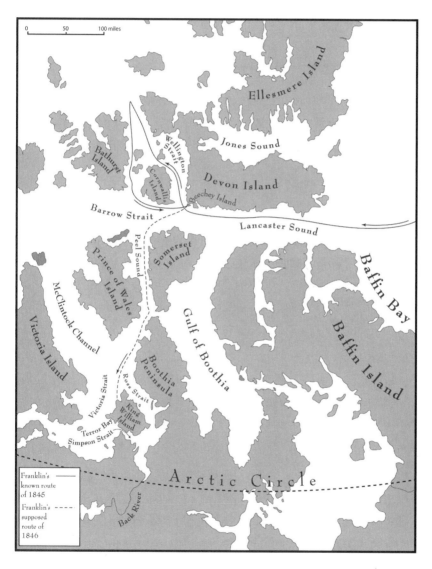

Franklin's route within the interior of the Canadian Arctic Archipelago from autumn 1845 to its tragic conclusion three years later on King William Island.

Map by Cameron McLeod Jones.

What came of the tossed bottles and copper cylinders is anyone's guess, for there is no record of any having been found. What little we do know of the fateful passage is pieced together from documents and other relics unearthed by subsequent search parties. From Baffin Island the two ships moved on in excellent weather and favourable winds, permitting Franklin to pass quickly through Lancaster Sound without incident. At the entrance to Barrow Strait, however, heavy ice brought it all to a halt and a sail west to Melville Island was made impossible. In his search for an open channel, Franklin boldly ordered a course north, up Wellington Strait, where he was again stymied by ice buildup. He turned back and, sailing south, Cornwallis Island was circumnavigated. With the developing winter bringing on freeze and ice buildup, he searched for a safe haven, which he found at Beechey. This tiny island six hundred miles north of the Arctic Circle lies just off Devon Island, which to this day holds its status as the world's largest uninhabited island. Here, the crews of the two ships passed their first winter locked in ice for ten months, attending to the requisite "magnetical and meteorological observations" ... and the burial of three of their shipmates. *[handwritten: lead poisoning from cans]*

By the end of October, the long polar night had taken root, the sun having disappeared beneath the horizon, not to be seen again until the end of January. Snow covered the iced decks and the eerie silence enveloping the ships was broken only by the hum of incessant winds. The sense of isolation is offered by Robert McClure, one of the many subsequent searchers for signs of Franklin: "No pen can tell of the unredeemed loneliness of an October evening in this polar world; the monotonous, rounded outline of the adjacent hills and the flat, meandering valleys were deadly white with snow."[7]

New Year's celebrations were dampened by the death of Petty Officer John Torrington, a twenty-year-old stoker on board the *Terror*. The young man had been confined to his bunk for weeks with lung complications thought to be tuberculosis. A wooden coffin was fabricated by the ship's carpenters and the body was lowered into a shallow grave within the permafrost. Under flickering lamps, the burial service was read by Franklin himself and the grave was closed and covered with a limestone slab carrying the chiselled name of the deceased.

Four days later, another death — that of Able Seaman John Hartnell, a twenty-five-year-old from the *Erebus*. Unlike Torrington's death, this one was sudden and unexpected for all as the sailor had appeared the picture of good health. An immediate autopsy was performed to determine the cause of death, but it proved inconclusive — pneumonia, perhaps. The body was wrapped, placed in a coffin, and laid side by side with Torrington. Hartnell's shipmates had nailed a small plaque on the coffin's lid, identifying the deceased and carrying the inscription: "Thus saith the Lord of Hosts, consider your ways" (Haggai, I, 7).

Then, within three months, a third death occurred, that of Marine Private William Braine, a thirty-two-year-old from the *Erebus*. Like Hartnell's death, this one also was sudden and unexpected. He was struck while on a hunting excursion at some distance from the ship. By the time the body was transported back it had begun to decompose, making an autopsy difficult, but since it bore signs of nascent scurvy it was presumed that the fearful disease was the cause of death — despite carefully taken dietary precautions. Hartnell was laid to rest near the other two deceased.

Three deaths within three months were confounding and an intimidating portent of things possibly to come. The winter proved long, but it was passed in reasonable comfort with hunting excursions, theatricals, and diversions of one sort or another, plus attention to scientific observations. The *Terror*, for example, carried a variety of musical instruments, including a hand organ and had a well-stocked library of 1,200 volumes. In the 120-square-foot wardroom situated on the upper deck, the ship's eleven officers gathered in the style to which they were accustomed. The dining table was laid with a linen tablecloth and silverware at each place, including initialled napkin rings. Food and drink was entirely satisfactory, particularly with the private reserves of upscale stocks brought aboard by individual officers. Dozens of punched metal discs were available for the organ to play music at any time and the games locker was stocked with chess sets, checker boards, and playing cards. Every officer, of course, had his own private cabin.

Below deck it was somewhat different. A thousand-square-foot space was allocated to forty-four men, not only for passing leisure hours, but as a place to eat and sling hammocks at night — privacy was non-existent.

To the modern eye, the startling contrast in the living arrangements of officers and men is dramatic, but those were Victorian times when officers were considered gentlemen of the upper class, and soldiers and sailors were commoners drawn from the masses. One description of the overcrowded conditions of the lower deck is given by the surgeon accompanying an Antarctic expedition in 1840 who fretted over contagion of diseases:

> ... if it was raining, snowing, the ship hemmed in by ice, there would be forty to sixty individuals in the orlop deck, spitting, drinking, eating, while all openings were tightly shut ... The smells from the hold, from the storeroom, the smoke, steam, and smells from the kitchen, the exhalation from lungs and skin were not dispersed by the faintest breath of fresh air; daylight was hardly encountered ...[8]

When summer came and the sea at last opened, everyone was delighted to quit Beechey, to leave behind the dreariness and monotony of "the isle of death." It was the beginning of the short Arctic season — summers last four to twelve weeks — and that particular summer was the warmest recorded by any previous expedition. Quick time was made in reaching the northern end of Somerset Island where Franklin was delighted to find the straits open, the same waters that were closed to him in the previous year. They were now free to follow Admiralty's instruction and the course was set south to King William Island, lying 280 miles away "as the crow flies." Their exact route is unclear and academics continue to fret over the question: did they sail past Prince of Wales Island on its west side through McClintock Strait or through Peel Sound on the east? (Majority opinion favours the latter.)

Within weeks of departure from Beechey their destination came into distant view with the mast-top lookouts reporting ice floes west of the island and clear waters to the east. In determining which direction they would take to sail around King William, the open eastern path would have been self-evident. The cartographers producing Franklin's flawed charts, however, had falsely indicated that an isthmus connected the island with nearby Boothia Peninsula, in other words, a blocked passageway. It wasn't therefore a matter of choice — only one route was viable, and as Jeannette Mirsky observes poignantly in *To the Arctic*, "his only choice — by reason of that mortal flaw in the map — lay in following to the west. To the west he sailed, right into the fatal spiderweb the Arctic had spun to trap the unwary ... never were they to get free."[9]

Initially, the *Erebus* and *Terror* sailed through new ice that was thin and sludgy, but in time they met thicker material. This too proved no hindrance to the heavy vessels with their iron-clad bows and reinforced keels. But the picture quickly changed when the ships began to encounter large blocks of the stuff being battered to and fro by angry currents. Some of the ice chunks were immense, floebergs as high as fifteen feet, but more worrisome still were their increasing numbers. The ships continued to bully their way through, but as the bergs began to knit together, progress was appreciably retarded. Sails had long given way to steam power, and now the stokers shovelled coal for all they were worth in order to build up a full head of steam for the engines, the struggle growing ever more challenging. On the night of September 15, 1846, the obdurate ice won and the expedition was decisively arrested. Twelve miles from shore, clamped in a vicelike grip, the "state of the art" *Erebus* and the *Terror* became prisoners of the floe ... and there would they remain for over a year and a half. Nature triumphed.

In the weeks that followed, the pack drifted slowly westward, no doubt raising hopes in the optimistically minded that the Northwest Passage might thus be completed. Eight months later, the warming rays of Arctic Spring provided no signs of thaw, and captivity continued. The fear was that should summer prove inordinately short they might well find themselves facing another winter locked up. Supplies were dwindling, especially coal, and food remained for just under a year. On May 26, Franklin sent out a sledging party to King William Island to scout out any sign of break in the surrounding waters. As they made landfall, the men deposited a message into the six-foot cairn erected and charted by William Parry[10] seventeen years earlier. The message

The opening of the cairn by Franklin's searchers in which a note had been deposited, dated April 25, 1848, recording the deaths of Franklin and those of twenty-three others.

gave particulars of the expedition's progress, including date, ships' names, route taken, and Sir John Franklin's name. It ended with the words, "all well." (The note was subsequently found in 1859 by one of the parties searching for evidence of the expedition.) When the sailors reached the island's east coast, they were no doubt startled to discover that the channel separating the island from Boothia Peninsula was free of ice. Not only that, but there was no evidence of an isthmus joining the two lands … oh, had they but taken this eastern route around the island! The party returned to the *Erebus* to make its report, but upon arrival the sailors were startled to find their sixty-one-year-old commander laying incapacitated in his cabin.

On June 11, 1847, Sir John Franklin died. He had taken to his bunk only days before and the decline had been rapid. The cause of death was uncertain. Fate, however, had been kind to the noble and ever-hopeful officer, for he went quietly to his death and was spared the agonies suffered by his shipmates in the calamitous events that followed.

Ten months later, a second note was deposited in the cairn on King William Island. Dated April 25, 1848, and signed by the captains of the *Erebus* and the *Terror*, it explained that they had "been beset" since September 12, 1846, and telling of Sir John's death, it went on to report that "the total loss of deaths in the Expedition had been to this date 9 officers and 15 men."

Franklin's one-time fear of yet another ice-locked year came to be and it was passed in abject misery, as the cairn's message partially evidences. Food had become dangerously short in supply; coal was severely rationed, causing even colder living quarters; the spectre of scurvy hung heavy; an additional, unidentified sickness had infected the ship, and boredom and ennui had given way to lassitude and despair. The dark angel of death was a familiar figure.

Francis Crozier, the *Terror's* captain and Franklin's second-in-command, had by then taken charge of the expedition. Faced with the grim realities, it was clear that the possibility of forcing a Northwest Passage was out of the question. Furthermore, there was no way that the group could survive a third winter of imprisonment. The only option appearing open was to abandon the vessels and make an 850-mile overland trek to Great Slave Lake where salvation would be had at the Hudson's Bay Company's outpost. Crozier, a veteran of four previous Arctic expeditions and well familiar with the Canadian North, no doubt realized that the intimidating march was a wholly uncertain risk.

In mid-April, preparations were launched for quitting the two ships. Since their departure from England two years earlier, twenty-eight men had perished and now the remaining 105 set to the tasks at hand. They realized that once they reached the limits of the ice floes, a traverse to the mainland would have to be made by boat and therefore four substantial ones were made ready and hauled onto the ice at some distance from the vessels. Up to thirty feet long and mounted on heavy oak sledges, they made for onerous dragging across rough, sometimes precipitous, ice. Each boat carried a complete repair kit, including such items as saw, hammer, nails, sheet metal, and canvas. Goggles and sharp cleats for boots were fabricated.

The large party required copious quantities of food for the estimated three-month passage, even with strict rationing and successful hunting. Barrels and casks containing such items as rolled oats, dried peas, tea, and sugar were emptied into canvas bags. Flour was baked into hard biscuit and salted meat was repacked into lighter containers. What little remained of lemon juice, rum, and vinegar was drained into smaller, more portable jugs. Hundreds of cans of prepared meat were also boarded. Taken together — boats, sledges, provisions, and equipment — the total weight is incalculable, amounting to several tons ... but after all, they were providing for the Arctic needs of 105 men for three months if not more.

On April 22, 1848, the signal was given for everyone to move ahead. Delighted as they must have been at leaving behind cloistered quarters, foul smells, shipboard sickness, attending despair, and sense of forlornness, the moment must also have been emotionally charged. The *Erebus* and *Terror* had faithfully served as their homes for two long years, and now they were bidding farewell to these dear friends. As Scott Cookman wrote so perceptively in *Iceblink*:

> More than almost any other bond, that between a sailor and his ship is extremely strong, and that between a captain and his ship even stronger still. There is a life-and-death dependency between them; neither can survive without the other. This affection, this love, may seem strange to those who have never gone to sea, but it is quite real, perhaps more real, as other kinds of love. No ship is a mere inanimate object; it lives in wind and water and light, and it moves, murmurs, complains, or shouts like everything living.[11]

The men, straining at the heavy burdens, moved farther and farther from their murmuring, complaining friends, and with every painful step they drew closer to their destiny. Soon a pitiable trail of abandoned equipment and unburied dead would litter the hopeless passage.

In England, there had been no word from Franklin for over two years, and public concern had swelled over the expedition's well-being.

The Admiralty, however, showed no anxiety — the ships after all were ultra-modern and provisioned for three years. With clamour of parliamentarians and journalists expanding, Lady Jane was spurred on in her standing efforts to persuade the government to expedite a search. In spring 1848 the Admiralty finally acquiesced — at the very time that Crozier and his men were abandoning the ships. Three expeditions were sent out, two by sea and one by land. One ship was to enter the Canadian archipelago from Lancaster Sound and the other, from the Pacific side via the Beaufort Sea. The overland search under the direction of Sir John Richardson and John Rae was to travel down the Mackenzie River to its mouth and then search out the coastline stretching east. As an incentive to private individuals, a £20,000 reward was posted to anyone successfully finding the missing men.

As noted, within two years, fourteen ships were in the Canadian archipelago scouring the area, and by 1850, forty-two recorded searches had been carried out. No sign of the missing men, but more than one Inuit reported having sighted them at one time or another. From the broad scattering of evidence gathered by these searches and those which followed, a reasonably authentic understanding has been pieced together of what happened.

Wreckage of boats and sledges were found as were cooking pots, hammers, tin cans, and countless personal items such as boots, buttons, eyeglasses, and toothbrushes. Searchers also came across human bones, skulls, and a complete skeleton, but perhaps the most interesting of all discoveries were the mummified remains of the three seamen interred in the permafrost of Beechey Island: Torrington, Hartnell, and Braine.

Causes of the expedition's deaths continue to captivate the imaginations of Franklinphiles. Exactly how did the desperate men of the *Erebus* and *Terror* finish their days? Of what precisely did they die? Scurvy quite naturally stands high on the list, but there's considerably more to it than that. It must be remembered that for two years the men had been cloistered in a hostile environ within the wooden confines of their immobile ships. Lacking the physical activity normally associated with ships under sail and able to do little during the months of darkness, they were naturally weakened and out of shape. Provisions were in short supply and since they were ice-bound "in the least favoured spot in the Canadian Arctic," game was scarce and certainly insufficient to make a difference to more than a hundred hungry men.

Scurvy did come to the ships. Sufficient lemon juice had been boarded in England to issue one ounce daily to each man for three years. The juice, of course, is an outstanding prophylactic, but when it freezes, much of the vitamin content is killed, and it's more than likely that this was the case by the time the two ships became icebound. The one-ounce-per-day calculation, furthermore, was made to meet the needs of men sailing in more temperate climates rather than those of the extreme Arctic cold. In short, Franklin's men suffered from an insufficiency of vitamin C, which when combined with their overall weakened conditions made scurvy inevitable.

Within the first year of ice-lock, living quarters on board the two ships deteriorated badly. Walls of the tightly closed cabins and messes dripped with condensation; the dwindling supply of fuel disallowed proper heating; smoke, humidity, and unhealthy fumes from the holds permeated the narrow confines. Pulmonary ailments of one sort or another struck the crew, especially pneumonia and tuberculosis.

Much of the food stores came from cans that had been improperly sealed by the purveyors and the contents had become unfit for consumption. Canned tomatoes, rich in vitamin C, and certain cooked meats suffered particularly and large quantities had to be discarded. Technology of food preservation at the time was in an embryonic stage and the techniques of canning not fully developed. Franklin's expedition carried tin cans the seams and seals of which had been soldered with toxic lead — some eight thousand of them containing over sixteen tons of preserved soup, vegetables, meat, and pemmican. In addition, tea, chocolate, tobacco, and other foods were stored in containers lined with lead foil.

In their book *Frozen in Time*, Professors Owen Beattie and John Geiger give an account of a study they made in 1981 of lead poisoning incurred by the crews. The bodies of the three Beechey Island seamen were exhumed, X-rays taken, and autopsies performed with body samples collected for pathological examination. Samples of hair from the nape of Torrington's head revealed that:

[H]e had been exposed to large amounts of lead. The hair was long enough to show levels of lead ingestion throughout the first eight months of the Franklin expedition ... lead levels in the hair exceeded 600 parts per million, levels indicating acute lead poisoning. Over the last few centimeters did the level of exposure drop, and then only slightly. This would have been due to a drop in the consumption of food during the last four to eight weeks of Torrington's life, when he was seriously ill.[12]

Lead content was found also in the bodies of Braine and Hartnell. It is clear that the toxic substance contributed to the deaths of these three men and most probably that of the others. It is unlikely that lead was the sole cause of any one death; the poisoning most probably acted in concert with starvation, scurvy, pneumonia, or typhus.

And so it was that on that April day, Crozier and his large party set off on their forlorn trek. Teams of sailors, harnessed like pharaohic slaves, hauled the loaded sledge-mounted boats. In their weakened state, the advance was slow, particularly when they had to traverse pressure ridges or the sharp hillocks of ice pushed upwards, called "hummockies." To proceed as they had was unrealistic; progress was so sluggish that the remaining rations would never see them to the mainland. Loads had to be lightened and at first only so much was abandoned. In the ensuing days and weeks, however, more and more was left behind, and for years to come, search parties scouring the area followed a veritable trail of discarded items, debris, and human remains.

In the meantime, Lady Jane continued in her unflagging efforts to locate her missing husband. As late as 1857, she purchased the 187-ton steamship *Fox*, and commissioned Francis McClintock, a naval officer, to carry out yet another search. McClintock was a veteran of the Canadian North, well familiar with the archipelago, and it was he who made the first substantive discoveries related to Franklin's ill-fated crews. Having passed the winter of 1858–59 on King William Island, he set out by sledge to carry out a thorough examination of that land and parts of the mainland coast to the south. Sixty-five miles south of where Franklin's ships

Francis McClintock, leading one of scores of parties sent out to search for the missing Franklin, came across the remains of a ship's boat on King William Island within which were portions of two skeletons. Among the numerous articles scattered about were "twenty-six pieces of plate, eight of which bore Sir John Franklin's crest."

had been abandoned, McClintock came across a twenty-eight-foot boat, "partially out of her cradle upon the sledge," within which were portions of two skeletons. "One was that of a slight young person; the other of a large, strongly-made, middle-aged man." Both were in "a disturbed state … large and powerful animals, probably wolves, had destroyed much of this skeleton, which may have been that of an officer." Both skulls were missing, except for the lower jaws of each. McClintock continued:

> [One] skeleton was in a somewhat more perfect state and was enveloped with clothes and furs; it lay across the boat, under the after-thwart. Close by it were found five watches; and there were two double-barrelled guns — one barrel in each loaded and cocked — standing muzzle upwards against the boat's side. It may be imagined with what deep interest these sad relics were scrutinized, and how anxiously every fragment of clothing was

turned over in search of pockets and pocketbooks, journals, and even names. Five or six small books were also found, all of the scriptural or devotional works, except "Vicar of Wakefield" ... besides these books, the covers of the New Testament and Prayerbook were found.[13]

The explorer goes on to inventory a list of over thirty articles found lying about close to the boat, including winter clothing, boots, cartridges, "silk handkerchiefs — black, white and figured ... [and] knives — clasp and dinner ones." Also found were a small quantity of tea, forty pounds of chocolate, and a tiny bit of tobacco. Within the boat near the skeletons were "twenty-six pieces of plate, eight bore Sir John Franklin's crest, the remainder had the crests or initials of nine different officers."

Four years before McClintock's foray, another Arctic explorer, John Rae, had also searched for Franklin. Although he found no physical traces of the Englishmen he did come in contact with Inuit who either had met or had seen them. On one occasion he spotted a native wearing a gold cap-band, and when asked where he got it, the answer was "where the dead white men were" — with no indication where that might have been. Reports were also had of "white men falling down and dying as they walked." One native told Rae of finding boots filled with cooked human flesh. Another reported that bodies had been found with the arms sawn off and others, with large amounts of flesh removed.

On returning home, Rae submitted a report on his findings to the Admiralty in which he spoke of the shocking and unwelcome evidence that the desperate survivors had engaged in cannibalism. He wrote, "From the mutilated state of many of the corpses and the contents of the kettles, it is evident that our wretched countrymen had been driven to the last resource — cannibalism — as a means of prolonging existence."[14]

A sensational story such as this rarely finds cover and Rae's did not take long to leak out to the press, which ran with it with fervour. The outraged Lady Jane was beside herself in indignation and rallied her friends and supporters in condemning Rae. After all, British naval officers are simply incapable of engaging in such heinous acts. Charles Dickens took up the pen against the story, but he exonerated Rae and even praised his "manly, conscientious and modest personal character."[15] He then railed vigorously against the Inuit for telling such absurd tales, and made clear his conviction that "every savage to be in his heart covetous, treacherous, and cruel." He praised the "noble conduct and example of [the expedition's] men, and of their great leader himself," and he condemned the Inuit and "the chatter of a gross handful of uncivilized people, with a domesticity of blood and blubber." The author concluded his essay: "Therefore, teach no one to shudder without reason at the history of the [survivors'] end. Therefore, confide with their own firmness, in their fortitude, their lofty sense of duty, their courage, and their religion." Certainly an eloquent and heart-rending outpouring by a literary genius, but a complete obfuscation.

Rae was the first to report on evidence of cannibalism, but subsequently others did the same, investigators like Charles Hall (1864), Frederick Schwarka (1879), and more recently Owen Beattie (1981). All found human bones that clearly show signs of having been cut with steel knives in efforts to de-flesh them, marks inconsistent with the gnawing of animals such as wolves. Skulls were found with gaping holes through which the brains were removed. Beattie tells of one human remain:

> Fracture lines also indicated that the skull had been forcibly broken; the face, including both jaws and all the teeth, was missing. Evidence that the body had been intentionally dismembered was further supported by the selective parts of the skeleton found: the head, arms and legs.[16]

Professor Anne Keenleyside of Trent University's Osteology Laboratory in her detailed study of the Franklin expedition bones offers a table of "Skeletal Elements with Cut Marks." She concludes from the examination results on 507 such bones that "the remains support 19th century Inuit accounts of cannibalism among Franklin's crew."[17] Horrifying as this may be to the modern reader and even more so to Dickens and the Victorians, it is not difficult to imagine the circumstances. There they were, the final remainder of the 130 — exhausted from the strain of hauling, frostbitten, feet swollen, bleeding, and sick, half wet and shivering yet blinded by ice glare; dead or dying mess-mates left behind with no sign of nearing the end of their miserable trek; crazed with hunger and too weak to hunt what little was about. The angel of death hovered. Repugnant as it may have been, those who died continued to serve their mates.

One wonders what went on in the minds of the pitiful valiants in their final days. Thoughts of wives and family left behind? Memories of laden tables and flaming hearths? Perhaps regrets of things done and not done, of unfinished lives? Bitter maybe or at peace with themselves, fearing or welcoming the approaching step into yet another unknown. The failed expedition has been called the greatest disaster in Arctic history. The men of the *Erebus* and *Terror*, however, had not failed. For three long years the crews lived in isolation, battling sickness and starvation, amid the most horrendous Arctic conditions. Even as they moved away from the abandoned ships they continued in faith and hope while stoically attending to their duties.

8

Americans of the Arctic

IN SUMMER 1987, AN extraordinary young woman from Los Alamitos, California, lowered herself gingerly into the frigid waters of the Bering Strait and set out to swim to Russia. Lynne Cox was her name. With long, persistent strokes, the stouthearted athlete pressed forward, eventually losing sight of the United States. She wore an ordinary swimsuit and bathing cap; incredibly no wet suit — only protective grease. In those 38°F waters, hypothermia might have been expected to overwhelm her, but she appeared immune to the cold. Steadily and forcefully, Lynne propelled herself through the choppy waters dancing about her, and after what seemed an interminable time, her feet finally scraped the rocky bottom. She was in Russia; she had made it. That the thirty-year-old succeeded in her goal was an unbelievable feat. Warmly bundled psychologists who monitored the swim from the comfort of the accompanying boat were as astonished as was the admiring public in Russia and the United States after they heard the news. In May 1990, at a White House summit conference, Presidents Reagan and Gorbachev raised a toast to the indefatigable Lynn, who "proved by her courage how closely to each other our peoples live."

It took Lynn two hours and sixteen minutes to cover the distance from Little Diomede Island (United States) to Big Diomede Island (Russia). For her, swimming in those near-freezing waters, the passage must at times have appeared endless. In reality, however, it is the shortest distance, a mere 2.7 miles separating the United States and Russia.

Canada and Mexico aside, Russia is America's closest neighbour. Had Lynn's swim taken place 120 years earlier, there would have been no question of neighbours; it was all Russian, the two Diomedes and Alaska. The United States at the time was simply not part of the equation.

How Alaska came to be American is an intriguing tale and important to us inasmuch as the United States became an Arctic country. The sale caused many Americans and Russians to wonder: what on earth prompted the tsar to transfer some six hundred thousand square miles of territory so rich in furs, timber, fisheries, and mineral resources for a paltry sum? Some view the sale as a shining example of Yankee ingenuity in hoodwinking naive Russians.

On the evening of March 29, 1867, Secretary of State Seward was at his Washington home, happily engaged in a game of whist with his wife by the fireplace. The doorbell sounded and an exhilarated Baron Stoeckl, the Russian ambassador and a friend of the family, burst into the room. He had just received a coded dispatch via the newly laid transatlantic telegraph cable, the contents of which he was simply unprepared to delay sharing until the next morning. The tsar had at last consented to the sale of Alaska. The two men had been meeting for four arduous months, discussing and negotiating for precisely this outcome and now it came to be. Stoeckl suggested that the two men meet in the morning at Seward's office to formalize the arrangement. But the impatient secretary would have none of that; he wanted the deed done immediately. Poor Mrs. Seward: she surrendered her winning hand, the cards were put away, apologies were made, and with that the two men parted company each to gather his staff. The assembled advisors worked hard into the night and by four o'clock in the morning the treaty lay on the desk of the secretary of state, ready for approval by congress and the president's signature. As one historian observes, "At a strange midnight conference, the two incredible international bedfellows, Russia and the United States, became close territorial neighbors. How close, no one was to realize until the dawn of the air age."[1]

But what is perhaps not appreciated is that it was Russia that wished to sell, not so much the United States wanting to buy. At the time of the negotiations, the very prospect of a positive outcome was dismaying for many Americans and caused much anger. One congressman bitterly summed up what others felt when he declared "that Alaska was created for *some* purpose I have little doubt. But our information is so limited that conjectures can assign *no* use to it, unless it is to demonstrate the folly which those in authority are capable of in the acquisition of useless territory."[2] It was only through the energy of expansionist-minded Seward that the talks on the purchase of Alaska were revived in the months before Stoeckl's precipitous return to St. Petersburg in 1866.

Years before becoming secretary of state, Seward openly reasoned that it was American destiny "to roll its restless waves to the icy barriers of the North, and to encounter oriental civilization on the Pacific." He argued not only for Alaska's annexation, but for a political union with Canada — little wonder that he has been called "the greatest of American expansionists." And even less wonder that he wished to act instantly on the tsar's decision.

Five months prior to Stoeckl's undoing of Mrs. Seward's whist game, the ambassador had taken leave of Washington to return to St. Petersburg. No sooner, however, did he reach home than Grand Duke Constantine, the tsar's younger brother, persuaded the envoy to go back to America. He wanted the sale of Alaska negotiated. Russia, he argued, had to focus on becoming more effective in dealing with the developing complexities of the Japanese-Chinese-Korean orbit, and Alaska was a drain on resources. "Our interests are on the Asiatic coast and that is where we must direct our energy," he wrote to Foreign Affairs Minister Gorchakov. "There we are in our own territory and have the possibility of exploiting a large, rich region ... we must not lose the opportunity to develop on this ocean a preeminent standing worthy of Russia." It was prudent to "gracefully yield" Alaska, thereby bringing the United States into an alliance that would provide Russia with a guardian to its Siberian back door.

The Alaskan sale came about not exclusively due to Seward's ambitions or through Constantine's strategic vision; the reasons were varied. By the mid-century the Russian-American Company was in collapse. The world market for furs had substantially bottomed out, added to which the fact that the Alaskan coastline was simply overhunted and the stocks of fur-bearing animals had withered. To add to the company's woes, the problem of defence loomed on the horizon. Historically, the company never gave much thought to the issue, for there was never any need. It had worked amicably with the Hudson's Bay Company and its relations with Americans were businesslike and, on the whole, neighbourly. The Crimean War, furthermore, caused the company to develop a dependency on the United States for its supply and shipping needs, and this resulted in an unfavourable balance of trade, which St. Petersburg found grating. By the middle of the century, global perspectives had changed. Given Britain's rapidly developing presence in British Columbia along Russian borders, and to the south, a mushrooming American economy, the tsar's government felt that some future territorial conflict along the eastern Pacific coastline appeared inevitable. If Russia was to continue in Alaska as it had in the past, then defence expenditures would have to be incurred, for honour's sake if nothing else. Under the circumstances, was it prudent to remain in Alaska? Grand Duke Constantine's forceful views on the issue were known and they found the support of the ministries.

It was clear that Russia was prepared to sell Alaska. But was the United States prepared to purchase it? In the years before the Stoeckl-Seward negotiations, American enthusiasm for Alaska was negligible at best, and it was viewed as a perfectly useless expanse, quite unnecessary for the already land-rich country. "A dreary waste of glaciers, icebergs, white bears and walrus fit only for Esquimaux," one politician opined.

As early as 1857, Stoeckl began to feel out possibilities of a sale. William Gwin of California initially rebuffed him, saying that he had no interest in Alaska — it was simply too far away to be of any value to his state and to the country. Vocal California lobbies, however, and others in the Washington territory gave him pause to reflect. The rich fishery potential of the Alaska coast, it was argued, should not to be overlooked and neither were the equally promising resources of inland furs. The senator eventually acquiesced and indifferently proposed that $5 million might be allocated for the purchase.

Russia was prepared and so seemed the United States — it was now a matter of price. President Johnson and the cabinet authorized Seward to offer the Russians $5 million, which is what he did. (This figure, coincidentally, matched the minimum amount Stoeckl was authorized by St. Petersburg to accept.) In December 1866, Seward presented the American offer, which Stoeckl agreed to take under consideration. It soon became clear to the Russian that his American counterpart was not only enthusiastic about the deal, but was also anxious to conclude it expeditiously. The wily Russian therefore determined to protract discussions, which he successfully did in the months that followed. Agreement was at last reached on a figure of $7 million but not without Steward's bitter complaint that he was exceeding all authorization. But Stoeckl, encouraged with the outcome of his bargaining, held out for more. To the agreed figure, he now insisted, must be added an additional sum to cover related expenses. Ostensibly, these included coverage of the Russian-American Company's debts and the cost of London banking houses, fees for carrying out the gold exchange transaction. In fact, "related expenses" were also a provision for the requisite bribes to certain members of Congress) if any hope was to be had of passing an Alaska purchase bill.

"I consider the price too high as it is," countered Seward. "I have gone far beyond the wishes of my Government in order to prevent unnecessary bickering. But I will not for one moment entertain any suggestion of taking over the obligations incurred by a chartered company. And my Government will not clear the transaction in London. We had our bellyful of London in the late war."[3] But, after continued deliberation, it was at last agreed to conclude the matter with a $7.2 million figure. Alaska at that price would become American, "free and unencumbered by any reservations, privileges, franchises, grants, etc." And this was the deal the two friends wrote into a treaty in the middle of that March night in the State Department offices.

Whatever Stoeckl's success, the Alaskan purchase price was a virtual giveaway. The tsar spent twice the amount annually merely to operate the imperial navy. A gift it was: American territory had expanded by 369,529,600 acres — at less than two cents an acre. A paltry sum it was if one considers that sixty years later United States purchased from Denmark three Caribbean islands for $25 million, or $249 an acre.

The bill providing for the purchase passed the Senate in record time, and after languishing in the House of Representatives for fifteen months, it was finally ratified. On October 18, 1867, the Stars and Stripes were ceremoniously raised in New Archangel (renamed Sitka) and United States became an Arctic land.

It didn't take long for southern-based entrepreneurs, tradesmen, and adventurers to begin shuffling into the newly acquired territory on one ambitious project or another. But even before the United States takeover of Alaska, Americans had been working not only in those Arctic and sub-Arctic wildernesses, but in Siberia, as well. One such hardy was a self-educated twenty-three-year-old from Norwalk, Ohio, bearing the same name as his great-nephew, George F. Kennan, the iconic twentieth-century American diplomat and historian. In 1865, the elder Kennan set off for northeastern point of Siberia, where he spent two and a half years working for the Russian-American Telegraph Company. In order to appreciate more fully the soul of the Arctic, it's essential to dwell a bit on George and his memoir, *Tent Life in Siberia*. But first, how did this young provincial find himself there?

In October 1861, an attempt was made to lay a telegraph cable between America and Europe. It failed, as did three subsequent tries, all checkmated by the seemingly invincible Atlantic; the technical challenges of the 1,600-mile distance and the wild ocean currents were judged insurmountable. Vast sums had been expended to no avail. The Western Union Company therefore decided to tackle the problem by passing through the west. It would hook up America with the capitals of Europe by establishing a telegraph via the Bering Strait. The plan called for a line that would move north from San Francisco, already connected with New York, through Oregon, British Columbia, and Alaska and then across the strait, down to the mouth of the Amur River in northeast Siberia. There it would meet the proposed extension of a Russian line that had already connected Europe with central Siberia. A continuous length of wire would thus be completed, circling nearly half the globe. An additional attraction of the proposed Bering Strait route was the easy possibility of extending service to Peking and the rich Chinese markets.

Thus it was that the Russian-American Telegraph Company came into being, with $10 million being raised within two months at a hefty price of $75 dollars per share. Not only was it the biggest public offering to that time, but it was the world's largest bilateral venture in its day — Yankee entrepreneurialism at its best. A call went out for manpower, with a special need for applicants having experience in telegraphic work. The eager Kennan unhesitatingly responded, volunteering his services as an "explorer" and announcing that he was ready "to leave for Russian-America [Alaska] within two hours."

George was born into a family of modest means, a precocious child who grew into an intelligent, quick-witted youngster with an abiding passion for books. He read voraciously and eclectically; but it was travel, adventure, and fantasy that attracted him most. The family's financial difficulties were such that at age twelve he was forced to quit school in order to help bring bread to the table, and he found a job with the Cleveland and Toledo Railway Company as a messenger in the telegraph office. He took to the world of telegraph quickly and at age seventeen was promoted to manager of the local office. Within two years, however, George became listless and utterly bored, not only with the repetitive nature of his work, but also with the parochial life of his small hometown. Thus it was that on July 8, 1865, he found himself on board the *Olga,* a Russian trading vessel setting sail north from San Francisco, excitedly waiting to start the adventure of a lifetime.

The first step of the ambitious project was to lay out the route of the proposed line and to fabricate and erect the required poles. For the implementation of the task, the path of the line was divided into four sectors, and Kennan was given the responsibility of joint command with a Russian counterpart of the northeastern Siberian segment, the most inhospitable and difficult of the four.

Twelve months later, George and his party of seventy-five Americans and scores of Natives found themselves isolated in the depths of the Siberian Arctic, incommunicado, unaware that transatlantic cable had been successfully laid and was in operation, and that the mega-project of the Russian-American Telegraph Company had been brought to a grinding halt. Blissfully oblivious of these developments they steadfastly pursued their now pointless mission for a further eighteen months. Before it was all over, he wrote bitterly on his return home, "We had explored and located the whole route of the line from the Amur River to the Bering

Strait. We had prepared altogether about 15,000 telegraph poles, built between forty to fifty station houses and magazines, cut nearly fifty miles of road through the forest in the vicinity of Gamsk and Okhotsk, and accomplished a great deal of preparatory work along the whole extent of the line."[4] It turned out to be a fool's mission.

There Kennan and his party lived in every imaginable condition of hardship with temperatures at times remaining steady at -35°F for days at a time (one midday temperature was recorded at -53°F). "For almost a month we had slept every night on the ground or the snow; had never seen a chair, a table, a bed or a mirror; had never been undressed night or day; and had washed our faces only three or four times in an equal number of weeks!" Imagine the joy of Kennan's party when, after weeks in the frozen steppe with no sign of human habitation and with depleted rations, the party arrived at Gizhiga, a tiny town south of the Arctic Circle, where they were able to rest for a few days in relative comfort.

The provincial administrator greeted George warmly and offered him the hospitality of his modest home. The first order of business was a luxuriating hot bath followed by a dinner the sort of which the young American had never experienced. "After the inevitable 'fifteen drops' of brandy [vodka]," he wrote:

> [A]nd the lunch of smoked fish, rye bread, and caviar, which always precede a Russian dinner, we took seats at the table and spent an hour and a half in getting through the numerous courses of cabbage soup, salmon pie, venison cutlets, game, small meat pies, pudding and pastry, which were successively set before us. We discussed the news of all the world, from the log villages of Kamtchatka to the imperial palaces of Moscow and St. Petersburg. Our hospitable host then ordered champagne, and over tall, slender glasses of cool beaded *Veuve Cliquot* we meditated upon the vicissitudes of Siberian life.

Premium French champagne in 1867 served in the shadow of the Arctic Circle sixteen thousand miles from Paris — Russian hospitality gone wild.

It was Kennan who brought to the west knowledge of the Koryaks, the peoples living south of the Bering Strait, closely related to the Chukchi. He described a home:

> The settlement resembled as much as anything a collection of Titanic wooden hour-glasses, which had been half shaken down and reduced to a state of rickety dilapidation by an earthquake. The houses — if houses they could be called — were about twenty feet in height, rudely constructed of driftwood which had been thrown up by the sea and could be compared in shape to nothing but hourglasses. They had no doors or windows of any kind and could only be entered by climbing up a pole on the outside, and sliding down another pole through the chimney — a mode of entrance whose practicability depended entirely upon the activity and intensity of the fire which burned underneath. The smoke and sparks, although sufficiently disagreeable, were trifles of comparative insignificance.
>
> The interior of a Korak *yourt* ... presents a strange and not very inviting appearance to one who has never become accustomed by long habit to its dirt, smoke, and frigid atmosphere. It receives its only light — and that of a cheerless, gloomy character — through the round hole, about twenty feet above the floor, which serves as window, door and chimney, and which is reached by a round log with holes in it, that stands perpendicularly in the centre. The beams, rafters, and logs which compose the *yourt* are all of a glossy blackness, from the smoke in which they are constantly enveloped. A wooden platform, raised about a foot from the earth, extends out from the walls on three sides to a width of

six feet, leaving an open spot eight or ten feet in diameter in the centre for the fire and a huge copper kettle of melting snow ... on the platform are pitched three or four square skin *pologs,* which serve as sleeping apartments for the inmates and as refuges from the smoke, which sometimes becomes almost unendurable. A little circle of flat stones on the ground, in the centre of the *yourt,* forms the fireplace, over which is usually simmering a kettle of fish or reindeer meat, which, with dried salmon, seal's blubber and rancid oil makes up the Korak bill of fare. Everything which you see or touch bears the distinguishing marks of Korak origin – grease and smoke.

We had not been twenty minutes in the settlement before the *yourt* which we occupied was completely crowded with stolid, brutal-looking men, dressed in spotted deer-skin clothes, wearing strings of colored beads in their ears and carrying heavy knives two feet in length in sheaths tied around their legs.

Further in his memoir, he wrote of a December midday some two hundred miles south of the Arctic Circle: "The sun although at its greatest altitude, glowed like a red ball of fire low down in the southern horizon, and a peculiar gloomy twilight hung over the wintry landscape." One day passed like the other and with the few exceptional overnights in isolated *yourts* the group lived on the steppe literally under the stars, and it is here that Kennan tells of the *aurora borealis.* Arctic literature is not well endowed with lyrical descriptions of surrounding nature although some travellers do pass comment on the spectacle of the *aurora.* No one, however, gives more thorough justice to the mystical beauty and hypnotic quality of this phenomenon than our young American. In the world of travel literature, does this school drop-out take back seat to the likes of Kipling or Trollop? Listen to him:

Among the few pleasures which reward the traveler for the hardships and dangers of life in the far north, there are none which are brighter or longer remembered than the magnificent auroral displays which occasionally illumine the darkness of the long polar night, and light up with a celestial glory the whole blue vault of heaven. No other natural phenomenon is so grand, so mysterious, so terrible in its unearthly splendor as this. Its veil conceals from mortal eyes the glory of the eternal throne seems drawn aside, and the awed beholder is lifted out of the atmosphere of his daily life into the immediate presence of God.

On the 26th of February, while we were all yet living together at Anadyrsk, there occurred one of the grandest displays of the Arctic aurora which had been observed there for more than fifty years, and which exhibited such unusual and extraordinary brilliancy that even the natives were astonished.

It was a cold, dark but clear winter's night, and the sky in the earlier part of the evening showed no signs of the magnificent illumination which was already being prepared. A few streamers wavered now and then in the North, and a faint radiance like that of the rising moon shone above the dark belt of shrubbery which bordered the river — but this was a common occurrence and it excited no notice or remark.

As we emerged into the open air, there burst suddenly upon our startled eyes the grandest exhibition of vivid dazzling light and color of which the mind can conceive. The whole universe seemed to be on fire. A broad arch of brilliant prismatic colors spanned the heavens from east to west like a gigantic rainbow, with a long fringe of crimson and yellow streamers stretching up from its convex edge to the very zenith. At short intervals of one or two seconds, wide, luminous bands parallel with the arch, rose suddenly out of the northern horizon and swept with a swift, steady majesty across the whole heavens, like long breakers of phosphorescent light rolling in from some limitless ocean of space....

Every portion of the vast arch was momentarily wavering, trembling and changing color, and the brilliant streamers which fringed its edge swept back and forth in great curves, like the fiery sword of the angel at the gate of Eden. In a moment the vast aurora rain how, with all its wavering streamers, began to move slowly up toward the zenith and a second arch of equal brilliancy stormed directly under it, shooting up another long seined row of slender colored lances toward the North Star, like a battalion of the celestial host presenting arms to its commanding angel.

I could not imagine any possible addition which even Almighty power could make to the grandeur of the aurora as it now appeared. The rapid alternations of crimson, blue, green and yellow in the sky were reflected so vividly from the white surface of the snow, that the whole world seemed now steeped in blood, and then quivering in an atmosphere of pale, ghastly green, through which shone the unspeakable glories of the mighty crimson and yellow....

Never had I even dreamed of such an aurora as this and I am not ashamed to confess that its magnificence at that moment overawed and frightened me. The whole sky, from zenith to horizon, was one molten mantling sea of color and fire, crimson and purple, and scarlet and green, and colors for which there are no words in language and no ideas in the mind — things which can only be conceived while they are visible.

I am painfully conscious of my inability to describe as they should be described the splendid phenomena of a great polar aurora, but such magnificent effects cannot be expressed in a mathematical formula, nor can an inexperienced artist reproduce, with a piece of charcoal, the brilliant coloring of a Turner landscape. I have given only faint hints, which the imagination of the reader must fill up. But be assured that no description, however faithful, no flight of the imagination, however exalted, can begin to do justice to a spectacle of such unearthly grandeur. Until man drops his vesture of flesh and stands in the presence of Deity, he will see no more striking manifestation of the "glory of the Lord, which is terrible," than that presented by a brilliant exhibition of the Arctic aurora.

The foregoing is an abridged version of the original, which runs nearly twice the length. Eventually Kennan's team arrived at the Amur River, their work completed. Here the men awaited the arrival of the company's ship from San Francisco to return them home. "It seemed hard to give up at once the object to which we had devoted three years of our lives, and for whose attainment we had suffered all possible hardships of cold, exile and starvation; but we had no alternative, and began at once to make preparations for our final departure ... [and soon thereafter] to close the book on our Siberian experience."[5]

Following the acquisition of Alaska, the trickle of Americans moving north swelled, and among the traders and entrepreneurs were also scientists and explorers, all seeking to learn more of the flora and fauna and of geological and geographic formations. The readily accessible coastal areas were a particular draw, as was the Bering Strait, with what lay beyond especially magnetic. The North Pole had hereto proven to be unreachable from the east, but access to it might be had from this western gateway.

Among the first to pass through that entrance on his way to the pole was Lieutenant Commander G.W. De Long. A resolute, strong-willed officer, De Long once sailed the waters off northern Greenland and had clearly heard the siren song of the Arctic. His story and that of his heroic crew are among the most dramatic in United States naval lore, indeed, of Arctic lore. And farfetched as it may be, it has its genesis at Lake Tanganyika in central Africa with the search for the celebrated Dr. Livingstone.

Livingstone was a Scottish missionary who in his twenties travelled to Africa to bring the word of the Lord to the natives. He spent the better portion of thirty years there not only preaching, but also exploring "the dark continent." At one point six years passed without word from him or knowledge of his whereabouts — he became lost to the world. The British press picked up the story and milked it for all it was worth, inflaming public imagination, as well as raising every sort of speculation.

The excitement over the mystery flowed to America via the *New York Herald*, a paper owned by James Bennett, a flamboyant millionaire reputed for his eccentricities. (At the home of one Fifth Avenue dowager and no worse for wear, he distinguished himself by urinating in the fireplace.) Bennett knew a good story when he saw it, and this one captivated him. He resolved to unravel the mystery by financing an expedition to find the missing man — the *Herald* would hold exclusive rights to the tale.[6] To head the search he appointed Henry Stanley, a journalist with a penchant for global adventure. Legend has it that when Stanley asked Bennett how much money was available for the project, the latter replied, "Draw £1,000 and when you have gone through that, draw another £1,000, and when that is spent, draw another £1,000, and when you have finished that, draw another £1,000, and so on … *but find Livingstone!*"

Stanley fulfilled his commission. Accompanied by two hundred porters, he travelled seven hundred miles through tropical forests in equatorial heat, and on November 10, 1871, he encountered the missing man. It was there that the alleged celebrated exchange took place. "Doctor Livingstone, I presume?" he asked with characteristic Victorian courtesy. To which the other replied with similar reserve, "Yes, that's my name." The story made headlines worldwide, and the *Herald* bathed in the glory. Its circulation skyrocketed to eighty-four thousand and before long the paper was styling itself as "The most largely circulated journal in the world." Such was Bennett's brilliant success that he schemed for an equally spectacular follow-up, and thus came to be De Long's ill-fated expedition to the North Pole.

Age-old wisdom had it that Arctic Ocean waters lying at a distance from coastal areas were ice-free. This assertion was forcefully endorsed by the eminent German cartographer of the time, August Petermann, Queen Victoria's Geographer Royal. He advised Bennett that once having cleared Bering Strait, an expeditionary vessel would find itself in open waters free to sail to the North Pole. The warm Kuso-Siwo current flowing north from the Philippines past Japan and into the Arctic through the straits, he claimed, made a relatively easy passage possible. The hare-brained expert went on to suggest that Wrangel Island — a large island in the Chukchi Sea, some ninety miles from mainland Siberia — was in fact an extension of the Eurasian landmass that stretched north to the pole.

His mind made up, Bennett lost little time in getting on with it. He searched out and engaged thirty-four-year-old De Long and sent him to Britain to acquire a suitable vessel. This the officer did — the 430-ton barque *Pandora*, a former Royal Navy gunboat, and then the personal yacht of Sir Allan Young. At $6,000, the price was right and Bennett bought it, renaming it the *Jeannette*. It was then sailed to San Francisco for refitting in the naval shipyard. The enterprising publisher by that time had worked his influential Washington connections and had successfully persuaded Congress to pass a bill bringing the expedition under the jurisdiction of the Navy. The ship's company was to be drawn from its ranks and the refit and procurement overseen by naval personnel. Bennett agreed to bear full costs of the project — an irregular partnership, indeed, one that was deeply resented by the Navy, which viewed the project as unwarranted civilian encroachment.

The *Jeannette* was a solid ship built to accommodate heavy cannons. With a length of 142 feet and a beam of twenty-five, she was powered by sail, but also capable of moving by steam. Shipyard carpenters pretty well gutted the vessel and set about reinforcing the hull with layer upon layer of pine planks — the finished hull grew to nineteen inches in thickness. Massive wooden beams, twelve by fourteen inches, were fitted athwart-ship to strengthen the sides; the old boiler was scrapped and replaced by a couple of new compact units; two updated engines were installed; coal storage capacity was increased by 50 percent; the quarters below-deck were renovated; and the entire ship was thoroughly insulated.

The ship's complement was made up of five officers and twenty-eight men. Lieutenant Charles Chipp, De Long's shipmate from a previous expedition to Greenland, was appointed second-in-command. Master John Danenhower came on board as navigator, George Melville as engineer, and James Ambler as the ship's surgeon. Attached to the wardroom were three others: Jerome Collins from the staff of the *Herald*, Raymond Newcomb, a naturalist and taxidermist, and William Dunbar, the ice-pilot. As for the lower deck, De Long had clear views on the sort of man he wanted, as seen in his instructions to Chipp:

> Single men, perfect health, considerable strength, perfect temperance, cheerfulness, ability to read and write English, prime seamen of course. Norwegians, Swedes and Danes preferred. Avoid English, Scotch and Irish. Refuse point-blank French, Italians and Spaniards. Pay to be Navy pay. Absolute and unhesitating obedience to every order, no matter what it may be.[7]

On July 8, 1878, following a week of banquets and farewells, the *Jeannette* put out to sea amid waving flags and cheering crowds. As she moved down the harbour, an Army band cheered them on with lively tunes, but a stony silence came from the Navy — not one ship saluted the Arctic-bound vessel. Thirty-five days later, they had reached St. Michael Island at the entrance of Bering Strait where they made their rendezvous with the *Fanny A. Hyde*. The supply schooner had been following the *Jeannette* in order to re-provision and re-coal her. The work was completed within a few days and a huge amount of other requirements was also brought on board: sixty-nine pairs of sealskin boots, three small native boats called *baideras*, forty Eskimo dogs, five dog sleds, forty sets of harness, and tons of compressed fish for dog food. Two Russian natives joined the ship, Alexsei and Aneguin, to attend the dogs and drive the sleds. The *Fanny A. Hyde* was ordered to follow a further distance in order to make one final refuelling down the line.

From the start, the dogs proved to be "the damnedest nuisance ever seen on board ship," roaming free on the decks, snarling and fighting in pairs and in groups. Alexsei and Aneguin had their hands full as they beat them apart. When gale winds hit the vessel, it would heel badly and churning water would pour over the wretched creatures, which then scurried about, tails between legs, in search of shelter. One particularly vicious storm carried a rushing wall of water that hit the vessel with force enough to smash the windows of De Long's cabin, flooding it and most of his belongings. That same wave also carried away the two toilets that had stood on the deck, a loss which subsequently proved to be more than distressing for the men.

By August 27, having passed the two Diomedes, the *Jeannette* was nearly clear of the Bering Strait and awaited the *Fanny A. Hyde* for a final transfer of coal. The refuelling process was backbreaking, but with the task completed, 132 tons of the stuff was stowed in the bunkers below and an additional twenty-eight tons piled on deck. With a final farewell and many "hurrahs," the supply schooner pushed off, carrying with it the last letters home from members of the crew. The *Jeannette* was now on its own at the gateway to the pole and ready to pursue its chosen path, and sail she did — to her doom.

As they progressed, Collins took daily readings of water temperature and to everyone's chagrin they gave no evidence of the warm Kuso-Siwo current; day after day the temperatures remained constant, the same at one fathom as at twenty-five fathoms. Newcomb put out a dredge, but found none of the gathered sea-life specimens were symptomatic of tropical waters. Furthermore, as they progressed west along the coastline, the formations of ice grew thicker and more widespread. Herr Petermann's assertions, it appeared, were dead wrong, and at this early stage more than one curse was thrown his way.

Early one September day with the mercury falling and ice building up all about, De Long gingerly squeezed and butted the *Jeannette* through the floes under steam. By four o'clock, a heavy fog had set in and visibility became nil; to proceed farther was folly. They would wait out twenty-four hours, hoping that the fog would clear. Orders were given for the ice anchors to be run out and in order to save coal, the boilers were shut down. During the night, the temperature fell to 23°F and as morning dawned they found themselves solidly encased and surrounded by ice as far as the eye could see. Once steam was gotten up again, effort was made to break the bond; engines were driven full ahead and then full astern with no result — the ship would not dislodge. By the evening of September 6, 1879, the helpless *Jeannette* was immobile, firmly frozen into the Arctic ice pack — and so it remained for nearly two years.

To make matters worse, on the following day a submerged tongue of ice projected below the hull and heaved up the port side, causing a nine degree list to starboard and making work hazardous on the slippery, ice-covered deck. The same underwater projection also immobilized the two-ton rudder by ramming it hard to starboard. The temperature fell to 16°F, the crew's efforts to free the vessel even more gruelling. Only so much work with drills, axes, and saws could be undertaken before having to break to warm up in the ship's 50°F interior. The ice continued to accumulate and by the week's end it measured nearly fifteen feet thick.

With currents carrying the imprisoning ice pack northwest and the *Jeannette's* hull continuing to withstand intense pressures, life on board for the men settled into a routine. Watches were kept; meteorological, astronomical, and magnetic observations recorded; dogs exercised; hunting expeditions organized on the floes; and daily positions taken. Weeks passed into months and by mid-December De Long began to worry over the possible appearance of scurvy — no Arctic expedition had yet been free of the dreaded illness. It was common knowledge that proper diet, salt-free water, and exercise were the best preventative measures. They had on board an ample reserve of lime juice, but that was not enough, he reckoned. Exercise was essential, and he issued the following order:

> Until the arrival of spring, and on each day without exception, when the temperature is above thirty degrees below zero, the ship will be cleared regularly by all hands from eleven a.m. till one p.m. During this period every officer and man will leave the ship for exercise

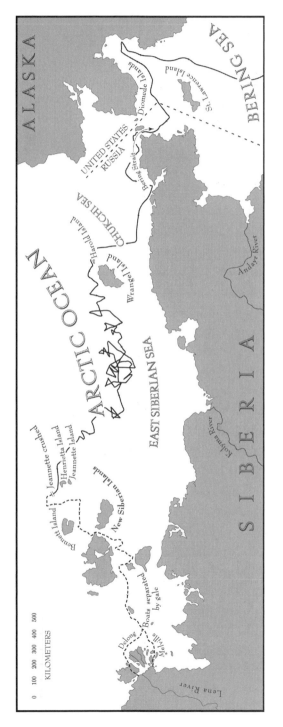

The path of the Jeannette as it was carried by the floes from September 6, 1879 to the time of its sinking two years later. The broken line traces the route the survivors took as they made their way to the Siberian mainland.

Map by Cameron McLeod Jones.

199

on the ice, which should be as vigorous as possible. No one except the officer entering the noon observations in the log will for any purpose during this period return to the ship

(signed) George Washington De Long, Commanding

Diarrhea, however, did hit the ship with a vengeance and incapacitated many. In addition to suffering from fatigue, which the sickness engenders, the unfortunate men had to endure the extreme discomfort of having to get up in the middle of the night to dash half-dressed across rough ice in sub-zero temperatures to the canvas privies set up at a distance — such was the pain inflicted by the wave that had swept away the two upper-deck toilets.

Dr. Ambler determined that the cause of the diarrhea was impure drinking water. By early December their supply of fresh water had been nearly depleted. Since Petermann had assured them that "beginning at a certain thickness the ice is almost free of salt" and therefore easily made into water, only so much had been brought on board. Having discovered that sea ice was in fact heavy with salt throughout, they turned to melting snow. What was consumed seemed clear and had an acceptable taste, but upon testing Dr. Ambler discovered an excessive saline content. Snowfall in those parts was paltry and the stuff they had been gathering lay too close to the sea ice. If snow was not the answer, distillation was, and in quick order Melville and his men fashioned an effective still. Its drawback was that for the generation of steam the ship's boilers consumed large amounts of coal. Only ninety tons of the "black diamonds" remained, and the needs of the cook were indisputable, as well as that of the heating plant — without heat, certain death. Furthermore with depleted bunkers, how would the *Jeannette* ever make it to the pole once it became freed? Coal had to be rationed. The question then: how much water was necessary to meet minimum requirements? The answer, Melville calculated, was forty gallons a day or about a gallon and a quarter per person, "the irreducible quantity."

Stored below deck was a small boiler designed to steam-power the generator for "Edison's newfangled carbon lamps." This was harnessed to a makeshift condenser and the flow of water began with minimal expenditure of coal. In their second Arctic winter, however, when the supply was near gone, the irreducible was reduced. The primitive windmill jerry-rigged to power the boiler did work, but it was insufficient.

Christmas: "the dreariest day I ever spent," wrote De Long. The officers gathered in the wardroom, a morose lot indeed, as thoughts turned to wives and family, to roaring fireplaces, bright decorations, and festive tables laden with fine foods. Overhead, the ceiling's insulating felt drooped with frost and moisture; the sloping deck was saturated with condensation dripping from the walls; the permeating smell of dampness and the unwashed hung heavy. A single flickering flame of a smoky lamp broke the gloom, as glasses of Irish whisky were raised in a toast to loved ones. De Long sent three quarts of the precious liquid to the deckhands below "to inject conviviality."

In early November, Danenhower had begun to complain to Ambler of an eye difficulty, which the surgeon tried by various mean to attend. The surgeon concluded that the condition was "syphilitic iritis," a deepseated inflammation of the inner eye. By New Year's, the swelling had grown severe enough to place the suffering navigator in a pitch-black cabin for total eye rest, but within days the painful condition intensified. The murky substance developing over the stricken eye was growing thicker and beginning to cause the iris to adhere to the lens. The situation grew critical enough for Ambler to contemplate cutting into the eye to relieve it from the sight-threatening viscidity.

As Ambler pondered the situation further, the heavy ice welded to the *Jeannette*'s hull heaved abruptly with a thunderous clap, throwing everyone on board into momentary panic. The noise had resounded unlike any other cracking of ice heard before, but then, just as suddenly an eerie silence descended and the crew breathed sighs of relief. The moment of relaxation, however, was shattered by the appearance of a stoker from below yelling that water was flooding the engine room. Despite the solidly reinforced hull and massive beams supporting it, the ship's sides had been punctured by the ramming ice. It was reckoned that the initial flow of water was sixty gallons per minute.

All hands sprung to work. Hand pumps were manned as the boiler was fired up to run the steam pumps. A bucket brigade was organized, and another group painstakingly hauled food stores and perishable goods from below. The outside temperature had fallen to -40°F, causing scuppers, hoses, and pipelines to choke. Since much of the labour involved handling iron, the freeze made work that much more painful. The men struggling in the bilge suffered most as they laboured in waist-high water to stem the flow by stuffing caulking into the openings. Eventually matters were brought under control and the immediate crises passed. Weeks earlier, De Long had taken precautionary measures in the event of having to abandon ship. A forty-day supply of food was assembled on deck, the ship's cutters and whaleboats were prepared for lowering, the dinghies secured to the sleds, and every man had a knapsack and sleeping bag at the ready. Thankfully the measures proved unnecessary for the moment.

While the men scurried about and pumps clanked and shuddered, Danenhower continued to suffer in dark isolation. Ambler visited him and found his condition considerably deteriorated, so much so that he informed De Long and the patient that unless surgery was performed immediately, sight in the left eye would be lost. The agonized officer agreed and the procedure got underway. Imagine the situation: Danenhower prone on the bunk of his dingy, feebly-heated cabin; deck at a nine-degree list with pumps clamouring; no ophthalmological equipment, merely a magnifying glass and scalpel; insufficient morphine and limited stock of brandy. Two sailors gripped the patient's arms and a third took his legs as Ambler's half-numbed fingers punctured the cornea to explore the inner eye.

It was a successful operation, as noted succinctly in Ambler's record: "Performed paracentesis and let out a lot of turbid fluid, operating on the temporal side." De Long's notation is more fulfilling: the operation "was beautifully performed by Doctor Ambler and borne with heroic endurance. I hardly know which to admire most, the skill and celerity of the surgeon or the nerve and endurance of Danenhower." Such was the mettle of the *Jeannette*'s men.

All the while, the ice-locked vessel drifted aimlessly about the ocean, with the currents carrying it round and about, but generally in a northwest direction some five hundred miles from Wrangel Island. Much excitement was had in the first days of June when two small islands loomed into sight, one with towering cliffs. A landing party was sent ashore by dogsled to the larger of the two and with a jigger of whisky it was christened Henrietta Island (the other, Jeannette Island). A flag was raised and "in the name of Great Jehovah and the President of the United States," claimed as American territory. Meanwhile the ship's pumps continued unceasingly to empty the bilges. Of the forty dogs — "our hoodlum gang" — seventeen had died or disappeared and the remainder had become personal pets of crew members.

Summer passed into autumn, autumn into winter with no change in their immobile situation. The deadly monotony of routine tasks was broken on occasion by the excitement of a hunt or a football game or an afternoon of kite-flying. A successful hunt brought welcomed luxury to the table: fillet of polar bear, side of seal, or perhaps roast goose. In periods of darkness, cabin fever became more apparent. Collins, who from the start showed himself not to be a team player, at one point rebelled outright against De Long's authority and was arrested and confined to quarters. Christmas came around again, but this time it was more jolly than the previous year. With all canned meat consumed, mince pies were made of pemmican laced with brandy. Rum was doled out and a talent show organized, complete with costumes and musical instruments. In their continued drift north, great joy was had on February 5, when after ninety-three days of night, the first glimpse of sun was had. In the weeks that followed, particularly fierce gales and winds battered the ship while screeching ice packs and the loud cracking of ice made sleep difficult. Early spring flights of noisy geese passed overhead and many were brought down. Sickness had once more taken hold, this time brought on by lead poisoning. Cans of tomatoes were found to have been improperly soldered and fragments of lead caused contamination. Lieutenant Chipp was struck particularly badly.

The strong rays of early summer wrought daily transformations to the world of ice and conditions changed hourly — "the changes going on all around, except in our isolated spot, were kaleidoscopic." That spot was in the middle of a floe measuring about a mile long and a half-mile wide. Far out, sporadic stretches of open water opened to view, but otherwise it was a panorama of tumbling "floebergs" thunderously crashing into one another and at times building into high craglike structures. Stronger currents now drove their little island at a faster clip.

Friday, June 10, passed as a bright pleasant day just it had been for many before. By ten that night most were asleep except for Melville, the officer on watch, who had taken up his position on deck. Shortly before midnight, the accustomed reverberations of ice action on the hull intensified as did the thumping and cracking of their surroundings. The vessel gave a sharp quiver, trembling sufficiently roughly to bring a hastily clad De Long on deck. Within moments his ship heaved abruptly and slid harshly from its iced cradle into the freedom of open water. Everyone appeared on deck to cheer their good fortune.

Jubilation was short-lived, however, for within hours the ice closed in once more. Floes as thick as sixteen feet and jagged floebergs came on rapidly to attack the ship's sides — a "contest between hallow hull and solid pack looked so unequal." The *Jeannette* screeched and howled as its bow slowly lifted and the entire mass heeled sharply to starboard. Ice penetrated the hull and then seawater, at first slight, but then in a torrent, filling the engine room and flooding the holds. The bow and bowsprit pointed high into the air with the stern almost buried. The list was nearing 30° and the men clung to rigging and davits to prevent themselves from sliding into the scuppers. Water poured into all the holds and it appeared that the keel had been torn out. The snapping and crackling sounds seemed to be coming from everywhere — it was clear that the *Jeannette* was breaking up. De Long issued the order to abandon ship.

Frenzied work began on removing provisions, equipment, dogs, and sleds onto the more stable, quieter spans of floes. Danenhower, eyes bandaged from a follow-up operation, was carried off the ship, as was the sick Chipp. Six nine-by-six-foot tents were set up two hundred yards from the stricken vessel with tons of stores piled about. Earlier, as a precaution, two cutters and a whaleboat had been removed together with eight sleds, three of which had been especially built to accommodate boats. When it

The death of the Jeannette. *With her hull staved in by the jagged ice and water pouring in, the vessel finally sank in the early morning of June 11, 1881, leaving her thirty-three men stranded on the ice packs.*

was all done, and despite the drama of it all, the exhausted men fell into their sleeping bags and by midnight all was quiet, save the continuous groaning of the dying ship. At four in the morning only two witnessed the *Jeannette*'s death pangs, when with a final heave she disappeared beneath the waters. The masts had crashed long before and as it went down, the yards snapped noisily, "like a great gaunt skeleton slapping its hands above its head." They were at 77°N, four hundred miles from the Siberian mainland and eight hundred miles from the North Pole.

By the end of the next day the salvaged clothing stores had been divided among the men and preparations begun for the next step. De Long noted in his diary, "… where the ship sank nothing is to be seen but a signal chest floating bottom up … we have provisions to live on for some time without impairing our sixty days' allowance for going south … all cheerful, with plenty to eat and wear. Lauterbach on the harmonica tonight. Keep the silk flag flying." Four days later, De Long wrote a few lines and left it in a waterproof keg: "Latitude 77°8' Longitude 153°25'. We break camp and start southward over the ice tomorrow evening, hoping with God's grace to reach the New Siberian Islands, and from there make our way by boats to the coast of Siberia. 17 June 1881."

Five hundred miles separated the party from their chosen destination, the delta of Siberia's Lena River. According to Dr. Petermann, villages dotted the area, and there they would find food and shelter. They would rest before proceeding onto the journey's next thousand-mile stretch to Yakutsk where communication with the outside world was available. The problem now: what to take and what things to leave behind? Baggage had to be hauled by sled and since thirty-three men and twenty-three dogs could do only so much, they were limited — piles of equipment and personal belongings would have to be abandoned.

Three specially reinforced sleds would each bear a twelve-foot boat and nine lesser sleds would carry provisions, two small dinghies, and the medicine chest. Essential camping gear including tents, cooking equipment, fur-lined sleeping bags, and knapsacks of personal items would be placed into the boats. The men were instructed to dress as warmly as possible, but all other outerwear had to remain behind (with the exception of three pairs of boots). A pile of furs, parkas, and blankets remained on the ice. In view of the harsh restrictions imposed on them, more than one man grumbled when De Long insisted that a barrel of lime juice and what appeared to be an inordinate quantity of pemmican be loaded together with certain books and the expedition's logs and records. By the time all was ready, the combined dead weight of the baggage train was estimated at eight tons. With everything in order, they set off in a joyous mood, relieved no longer to be cloistered in cramped, foul-smelling quarters and buoyed by the prospect of a safe haven on the mainland. The brilliancy — not necessarily the warmth — of the summer sun no doubt added to the lifting of spirits.

But what followed in the next months was anything but joyous; a nightmare journey across treacherous floes and violent waters, a passage that became littered by a trail of abandoned items, dead dogs, and human bodies. De Long recorded only a part of the tale for his notebook entries cease on October 30, 140 days after abandoning ship. He died immediately thereafter. Of the thirty-three men who set out on that sunny June day, seven survived the ordeal. Danenhower and Melville were the two officers among them, and it is from the latter that we learn of the expedition's final days. With canvas harnesses strapped across their chests, twelve men were hitched to the drag ropes attached to a sled or cutter and the heavy thing was hauled forward as others steadied the sides. After five hundred yards they unhitched, returned to where they had begun and repeated the process on the next load. Ice-pilot Dunbar proceeded well ahead of the troop, laying out the route with small black flags. By mid-afternoon the indicated path had become rutted, the ice had turned into slush and by the time it came to the final load, the team was in ankle-deep water. Sliding downhill, the loads sometimes over-turned, causing delays and havoc among the dog-pulled sleds. At the close of the day they had covered a mile and a half. Ambler did what he could to attend blistered and skinned hands. Days later, they thought that ninety miles had been covered, but when De Long took careful sex-tant readings he was chagrined to find that the true distance travelled was a mere twenty-eight miles — as the group progressed south, the cur-rent had been driving their floe north.

At one point Ambler fell into the water during a sleet storm and after swimming from floe to floe he managed to pull himself out. He rummaged in his knapsack for dry clothing, stripped, and changed — the temperature was 21°F. On July 4, cheers went up from the men as "all flags were flown" to celebrate the American national day. Signs of extreme fatigue began showing and feet had become blistered as moc-casins rotted and sodden stockings tore apart. Sleep was often had "in wet clothes in a wet bag on wet ice … every bone and every separate muscle" aching. Yet Ambler's diary noted, "For forty days we have been under way in all kinds of hardships; but not a murmur, and tonight after nineteen hours work, many of the men having been overboard, they are cheerful and come up smiling." The ailing Chipp continued in his physical agony and for the first part of the journey had to be transported by sled. He was so distraught over his condition and from the worry of being a burden to others that he begged to be abandoned so he could suffer a natural death, but De Long would have no part of that and the "hospital sled" continued to be dragged along. On July 19, landfall was made on a barren, rocky island at the eastern tip of the New Siberian

The men of the Jeannette, *having abandoned their lost vessel, struggle in hauling boats over the ice as they head to the Siberian mainland, June–September 1881.*
© Naval History and Heritage Command.

Islands, which, with ceremony, was named Bennett Island and claimed for the United States. Here they rested for nine days and before quitting the place, De Long left the following message in a cairn:

> It is my intention to proceed from here at the first opportunity towards New Siberian Islands and thence towards the settlements on the Lena River. We have three boats, thirty days of provisions, 23 dogs and sufficient clothing, and are in excellent health. Having rested here a few days, we are now detained by a westerly gale and fog …

When the weather cleared, they set off by boats, but not before shooting ten of the most "broken-down" dogs. Supply of pemmican had been depleting and the dogs were deemed a luxurious drain on the supply. During their island sojourn and in anticipation of clear waters, De Long rearranged the "order of march." The expedition would proceed by water in three boats: himself commanding one cutter with Ambler, Collins and ten men; a second cutter under Chipp's command with Dunbar and eight men, and the whaleboat with Melville commanding, carrying Danenhower, Newcomb, and seven men.

The over-packed boats stood low in the water and made slow progress — forty miles in nine days. Arriving at the next island after long stretches on the water the excited dogs ran off and disappeared into the interior not to be seen again — only their pet "Snoozer" deigned to remain behind. The boats' loads lessened by that much, but it was not sufficient to noticeably increase the sailing speed. Time was passing, the season changing, food supplies diminishing, and there was far to go. Better time had to be made; to lighten loads further, De Long ordered the sledges destroyed and with that the rate of progress increased dramatically.

Days of sailing, days of camping on ice floes, days of gales, snow and heavy fog. Provisions ran low; only pemmican and tea were left. The mouth of the Lena Delta was reached, but, contrary to Petermann's assurances, they found no settlements. A particularly vicious gale struck the three small boats and they became separated. Chipp's cutter was lost and never heard from again. Melville made his way to the east coast of the Lena, where a village was found in which a Russian exile resided, and here the broken men found food and shelter.

De Long reached the Delta's northern tip, where he was stopped by silted shoals. With all food gone, the faithful Snoozer was shot, and dog stew nourished the crew for the following days. On October 6, De Long noted, "At 8:45 a.m. our messmate Ericksen departed this life," a victim of hypothermia. On the next day, "Breakfast, consisting of our last pound of dog meat and … our last grain of tea." The entry for Wednesday, October 12, noted:

> One hundred and twenty-second day. Breakfast; last spoonful glycerine and hot water. For dinner we tried a couple of handfuls of Arctic willow in a pot of water and drank the infusion. Everybody getting weaker and weaker. Hardly strength to get firewood. S.W. gale with snow.

A week later, the last strips of their boiled deerskin moccasins were consumed. On the 30th, the totality of De Long's final notation: "One hundred and fortieth day. Boyd and Gortz died during night. Mr. Collins dying." The death of the two seamen were the sixth and seventh of his small crew, and Collins must have followed immediately thereafter, as did the *Jeannette*'s commanding officer and the rest.

By summer 1881, world anxiety over the whereabouts of the *Jeannette* deepened into alarm. Two expeditions were sent out by the United States government to seek signs of the ship or its survivors, but to no avail; it seemed that the ship had been swallowed up by the trackless Arctic. The following year, preparations were underway for a renewed search, but this time it was to be a concerted effort involving the navies of England, Russia, and Sweden. It was at that point that Melville's haggard group appeared in Ikutsk, where word of the astonishing survival was telegraphed to an amazed world.

Plans for an international search were put aside, but Melville, with a small select group, returned to the Delta to continue the search. One frozen tributary after another was travelled; streams, large and small, were explored. Then, by serendipity, they stumbled upon a Remington rifle, eight inches of its muzzle protruding from the snow. At a short distance from the find, a copper kettle resting incongruously on the snow, and as Melville approached to retrieve it, he spotted a human arm, stiff and stark, stretching skyward from the snow. It was De Long and near his frozen corpse were the bodies of Dr. Ambler and Ah Sam, the Chinese cook. Further digging uncovered the journal that De Long kept from the time of abandoning ship, and subsequently, Ambler's notebook.

The rigid, emaciated bodies were buried and prayers said over them. Months later, they were retrieved by the naval expedition and brought home for an interment with full honours in Woodlawn Cemetery, New York — a ceremony held in a blinding snowstorm and blistering wind.

9

The Scandinavians

BETWEEN GREENLAND AND Norway, in the uppermost reaches of the North Sea, lies the Svalbard Archipelago, where the four Pomors passed their six desolate years on Edgeøya Island. It is certain that the early Scandinavians discovered this cluster of islands in the twelfth century, although definitive such evidence escapes us. It is, however, known that Pomori had hunted in the area as early as the fourteenth or fifteenth centuries, but knowledge of it remained unknown in Western Europe.

The first definitive record of the islands' discovery lies with Willem Barents, who came across the archipelago in 1596 as he searched for the Northeast Passage. The largest of the islands — some fifteen thousand square miles in size — he found "nothing more than mountains and pointed peaks, therefore we called it Spitzbergen." His expedition, however, encountered whales, many of them, and word of this find quickly spread. Whale oil in those days seems to have been more eagerly sought than fossil oil of today — Thomas Jefferson is said to have remarked, "next in value to bread is oil."

By 1615, Spitzbergen had developed into a centre for whaling, and opposing claims to the place had been staked by King Christian IV of Denmark and the Muscovy Company. The English stuck to their dubious assertion that Hugh Willoughby had discovered the island in 1533 and that therefore the land was rightfully theirs. Within a couple of decades, whalers from a bevy of nations were operating in the rich hunting grounds, principally the English, Danes, Dutch, French, Spaniards, and the Basques. In a setting of wild lawlessness, clashes between these groups were frequent and often bloody, particularly between the Danes and the English.

The shallow waters along the archipelago's western edges are rich with krill, squid, and cod, thanks to the turbulence created by the confluence of the warm nutrient-rich Gulf Stream current and the cold currents flowing southward from Greenland. The waters therefore abound not only with whales but with seals, walrus, and bears. Little wonder that hunters and fishermen were attracted to the area in pursuit of ivory, baleen, furs, and oil.

Denmark was the first to establish a settlement on the island cluster, but within six years the Danes were ousted by the Dutch, who in 1625 set about creating the town of Smeerenburg ("blubbertown") on Amsterdamøya Island at the archipelago's northwest corner. By the time it had grown into its own, there were twenty cookeries for the making of oil, warehouses, dormitories for over two hundred workers, bakeries, taverns, and, to ward off the Danes, a fort — a remote frontier town eight hundred miles from the North Pole. In the ensuing half century, whaling technology underwent significant changes, with hunts moving away from coastal areas into the high seas and blubber becoming processed at home ports. By 1670 activity in Smeerenburg had died out and the town was abandoned and left to decay.

In the decades that followed, Svalbard continued to attract English, Danish, and Basque whalers, plus Russian and Norwegian hunters, but apart from isolated outposts, no settlements came to be. In the nineteenth century, a coal-mining operation blossomed, financed principally by British and American interests. All the while, the archipelago had been variously claimed by England, Holland, and Denmark-Norway, and it was only in the twentieth century that the matter resolved. The 1920 Peace Treaty of Paris that ended the First World War assigned sovereignty over the island group to Norway (with the proviso that citizens of other nations could freely reside and work there). Historically, the archipelago has been called Svalbard, with Spitzbergen the largest island at the hub, but when it was incorporated by Norway, the whole came to be named after the principal island.

Today, the administrative centre of the archipelago is Longyearbyen, where three-quarters of the archipelago's 2,800 inhabitants reside, the world's northernmost town of size and where coal mining continues to be the major industry, in addition to tourism. The most notable feature of Spitzbergen attracting world attention is the Svalbard Global Seed Vault on the outskirts of Longyearbyen. Created and financed initially by the Norwegian government, the project's mission is to collect and store seeds from up to 3 million known varieties of the world's crops. The "dooms-day vault," as it's popularly called, is constructed to withstand any nuclear or natural disaster that might threaten the planet's sources of food. The location was chosen for its virtual freedom from tectonic activity, but more important, for its naturally frozen environment, boosted by locally mined coal-powered refrigeration units that help maintain a constant temperature of 0°F. Two chambers house the collection deep in the bed-rock of a sandstone mountain at the end of a specially fortified 390-foot tunnel. The entire construction is lined with steel-reinforced concrete and the facility is equipped with a variety of robot systems that control blast-proof doors, motion sensors, and air locks. The seeds are envel-oped in specially designed moisture-proof packets.

Sharing the North Sea waters is another Norwegian territory, a thirty-four-mile-long volcanic island lying at 71°N called Jan Mayen. Legend has it that in the sixth century, an Irish monk, St. Brendan "the Navigator," travelled into the North Sea in a continuing search for the Garden of Eden. He did not find Eden, but he did come across a "black island" that was on fire and from which terrible noise emanated, and this, it is believed, was Jan Mayen. The venturesome Vikings no doubt knew of the island, but the sagas fail to offer such confirmation. The most likely record of European discovery of the place points to Henry Hudson, who, on his second voyage into Arctic waters, came across it as he sailed from Novaya Zemlya. For whatever reason, the explorer gutted parts of his journal and because the concerned segment of the log was missing, con-firmation may not be had that it was he who uncovered Jan Mayen.

In 1614, the Dutch took possession of the island and set up whaling stations along the northwest coast. The waters around the island at the time teemed with bowhead whales, and these animals were particularly prized for the high-quality oil they provided. By melting down the blubber of a medium-sized bowhead of fifty to sixty feet, some twenty-five tons of high-value oil could be harvested. In one exceptional season, forty-four bowheads were processed in its furnaces. As with Smeerenburg, the whaling stations at Jan Mayen in their day had complete infrastructures and were worked by hundreds of men. And, as with Svalbard, the place beehived with activity for only a few decades before being abandoned. The oil rush had been so successful that by 1640 Jan Mayen's whale herds had been hunted out and were no more.[1]

The island remained uninhabited for nearly two-and-a-half centuries, when in 1882, an eccentric Austrian nobleman, Count Johann Wilczek, founded a short-lived polar station, the purpose of which was to further the study of meteorology, astronomy, magnetism, and the *aurora borealis.*

In 1921, the Norwegians took possession of Jan Mayen and established a meteorological station that continues to operate to this day. The island enjoys a population of eighteen (thirty-five in the summer) — employees of either the Norwegian Meteorological Institute or members of the armed forces.

From earliest times, Scandinavians have been wed to the sea, and it was natural for these Nordic peoples to venture out beyond their coastlines into distant polar waters. By the tenth century, as we have seen, their settlements dotted the Greenland coastline, and in the seventeenth century, Jens Munk made his epic exploration of Hudson Bay. In the pantheon of Arctic history there stand a number of other Scandinavians — among the more notable of whom are Adolf Nordenskiöld, the first to navigate the Northern Sea Route, and Roald Amundsen, the first to traverse the Northwest Passage. The fame of Fridtjof Nansen lies not only in his explorations of Greenland, but in his global humanitarian achievements. The work of Otto Sverdrup was focused on Greenland and the Canadian Arctic Archipelago, as was that of Knud Rasmussen. One might legitimately add to this list a Canadian of Icelandic blood, Vilhjalmur Stefansson.

Nordenskiöld was born in Finland into a Swedish noble family and in 1858, at the age of twenty-six, he undertook his first Arctic voyage as a mineralogist attached to a scientific expedition to Spitzbergen. In the quarter century that followed, the untiring explorer accompanied or led nine more expeditions into polar regions, principally to Spitzbergen and Greenland, in continued mineralogical and geological research. In 1875, he chalked up one notable achievement by reaching the highest northern latitude then attained in the eastern hemisphere, 81°42' N. But it was for his memorable voyage on board the 357-ton whaling ship, the *Vega*, that Nordenskiöld garnered his ~~notoriety~~. fame.

In July 1877, the seasoned Arctic hand presented to Oscar II, king of Sweden and Norway, his plan for an ambitious expedition, the principal purpose of which was to investigate the geography, hydrography, and natural history of the North Polar Sea beyond the mouth of the Yenisej, if possible as far as Behring's Straits … if only the state of the ice permit a suitable steamer to force a passage of that sea.[21]

His Majesty approved the project and preparations were set in motion to get the expedition underway. The steam-driven, massively reinforced *Vega* was outfitted in the admiralty shipyards and two officers and seventeen ratings from the Royal Swedish Navy volunteered to form the complement. For whatever reason, the ship was denied the privilege of sailing under the naval ensign and it therefore put out to sea flying the colours of the Swedish Yacht Club. In spring 1878, it sailed out of Tromsø in northernmost Norway in and headed east.

Nordenskiöld was, first and foremost, a scientist, and the expedition he proposed to the king was of a scientific nature. Let there be no doubt, however, that of equal interest to him, to King Oscar and to the Swedish Academy was the prospect of a successful traverse of the Northern Sea Route, the linking of the Atlantic and Pacific Oceans. Where Willoughby, Brunel, Hudson, and others had failed, he would succeed. The project called for the *Vega* to cross the Barents Sea, round Novaya Zemlya, sail the Kara Sea, and reach the mouth of the Lena by August. There the expedition would winter and in the following spring it would continue on to the Bering Strait.

Unlucky as the early explorers had been with impassible ice conditions on the Kara Sea, Nordenskiöld was favoured by open waters, and with virtually no difficulty or undue incident he sailed through and reached the Lena as planned. Lady Luck continued to smile on him by providing exceptionally favourable weather and winds, together with mild, non-hazardous ice conditions — so much so that the explorer forwent plans for wintering at the Lena and sailed on. By mid-September, with the weather changing for the worse, and heavy ice forming, progress was appreciably slowed, and finally on the 28th the *Vega* was beset at its anchorage along the Chukotka coastline, a mere 190 miles from the Bering Strait.

In his 758-page journal, Nordenskiöld gives every sort of detail concerning the flora and fauna encountered, geographic and hydrographic information, magnetic and meteorological data, and observations on the peoples met en route, especially the Chukchi, with whom the Scandinavians came in frequent contact during their long winter of ice captivity. The modern-day reader might be interested in one vignette that reflects on the times. While outdoor temperature fluctuated from -22°F to -40°F, temperatures within the vessel hovered from the low minus forties to 55°F, "that is to say about the same as we in the north are wont to have indoors in winter, and certainly higher than the temperatures of rooms during the coldest days of the year in many cities in the south, for instance in Paris and Vienna."

"Christmas Eve was celebrated in the usual northern fashion." A makeshift Christmas tree was fashioned out of wood and small twigs brought by the Chukchi, and festooned with tinsel and decorations, around which "thundering polkas" were danced by the happy celebrants.

At supper neither Christmas ale nor ham was wanting, and later in the evening there made their appearance in the 'tween decks five punch bowls which were emptied with songs and toasts for King and Fatherland, for the objects of the Expedition, for its officers and men, for the families at home, for relatives and friends, and finally for those who decked and arranged the Christmas tree.[3]

As the men of the *Vega* cavorted around the Christmas tree and quaffed the sequence of toasts, the world outside fretted and worried. Nothing had been heard of the expedition for some time and no sign of the Swedes had been had at the mouth of the Lena. The Swedish government sent out messages to world capitals requesting co-operation in locating the missing vessel. The *New York Herald* picked upon the story and Bennett, as sponsor of the De Long's expedition, made the search for Nordenskiöld an add-on condition of the naval officer's mission. This last-minute assignment, noble and worthy as it was, threatened to skew De Long's tight timetable; he was less than pleased. He noted that in the previous winter Nordenskiöld had reached Cape Serdze Kamen, well along the Siberian coastline, and so, he writes:

> I decided to go there and make inquiry, and if I find the Swedes were there and left, I shall push to Wrangel Island at once; if not — and there is the sticker — I suppose I shall have to grope along until I find where they did winter.[4]

At the very time that De Long was worrying about Nordenskiöld, the Swede, quite oblivious to the anxiety of the outside world as to his whereabouts, was happily sailing the Pacific. The *Vega* had spent ten captive months on the Siberian coastline until the spring melt and favourable south winds finally set it free on July 20. In continuing fair weather and with steady winds Nordenskiöld arrived at the entrance to Bering Strait shortly thereafter and sailed through it serenely, making a brief stop at the Diomede Islands. The *Vega*, he noted in his journal, "is thus the first vessel that has penetrated by the north from one of the great world-oceans to the other."[5] Contrary to previous attempts to complete the northern passage from Europe, the Swede finished his journey almost as though it was a holiday excursion. It had been a smooth sail with no loss of life or equipment — anticlimactic, really.

From the Diomedes, the Swede continued on to Japan, the Gulf of Aden, and around Africa, making it back to Stockholm on April 24, 1860. It had been a journey of 22,189 miles — the first circumnavigation of the eastern hemisphere. On his arrival home, Nordenskiöld was wined and dined by the admiring nation and a variety of honours befell him, including being made a baron and an induction to the Swedish Academy. His massive tome describing the journey became a bestseller, richly detailing virtually all he saw about him. Marcel Proust must have had

Fridtjof Nansen (1861–1930), the Norwegian Arctic explorer, scientist, diplomat, humanitarian, and Nobel laureate.

Nordenskiöld in mind when he wrote, "the only true voyage of discovery consists not in seeking new landscapes, but in having new eyes." A charmed life indeed.

The fearless Fridtjof Nansen stands unique amid Scandinavian Arctic explorers, for his fame transcends his impressive accomplishments in the world of exploration and science. He is perhaps even better known for the astonishing range of achievements following his withdrawal from Arctic activity. As one biographer puts it adroitly, "there is a timelessness about great men; and in Norway, and indeed the world, Nansen was among the greatest." Explorer, oceanographer, zoologist, geologist, athlete, author, statesman, and humanitarian — all that, plus Nobel Peace Prize laureate. When one wonders at what manner of men were those who were challenged by the Arctic Siren, Nansen confounds accurate depiction. As New York's *Herald Tribune* noted in 1932, he "should have been born in the Renaissance, before specialists became civilization's heroes."[6]

Born near Oslo of a prosperous professional family in 1861, as a tall, slim schoolboy he was a brilliant athlete and a prize-winner in swimming, gymnastics, and skating. For twelve consecutive years, he won the Norwegian national cross-country race and it was his extraordinary prowess at this sport that helped mould his life. At age nineteen he made his first trip to Greenland as a note-taker and artist for a scientific expedition. It was an eye-opening experience for the young man. The mist-covered snowfields of the great glacier so captivated him that he resolved some day to return and explore that unknown land. The following six years he spent in intensive study of zoology, which culminated in a doctorate from the University of Oslo.[7]

In 1883, Nordenskiöld capped his earlier successes by making a final voyage to Greenland where he succeeded in breaking through the almost impenetrable ice barrier of the east coast, a feat that had thwarted explorers for over three centuries. The twenty-seven-year-old Nansen was so inspired by this that he immediately embarked on preparations for his dream exploration of the Greenland interior. The plan he had in mind was to land on the uninhabited east coast and then ski across the island to the peopled west coast. Once his party was deposited on Greenland's shores, therefore, there would be no turning back and only one way to go — forward. On more than one occasion, he urged students to burn bridges behind themselves so that no alternative would remain but to move forward. His actual words: "Never keep a line of retreat; it is a wretched invention."

Nansen's party of six was duly transported to Greenland and on August 11, 1888, the men found themselves ashore, ready to set off on the trek across the glacial island. It was a gruelling hike with a climb to nine thousand feet above sea level, over roughest ice and deep crevasses, all the while hauling sledges heavily laden with equipment and supplies. The September temperatures hit lows of -50°F, "these temperatures," wrote Nansen, "are without any comparison the lowest that have ever been recorded at this time of year anywhere on the face of the globe."[8] He continued, "Constant exposure to the cold was by no means pleasant. The ice often formed so heavily on our faces that our beards and hair froze to the coverings of our heads and it was difficult to open the lips to speak. This inconvenience had to be endured because we had no way of shaving."

Two months later, Nansen's party arrived on Greenland's west coast, but too late to catch the season's last vessel sailing for home. He therefore spent the winter living among the Inuit, learning about them and studying their ways. In 1893, he brought out a book on these studies, *Eskimo Life*, one of six works he authored in his lifetime. Shortly after returning home in the spring, he began plotting his next project.

In his studies of Arctic pioneers, Nansen was captivated by the saga of the *Jeannette*. He wrote:

> It was in the autumn of 1884 that I happened to see an article by Professor Mohn ... in which it was stated that sundry articles which must have come from the *Jeannette* had been found on the southwest coast of Greenland. He conjectured that they must have drifted on a floe right across the Polar Sea. It immediately occurred to me that here lay the route ready at hand. If a floe could drift right across an unknown region, that drift might be enlisted in the service of exploration — and my plan laid.

Nansen now set about raising funds for the construction of a special ship, the hull of which would be impervious to pressures of ice. He planned to sail it out from the Siberian coastline until it became icebound, and then allow it to drift westward with the currents toward the North Pole and on to Greenland. Some members of the Swedish Academy thought him quite mad and would have no part in the harebrained scheme. Others, however, believed in their enterprising hero and readily subscribed funds for the project, the king among the first.

A certain Colin Archer, a Scottish naval architect of Norwegian descent, was commissioned to design the vessel, and in 1892, the *Fram* ("Forward") was launched. It was a four-hundred-ton tri-mast, steam-powered sailing ship, 127 feet long, made of exceptionally hard wood from Guyana, with a smooth, rounded hull bearing virtually no keel. It had retractable propellers and rudder and it carried a built-in windmill for the generation of electricity. When heavy ice would press the vessel, the cunning design of the iron-clad hull would disallow it to grip the sides, and as the pressure build up from beneath, the ship would be squeezed upward rather than being crushed inward by an unrelenting

The 127-foot Fram, *used in passages to the North Pole by Nansen and by Sverdrup, and by Amundsen to the South Pole.*

221

grip. In Nansen's words, she would slip upward "like an eel out of the embraces of the ice."

Twelve men signed on to the bold expedition, including Otto Sverdrup, selected as the *Fram*'s captain. The seasoned sailor was a close companion to Nansen and had accompanied him on the momentous cross-Greenland ski expedition. Although Nansen calculated that this fresh journey would take two years, when the expedition finally left Christina harbour (known today as Oslo) on June 24, 1893, it carried provisions for six years and fuel for eight. As Jeannette Mirsky observed in *To the Arctic!*, "The magnificent and novel adventure had begun. Not only was the *Fram* to be subjected to every whim of the pressed-up ice-fields, but thirteen men were to face the test of three — or five — years of monotonous life, surrounded by monotonous icy wastes, severed entirely from all outside contacts."

They set off east on Nordenskiöld's route through the Northern Passage. The expedition passed the Kara Sea to the New Siberian Islands and by the end of September found itself off Bennett Island where it was beset by ice, frozen in, and riding the currents. "The *Fram* behaved beautifully. On pushed the ice, but down under us it had to go, and we were lifted up … the men have grown so indifferent to the pressure that they do not even get up to look, let it thunder ever so hard." The boredom of long days was punctuated by astronomical and magnetic studies and by the systematic taking of ocean temperatures and water samples at various levels.[9] From time to time a confrontation was had with a polar bear, but otherwise ennui seems to have been the order of the day.

For over a year, the *Fram* had been drifting slowly but steadily north and west. In November 1894, however, by the time they had reached 83°N, the troubling realization came to Nansen that their direction had changed imperceptibly to a southward direction, past the pole. Months of inaction, and now they were moving away from his objective: it was too much for the restless man and he would cope with the situation no more. As soon as sufficient daylight was had in spring, he decided, he would quit his ship, and, with a willing companion, make a dash for the pole by ski and snowshoe. The *Fram* would be left to return home under Sverdrup's capable command.

In his book, *Farthest North,* Nansen gives lively details of the trek he and Hjalmar Johansen undertook in those frozen wasteland. Setting out on March 14 with sledges, kayaks, and twenty-eight dogs, every sort of adventure befell the two as they pressed forward … ever forward. Sledges overturned, kayaks were pierced by ice, steep pressure ridges were surmounted, dogs were overcome and had to be put down. Frequent gales detained them, as did pockets of knee-high snow. Once they were ambushed by an attacking bear, which at the last moment Nansen was able to shoot "just as the bear was about to bite [the prone] Johansen in the head … a shot behind the ear, and it fell down dead between us …"

One by one, the dogs were killed to feed those that survived until finally none remained. Heavy perspiration froze clothes "which were now a mass of ice and transformed into complete suits of ice-armour." The overall situation became dire, viewed by Nansen with despair. His entry for April 8:

> No, the ice grew worse and worse, and we got no way. Ridge after ridge, and nothing but rubble to travel over. We made a start at two o'clock or so this morning, and kept at it as long as we could, lifting the sledges all the time; but it grew too bad at last. I went on a good way ahead on snow-shoes, but saw no reasonable prospect of advance, and from the highest hammocks only the same kind of ice to be seen. It was as veritable chaos of ice-blocks, stretching as far as the horizon. There is not much sense in keeping on longer; we are sacrificing valuable time and doing little. If there be much more such ice between here and Franz Josef Land, we shall, indeed, want all the time to have.

The two men had been out for twenty-six days and had reached 86°14' N, but were no closer to the pole. Nansen concluded his entry, "I therefore determined to stop, and shape our course for Cape Fligely [at Franz Joseph Land, Europe's northern-most point]."

Changing direction, they pushed steadily on, with the days becoming weeks. Then, on July 24: "At last the marvel has come to pass — land, land, and after we had almost given up our belief in it! After nearly two years we again see something rising above the never-ending white line on the horizon yonder — a white line which for countless ages has stretched over this lonely sea, and *which for millenniums to come shall stretch in the same way*" [author's italics]. Unrealized by them, the island they had reached was part of the Franz Joseph archipelago within a hundred miles of Cape Fligely.

By the end of August, with temperatures rapidly falling and the weather turning for the worse, it became clear that it would be impossible to make their destination before the onset of full winter. They would have to stop where they were, create a shelter and patiently sit out the months ahead.

Using a makeshift spade made of a walrus shoulder blade, the two men excavated a hole in the frozen ground. Around this primitive foundation walls carefully placed stones were built and the joints were "plastered in" with moss and earth. Driftwood was found in large quantities, which they gathered and of the larger branches formed "trusses" to

The tiny semi-underground shelter hastily constructed by Nansen and Johanssen in which they spent the winter of 1884–85. Sleep was their greatest comfort, and "we carried this art in a high pitch of perfection."

support a roof of walrus hides. Fortunately game was plentiful, particularly walrus and the occasional intruding polar bear, therefore not only was there a supply of food at hand, but the melted fat from these animals brought heat and light to the hut. "By the aid of lamps we succeeded in keeping the temperature at about the freezing-point in the middle of the hut, while it was, of course, colder at the walls." Here the men spent nine mostly dark months, awaiting the daylight of spring with much of the time being spent in sleep. "We carried this art to a high pitch of perfection, and could sometimes put in as much as 20 hours' sleep in 24."

It is hard to imagine the men's primitive living conditions and the hardships and vicissitudes of daily life, all within permeating cold and profound solitude. Nansen seemed to have risen above it all and in places of his journal he reflected a measure of joy and of poetic wonder:

> *Sunday, 1 December, 1895.* Wonderfully beautiful weather for the last few days, one can never weary of going up and down outside, while the moon transforms the whole of this ice world into a fairey-land. The hut is still in shadow under the mountain which hangs above, dark and lowering; the moonlight floats over ice and fjord, and is cast back glittering from every snowy ridge and hill. A weird beauty, without feeling, as though of a dead planet, built of shining white marble. Just so must the mountains stand there, frozen and icy cold; just so must the lakes lie congealed beneath their snowy covering; and now as ever the moon sails silently and slowly on her endless course through the lifeless space. And everything is so still, so awfully still, with the silence that shall one day reign, when the earth again becomes desolate and empty, when the fox will no more haunt those moraines, when the bear will no longer wander about the ice out there; when even the wind will not rage — infinite silence! In the flaming aurora borealis, the spirit of space hovers over the frozen waters. The soul bows down before majesty of night and death ...

With the coming of spring and daylight, the two men set out again, once more harnessed to their sledges. Alternating between snowshoes, skis, and kayaks, the couple progressed steadily south along their laborious path when entirely by chance, almost miraculously, they were delivered from their sorrowful situation. Encamped one day in a "land I believed to be unseen by any human eye and untrodden by any human foot, reposing in Arctic majesty behind its mantle of mist ... a sound suddenly reached my ear so like the barking of a dog ..."

The barking was indeed that of a dog, one that was accompanying Frederick Jackson to Franz Joseph Land on a British scientific expedition sponsored by the Royal Geographic Society. With waves of hats, the two men came together — Nansen described the scene:

> [O]n one side the civilized European in an English check suit and high rubber boots, well shaved, well groomed, bringing with him a perfume of scented soap, perceptible to the wild man's sharpened senses; on the other side the wild man clad only in dirty rags, black with oil and soot, with long uncombed hair and shaggy beard, black with smoke, with a face in which the natural fair complexion could not possibly be discerned through the thick layer of fat and soot which a winter's endeavours with warm water, moss, rags, and at last a knife had sought in vain to remove. No one suspected who he was or whence he came.

There followed a replay of the Stanley-Livingstone African encounter:

> Jackson stopped, looked me full in the face, and said quickly, "Aren't you Nansen?"
> "Yes, I am."
> "By Jove! I am glad to see you!"

The two elatedly exchanged information with one another. Nansen and Johansen were then taken to the British base camp, and, a couple of months later, on August 13, 1896, the two came ashore at Vardø in easternmost Norway, close to the Russian border. Within days of their return, they found themselves reunited with their companions on board the *Fram*. Following Nansen's abandonment of the ship months earlier, the vessel continued in its ice-lock until June, by which time it had been borne north of Spitzbergen. At that point, after nearly three years of captivity, Sverdrup was successful in blasting the ship free from the melting pack and the *Fram* found itself under sail once again. The expedition was now safely reunited. "The meeting which followed," wrote Nansen, "I shall not try to describe. I don't think any of us knew anything clearly, except that we were all together again — we were in Norway — and the expedition had fulfilled its task … in my heart I sobbed and wept for joy and thankfulness." Although the North Pole had not been reached, the voyage had been one of high adventure, but more importantly, the meteorological, biological, and oceanographic data that was brought home added generously to the knowledge of the Arctic Ocean.

The laurels belonged to Nansen. Appointed a professor at the University of Oslo, he took to compiling the six-volume record of his extraordinary trip. But he didn't stop there — always "forward!" Tales of his heroic exploits had spread throughout the country and his popularity had grown so significantly that involvement in national affairs seemed an inevitable encore. In 1905, the Norwegian parliament unilaterally broke the personal union it had with Sweden, and in the negotiations that followed, received full autonomy. Standing behind the independence movement was the tireless Nansen. With self-government granted, the country fell into debate as to the next step — was it to be a monarchy or a republic? A plebiscite gave a 79 percent majority to the monarchists, and here Nansen once more came to the fore. It was largely through his efforts that Prince Carl of Denmark was selected as Haakon VII, King of Norway. (It might be added that as the debate over the government issue raged, Nansen reportedly was asked to become the country's first king or president. He declined the offers, declaring that science and exploration were his vocations. He did take on, however, a two-year appointment as Norway's first ambassador to Britain.)

In the chaotic aftermath of the First World War, Nansen once again plunged himself into public affairs, but this time at an international level.

In the years 1917–29, he served as a lobbyist at the Peace Conference of Paris, then as Norway's delegate to the League of Nations, and finally as the League's Commissioner for Refugees. Among his achievements are the postwar repatriation of 450,000 prisoners; the creation of the "Nansen Passport," recognized by fifty-two nations, by which stateless refugees received a document of identification; the repatriation and rehabilitation of hundreds of thousands of Russian, Turkish, and Armenian refugees; relief supplies for Russians during the disastrous 1921–22 famine, and the drawing up of a plan for the foundation of the Armenian state. The Norwegian patriot had become an internationalist and perhaps Schumann, Adenauer, and de Gasperi — the fathers of modern Europe — received their cue from Nansen, who, after the First World War, warned that unless Europeans shed their nationalistic mindsets, another war would be hard to avoid. "The only policy an international economic point of view."[10] Such was the uncommon son of the Arctic and the mettle of a man who lived by what he preached: "The difficult is what takes a little time; the impossible is what takes a little longer."

One of Nansen's closest companions was Otto Sverdrup who, had accompanied the explorer on the cross-country trek of Greenland and on the odyssey of the *Fram*. Whereas in later life, Nansen gravitated to academia and politics, Sverdrup continued in the world of Arctic exploration, and in the years 1898–1902, he took the *Fram* on four expeditions into the Canadian Arctic, each time wintering on Ellesmere Island. To him goes credit for the discovery of three major islands in the archipelago lying west of Ellesmere, including the most prominent, Axel Heiberg. It was on this uninhabited island in 1985 that a sharp-eyed helicopter pilot flying over the land spotted the "fossil forest," or more accurately, mummified remains of tree stumps. Over 45 million years ago when Arctic climatic conditions were radically different, forests blanketed much of the region and dinosaurs walked the lands. The stumps on Axel Heiberg are the remains of trees that once towered at heights up to 130 feet, relatives of the redwoods of the American West. Scattered about the stumps are beautifully preserved flattened leaves, feathery and easily recognizable as conifer.

Sverdrup's Arctic achievements have been eclipsed by the likes of Nansen and Amundsen, but at an unveiling of a monument in his hometown of Steinkjer, Norway, he was referred to as "a prince of polar navigators … the most competent and practical of Norwegian polar explorers."

Standing shoulder to shoulder with Nansen at the top of the dais of Scandinavian Arctic explorers is Roald Amundsen, the first man to have reached the South Pole. In 1911, Amundsen sailed the *Fram* into the Antarctic and after a dangerous and gruelling passage, reached the pole on December 12. It must have been a euphoric moment for him, yet he wrote in his account of the event:

> The goal was reached, the journey ended. I cannot say
> — though I know it would sound much more effective
> — that the object of my life was attained. I had better be
> honest and admit strait out that I have never known any
> man to be placed in such a diametrically opposite posi-
> tion to the goal of his desires as I was at that moment.
> The regions around the North Pole — well, yes, the
> North Pole itself — had attracted me from childhood,
> and here I was at the South Pole. Can anything more
> topsy-turvy be imagined?[11]

Amundsen was indeed a child of the North, notwithstanding his historic Antarctic achievement. The first to reach the South Pole, but the kudos of being the first to the North Pole would not be his — the American explorer Robert Peary had reached it two years earlier. MAYBE Amundsen, however, was not to be totally undone. In May 1926, he set off from Norway in an airship, the *Norge*, determined to be the first to reach the pole by air. Accompanying him was a crew of fifteen, including Umberto Nobile, the Italian builder of the dirigible and Lincoln Ellsworth, the wealthy American sponsor of the expedition who spent $100,000 for the privilege of the flight.

Crossing the Barents Sea, Amundsen's flight stopped briefly at Svalbard, where on Spitzbergen Island he met Richard Byrd of the United States Navy who was in the final stages of preparation to fly his tri-motor

Fokker airplane over the same destination. On May 12 at 1:25 a.m., the *Norge* reached the North Pole, where the flags of Norway, Italy, and the United States were dropped onto the ice. (Within minutes of the deposit, acrimony broke out between Amundsen and Nobile, with the former accusing the latter of providing an Italian banner larger than the others, an incident that coloured their relations for years thereafter.) Three days earlier, Byrd had successfully flown over the pole, the first to have done so. Subsequently, his claim came to be questioned for the flight's log of sextant readings appeared in variance with those recorded by the aviator in his official report to the National Geographic Society, and to this day some refuse to recognize the American's achievement. The *Norge*'s mission having been achieved, it continued on its way and headed to Alaska, where eventually it landed in Nome after a 3,180-mile fight. The crew was enthusiastically greeted as being the first to have flown from Europe to America.

The South Pole and the *Norge*, two significant accomplishments. But it is not for these successes that Amundsen stands high among polar achievements. At the turn of the twentieth century, after the likes of Franklin, Frobisher, Cabot, and Columbus had failed for over five centuries, he succeeded in completing the entire length of the Northwest Passage, sailing from one end to the other. On June 16, 1903, Amundsen put out of Oslo with a six-man crew on board the *Gjøa*, a small forty-eight-ton seal hunting vessel built thirty years earlier. The objective of the expedition was to pinpoint the magnetic North Pole and to carry out studies of its forces. Passing the coasts of Greenland and Baffin Island, he sailed through Lancaster Sound, and, after a hazardous passage of violent storms and inordinately thick ice floes, they arrived at King William Island, on the opposite side from where Franklin's expedition had been abandoned fifty-five years earlier. Here the *Gjøa* found suitable anchorage and for the next two years it remained on the spot. An observatory was constructed, equipped with the finest instruments of the time, and for the length of their stay the men engaged in magnetic measurements and observations. While those primarily skilled in magnetism attended to their work, Amundsen befriended the local population and went on to study their ways, their arts, and their spiritual lives. In *The New Passage*, he gives the most comprehensive overview of those remarkable people that was had up to that time.

In the process he took to Inuit dress, diet, and hunting methods and in short order "became virtually an Eskimo himself."

With its scientific mission completed and the ship freed from its winter ice lockup, the *Gjøa* continued on its journey west. Fogs, drift ice, and shallow waters made navigation difficult — at one point, the water beneath the keel was reportedly one inch deep. After three such weeks, Amundsen finally entered known waters, regions that had been navigated and chartered in Alaska by explorers entering from the west. That which had been denied travellers for half a millennium, had at last been gained: the traverse of the passage. Amundsen nonchalantly described the milestone accomplishment:

> ... the final accomplishment of the North West Passage by ship. I had hoped to have a little festivity to mark the notable event, but the weather did not permit. The event was celebrated by a simple toast, nothing more. We could not even hoist the flag, as it would have been blown to tatters.

This seemingly casual attitude toward his success was not altogether genuine; in fact, the explorer itched to inform the world of the triumph. Unfortunately for him, however, the *Gjøa* became frozen in by early winter and contact with the outside world was denied. Undaunted, Amundsen set off on October 5 with a native companion by dog team to reach Eagle City, some five hundred miles inland where, he was assured, there was a telegraph station. He reached his destination two months later, after a laborious passage through a mountain range with peaks as high as nine thousand feet. Eagle City, it turned out, was a hamlet of 130 isolated inhabitants, but it did have a telegraph connection — and the news went out. Shortly thereafter he returned home where he was rejoined by his companions of the *Gjøa*.

Soon after Amundsen's return, his one-time flight companion, Umberto Nobile, found himself in mortal Arctic peril. Determined to make another dirigible flight over the North Pole, he enlisted a sixteen-man crew and set off from Svalbard on board the airship *Italia* on May 23, 1928, and headed north. Within twenty-four hours, the dirigible crashed and most of the crew was killed or severely injured. Nobile, himself, sustained a broken arm, a broken leg, and a broken rib, as well as head injuries. Fortunately, the ship's signals operator was able to repair the damaged radio and his SOS signals were picked up by an amateur in Russia. Word of the tragedy quickly spread and in short order search parties set off to locate the survivors. By the time it was all over, thirty different rescue teams from six countries had become involved with the operation one way or another. Putting aside his differences with Nobile, one of the first to volunteer in the search was Roald Amundsen. In quick order, he organized a rescue flight aboard a French seaplane with a four-man crew. On June 18, the aircraft took off from Trømso into the timeless white yonder beyond and it was not heard from again. More than likely it went down, possibly in heavy fog, somewhere in the Barents Sea — some

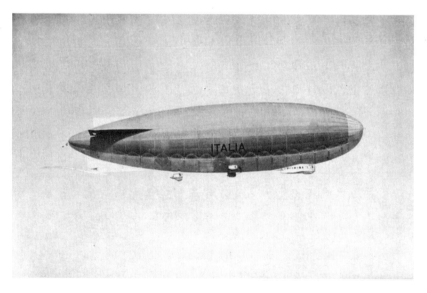

Umberto Nobile's dirigible, the Italia. *On May 28, 1928, the Italian adventurer set out for the North Pole, but the airship soon crashed. In search of his former colleague, Amundsen lost his life when his own plane crashed somewhere into the Barents Sea.*

of its wreckage was found floating, but not the bodies. Amundsen had succumbed to the Arctic Siren's beguiling song.

The fame of Knud Rasmussen, the so-called "father of Eskimology," rests on his studies of Inuit culture. In 1902, he participated in the Danish Literary Greenland Expedition in a two-year study of native folklore and legends. Since he was born and raised in Greenland he was totally at home with the Inuit and fluent in their language. "My playmates were native Greenlanders; from earliest boyhood I played and worked with the hunters, so even the hardships of the most strenuous sledge-trips became pleasant routine for me." On this particular journey, the twenty-three-year-old served as translator and interpreter to the academics from Copenhagen.

In 1910 Rasmussen was joined by others — including his friend, the accomplished Arctic traveller Peter Freuchen — in establishing the Thule Trading Station on the island's far northwest coast, opposite Ellesmere Island, the most northern outpost in the world. A flourishing trade with the Inuit blossomed there with pipes and tobacco, knives, rifles and ammunition, and other manufactured items being exchanged for Arctic furs. So successful was the enterprise in the following two decades that Rasmussen was able to help finance seven Thule Expeditions between 1912 and 1933. The object of these missions was to study intensively the culture, traditions, and history of Inuit everywhere, from Greenland to the Bering Sea. The most notable of the expeditions was the fifth, undertaken from 1921–24, which set out to "attack the great primary problem of the origin of the Eskimo race." Upon its completion, a ten-volume account was published of the collected ethnographic, archaeological, and biological data, an important record of native folklore and history at a time when the Inuit still remained in their primitive state, unaffected by the introduction of commercially produced foods, Christianity, and European laws and ways.

While seven experts continued the work of interviewing, recording, excavating, and collecting specimens, Rasmussen, with two Inuit hunters, left the expedition's main body, and travelled by dogsled across the North

American continent. For sixteen months the trio coped with all the hazards such a journey might entail and with whatever the elements might throw their way, all the time living off the land or sharing the hospitality of Inuit met along the way. The passage was completed with their arrival at Nome, Alaska — the first crossing of the Northwest Passage by dogsled. One might have thought that Rasmussen would have been content to rest on his laurels, but that was not to be. He immediately began planning for a continuation of his path, across the Bering Strait and Siberia, but was thwarted by Soviet authorities, who denied him the requested visa.

The sixth and seventh Thule Expeditions were continuations of the earlier ones, always in the furthering of knowledge and recording the ways of the admirable indigenous people of the North. On the final tour in 1933, he fell ill with food poisoning and, transferred to Copenhagen, he contracted influenza and pneumonia and died. The crossings of Greenland and America and his insightful studies of Inuit form the basis of his fame. By his work the "father of Eskimology" is also largely responsible for establishing Danish sovereignty over that huge island.

To encourage settlement in its west, in 1877 the Canadian government persuaded 250 Icelanders from the north of the island to quit their country and move outside of Winnipeg, Manitoba, and it was there that Vilhjalmur Stefansson was born in 1879. An anthropologist by training and an advocate of the Arctic by vocation, he came to be known as "The Prophet of the North" — so reads the epitaph on his tombstone near Dartmouth College, New Hampshire. At age eighteen he left home to study at the University of Iowa, then moved on to the University of North Dakota and finally ended up at Harvard where he became affiliated with the department of anthropology and also the Peabody Museum. In 1905, he undertook the first of his Arctic expeditions, one of three journeys into northernmost Canada and Alaska, each lasting from sixteen months to five years. By the end of his career, he had published twenty-four books and more than four hundred articles on his travels and studies of native peoples.

But even at age twenty-seven, Stefansson had already become recognized as a serious anthropologist, having published the results of his one-year study in Iceland of the relationship between diet and health. Harvard took him on as a teaching fellow where he was valued by the department of anthropology as an authority on the Arctic. In 1906–12 he worked with the Peabody and the American Museum of Natural History, living with and studying the Mackenzie River Indians and the far north Inuit. Like Rasmussen, Stefansson believed that the most efficacious way of acquiring knowledge of the Inuit was to live among them and to fully embrace their ways — their dress, their shelter, and their diet. "Living with [the Inuit] was much better from an ethnological point of view than merely living amongst them, as other white men had done," he declared. One statement of mission by the American Museum clearly sets out that "the present expedition ... differs essentially from ordinary Arctic ventures in this, that where it is usual to take along with the party everything that the party is expected to need during their stay in the field, in this case there will be taken neither food, clothing nor housing materials, and there will be complete dependence on local resources."

On his first venture into the Canadian North, Stefansson heard of the rumoured existence of a mysterious tribe of blond-haired Inuit living west of the Coppermine River in a region supposed by geographers to be uninhabited. It was said that these people were exceptionally primitive and that they had never known white men, yet themselves looked like white men. If true, the finding of such peoples would be sensational not only for the scientific world, but for the general public — tales of lost tribes invariably excited imaginations. In 1908, with the backing of the American Museum, Stefansson embarked on his second Arctic expedition, this one lasting four years, during which he did in fact come across the "lost tribe" of blond Inuit. The small community consisted of primitive peoples who until then had had no contact with Europeans — rifles and butchering knives proved to be objects of amazement. He was struck not only by their physical appearance, particularly the light-coloured hair of some, but by their manner of speech that sparkled with philological similarities to Icelandic. "These are two points," he notes, "that suggest, as far as they go, the possibility of some connection with the three thousand lost Greenland colonists."

In 1913–18, on his final expedition into the Arctic, Stefansson spent five-and-a-half years living with the Inuit, during which time he expanded further his studies of them. Equally impressive, however, were his other achievements, best described by Major-General Aldophus Greely, himself an Arctic explorer, in a tribute before the National Geographic Society:

[H]e has made inroads into the million square miles of unknown Arctic regions, the largest for many years. His hydrographic work is specially important, in surveys and in magnetic declinations. His numerous soundings not only outline the continental shelf from Alaska to Prince Patrick Island, but also disclose the submarine mountains and valleys of the Beaufort Sea.[12]

From the unknown regions of Arctic lands and sea he has drawn areas amounting to approximately 100,000 square miles … three large islands and other small islands were discovered … [which] unquestionably fill in the last gap in the hitherto unknown seaward limits of the great Arctic archipelago in the north of the continent of America.

These accomplishments notwithstanding, the "prophet of the North" is best remembered for his advocacy of the North. Stefansson consistently regarded the Arctic as a benign place — witness the fact that one of his books is entitled *The Friendly Arctic*. "It is human nature to undervalue whatever lands that are distant and to consider disagreeable whatever is different," he wrote, and he chastises southerners for viewing the North as hostile. In his life's work, he took satisfaction in having brought the Arctic and its inhabitants closer to the world and to having made it look more like "a commonplace country … like Michigan or Switzerland." The Arctic, he argued, is misunderstood chiefly through "our unwillingness to change minds that prevents the North from changing into a country to be used and lived in just like the rest of the world."

"The place that God had secreted for himself," the pristine land of the peaceable Inuit had taken sizeable steps in the twentieth century to becoming "just like the rest of the world" … including defilement by war. One might have thought that major powers in conflict with one another would have little cause to bring war to those remote, largely uninhabited northern regions. This was not the case, however, and as early as 1854, during the Crimean War, gunfire was exchanged between the British and the Russians well above the Arctic Circle along the Kola Peninsula and the White Sea. In the earliest stage of the war, a small squadron of British ships rounded North Cape to bombard and put a torch to the town of Kola, thirteen miles east of the Norwegian border. They then moved on to the White Sea where they fired on Solovetsky Monastery. Some rounds were returned from the feebly fortified stronghold without major damage to the ships, but with casualties among the crews. The British withdrew, sailed for home, and that was the extent of it. Among the felled attackers was a certain Seaman Ordenz from Jamaica — it might be said therefore that one of the earliest casualties of the world's most curious and unnecessary struggles was not a white man on the Black Sea, but a black man on the White Sea.

But it was the Second World War that saw meaningful incursion of warfare into the Arctic, including actual combat. As early as 1941, the Allies had committed to the policy of supporting in any way possible Soviet armies fighting on the Eastern Front — a two-front division of Hitler's resources was fundamental strategy. War material of every sort flowed east from America under the Lend-Lease program, principally tanks, fighter planes, and trucks, and, to bolster infrastructure, locomotives and railway cars. Convoys of ships assembled at staging areas along the North American coast, sailed northeast under naval protection to Iceland, and continued north of Jan Mayen Island to arrive at Murmansk or, in adverse ice conditions, at Arkhangelsk. In the four-year period,

August 1941 to May 1945, seventy-eight convoys made the "Murmansk Run," and by the time it was all over 1,400 vessels had been escorted to the USSR by British, American, and Canadian naval vessels.

Germany quite naturally made strenuous efforts to stem the flow of Allied materiel from reaching its Soviet enemy; its cruisers, destroyers, submarines, and aircraft harassed and engaged the Allies at every point. In July 1942, the convoy that suffered the greatest losses of the entire war was the seventeenth to make the crossing. As it entered Arctic waters it came under heavy attack by German aircraft and submarines. As the fighting progressed, a signal was received that a battle group was on its way to intercept the convoy and that among the ships was the fabled battleship *Tirpitz*. The ships were ordered to scatter, and in the confusion that followed, twenty-four of the thirty-five transports were sunk. The eleven that made it through barely limped into port and carried hundreds of the dead or wounded. Five months later, the Allies won a victory of sorts at the Battle of Barents Sea when the enemy suffered punishing losses and was driven off by a combined force of destroyers and cruisers.

The "Arctic front" insofar as the Navy was concerned, was not exclusively a matter of convoy duty. A successful war effort is much dependent on authentic weather prediction. The supply convoys on the Murmansk run relied heavily on them, as did most land and air operations in northern Europe — Allied or German. (Never more so than in early June 1941 when General Eisenhower signalled the launch of D-day invasion.) To feed military experts data with which to make weather predictions, a number of meteorological stations dotted the Arctic, which, understandably, one side or the other was determined to destroy or take over — in Greenland, on Jan Mayen Island, in Spitzbergen, and even on Bear Island. Following the capitulation of Denmark and Norway in April 1940 the "war of the weather stations" began in earnest.

Typical of that "war" was a relatively minor incident, but one that is illustrative of the sort of engagements that occurred in various corners of the Arctic. With Norway's fall, Spitzbergen became vulnerable and under threat of German attack. The Allies sent in a flotilla of ships and evacuated some three thousand Norwegian and Russian coal miners from the vicinity of Longyearbyen. No sooner had the evacuation been completed, than the Germans rushed in to set up a meteorological station supported and supplied by U-boats. As soon as British intelligence informed the Norwegian forces in exile in Britain of the station's existence and approximate location, a select team of ten men was dispatched to deal with it. The hut with a high radio mast was quickly spotted and the commandos approached it cautiously to find it unoccupied, but well-equipped and provisioned. The Norwegians then withdrew to await the enemy's appearance — in *The Arctic, a History*, Richard Vaughan picks up the story — just as they were concealing themselves:

> A man came walking toward them. It was Heinz Köhler, second-in-command of the German weather station, returning from photographing the bird life in the neighboring marsh. As soon as he came within earshot, the Norwegians shouted for him to put his hands up and surrender. But Köhler turned and ran off, zig-zagging and firing a pistol at the pursuing Norwegians, who returned the fire with their rifles. Then he disappeared, and later the Norwegians heard a single shot. After waiting an hour, two of them warily approached, covered by the others. They found that Köhler had crouched behind a rock, pointed his pistol at his temple, and shot himself.[13]

Köhler's five colleagues discovered what was going on and radioed for assistance. A U-boat arrived the following day, boarded the surviving Germans, and then opened fire on the station and on the Norwegian motorboat, killing one man.

In the scale of things, the skirmish was a relatively trifling incident, incomparable to one that followed five months later when the *Tirpitz* appeared off the coast to shell Norwegian positions with its heavy guns. It then landed troops to attack the 152-man garrison and in the exchange that followed, six defenders were killed and forty-two taken prisoner while the remainder took to the mountains.

As noted earlier, during the Cold War, the Soviets used the North for nuclear testing. Not only was the Tsar Bomba detonated in 1969, but scores of other detonations took place. Estimates have it that since 1949 more than two hundred nuclear detonations or accidents have occurred inside the Arctic Circle with quantities of nuclear waste being deposited in the region. It is known, for example, that at least six nuclear reactors have been dumped into offshore waters, off the coast of Russia and tales of Russian nuclear submarines sinking in Arctic waters are not unfamiliar to the modern reader.

10

Canary in the Cage

THE ARCTIC OF YESTERDAY'S explorers and adventurers is not the Arctic of today. The seemingly limitless distances and the inhospitable climate those early hardies encountered, coupled with oppressive winter darkness and ever-changing and deadly ice conditions, remain unchanged. But the impact of climate change, the demand for natural resources — oil and gas above all — and political jockeying of nations for strategic advantage have brought dramatic transformations to the Arctic landscape. Nothing has changed; everything has changed. The song of the Arctic Siren has been deafened by the din of mining drills, the hum of oil pumps, and the drone of exploratory aircraft, ships, and submarines. Modern technology has immunized today's explorers from her beguilement.

The pristine, unchanging Arctic we have inherited is on its deathbed — and the heart of the matter lies in man's insatiable thirst for energy and in its abuse. Eighty percent of the world's energy is derived from the burning of coal, oil, and natural gas, and the record of carbon dioxide fallout becomes locked in Antarctic ice cores. The analysis of these cores describes snowfall conditions over the millennia — reaching back as far as 160,000 years — and the evidence clearly demonstrates that since the industrial revolution concentration of atmospheric carbons has increased 35 percent. The Arctic is extremely vulnerable to observed and projected climatic change and what's happening in the world at large is happening at twice the speed in those northern reaches.

While debate rages over the issue of fossil fuels, our civilization's demands for them burgeon, deposits deplete, and pressures to secure fresh sources become almost frenzied. Historically, the Organization of Oil Exporting Countries (OPEC) has been the world's principal purveyors of oil, joined by such countries as United States, Canada, and Norway. More recently, others have come onto the market — places such as Kazakhstan, Brazil, Mexico, and even Barbados and Ethiopia. But it seems never enough and the hunt for new sources is unflagging. The Arctic is known to be rich in oil and gas, although estimates of quantity do vary. In May 2009, the United States Geological Survey reported on its comprehensive review of the regions within the Arctic Circle, and using "probabilistic geology-based methodology," it concluded that 30 percent of the world's undiscovered gas reserves and 13 percent of the earth's oil reserves lie within that boundary. If the estimates are correct, they are nearly equivalent to today's proven reserves of Saudi Arabia and the nearby Gulf States combined. Additionally, USGS reported that 84 percent of this wealth lies offshore in shallow waters not exceeding 1,700 feet — accessibility is that much less arduous. Approximately sixty large oil and natural gas fields have been discovered in the Arctic, over half of which are in Russia, and 80 percent of them are already in production, while the remainder awaits development. Norway has developed a state-of-the-art processing plant 235 miles north of the Arctic Circle, which receives gas from huge off-shore platforms and then transports it on specially designed ships to feed American east coast pipelines. With sharp increases of demand, it is expected that by 2030, such imports will account for a fifth of that country's needs.

The USGS survey encompasses the areas within the Arctic Circle only; "the Arctic," in this case, falls within the narrower latitudinal definition, rather the broader isothermal definition. What the estimates of reserves might be for the *greater* Arctic region are not clearly defined, but certainly they exceed those of the immediate USGS survey. Venerable oil giants such as Royal Dutch Shell, Total, Exxon Mobil, and ConocoPhillips, joined by newcomers such as Russia's Gazprom and Norway's StatoilHydro, are exploring drilling possibilities in those far-off regions. "If you're a serious oil and gas player ... then this is a long-term, natural place to look," gushed one enthusiastic oil executive. Oil deposits for the most part are centred in the western hemisphere — eastern Alaska, the Canadian North, and east Greenland, whereas an estimated 70 percent of gas deposits occur in the Barents Sea, western Siberia, and western Alaska.

The manifold problems of drilling in the Arctic are self-evident and costs of extraction are high. To transport and erect an oil rig and then to man and operate it in temperate, more readily accessible places, such as Venezuela or Nigeria is one thing — to accomplish the same in the far-off, forbidding Arctic is quite another matter. The real challenge, however, lies not in the extraction of the product, but in its transportation to the marketplace. Nothing new in this problem — Munk, Hudson, and scores of other lost their lives in seeking routes of transport through the Arctic, but despite heroic efforts, they were universally stymied by ice, ice, and more ice. But now the ice is disappearing at a startling rate and avenues are opening.

Under normal circumstances, the Arctic should have been undergoing a cooling over the past two thousand years because of a wobble in the earth's orbit that causes a reduction in sunlight intensity reaching the polar region in the summer. This natural progression had indeed been taking place — hark back to the onset of the "new ice age" suffered by Greenlanders in the Middle Ages. But within the past century a sharp reversal has occurred and the Arctic has grown warmer, a turnabout that has man's fingerprints all over it. The ten-year period 1999 to 2009 was the warmest of the past two millennia, with Arctic summer temperatures rising on average 6.8°F higher than might have been expected had cooling followed its natural progression. Tundra is thawing and trees are germinating, polar bears are becoming endangered, permafrost is melting, new species of fish are finding their way into warming northern waters. And Arctic ice has dramatically shrunk. Studies show that from 1979 to 1996, the average per decade decline in entire ice coverage was 2.2 percent. For the following decade it was 10.1 percent. The National Snow and Ice Data Center (NSIDC), an organization partially sponsored by NASA, reports in its October 2010 findings that "the linear decline of September ice extending over the period 1979 to 2010 is now 31,400 square miles per year, or 11.5% per decade relative to the 1979–2000 average. NASA satellite measurements show that in one four-year period of 2004–08 the decrease was 42 percent."

The effect of the melting, coupled with technological advances in weather prediction, information-gathering, and ship construction, is making possible the prospect of commercial navigation through the top of the world. The elusive goal is being won not so much through man's noble efforts, but through his careless disregard of the environment. Today icebreakers, research ships, drilling ships, cruise ships, and even private yachts sail through the Northwest Passage during summer months. In summer 2009, two German merchant ships loaded with construction material, MV *Beluga Foresight* and MV *Beluga Fraternity*, passed through Arctic waters from Ulsan, South Korea to Rotterdam — the first commercial transit of the Northern Sea Route. By completing that route rather than the 12,700-nautical-mile voyage around the Malay Peninsula, Suez Canal, and Mediterranean, the ships cut the distance by nearly 40 percent (and avoided the perils of Malay piracy). A voyage from Seattle to Rotterdam through the Northwest can be shortened by two thousand nautical miles, a 25 percent saving over a Panama Canal route. Marine engineers are busily developing new models of ice-capable ships, designed to avoid the necessity of accompanying icebreakers.

Exciting as these prospects may appear, a word of caution. Whatever the melt, experts tell us, there is no such thing as completely ice-free Arctic waters. Sailing distances may be shorter, but navigation through icebergs, floes, and "growlers" — dark-coloured, low-lying masses of ice that are difficult to spot — will inevitably be slower. Getting caught in the floes of late season or heavy fog is an additional risk. When the specially reinforced supertanker SS *Manhattan* journeyed through Arctic waters in 1969 to test the viability of the passage for oil transport, it required the assistance of a Canadian icebreaker. A free passage through those waters may one day come to be, but the Northwest Passage will not become a Panama Canal in the immediate future.

In addition to oil and gas, the Arctic offers a trove of minerals and ores. In Canada, operating mines or projected mines centre on copper, nickel, lead, zinc, and uranium. The country is the world's largest

producer of uranium, and the deposits at Kiggavik in Nunavut are especially promising. Since 1991, Canada has become the third-largest producer of diamonds from major mines in the Northwest Territories and
Nunavut. Just south of the Arctic Circle lie the two largest such facilities,
Ekati and Diavik, each operating open pits that are among the world's
largest. Resolute, Canada's northern-most community at 74°43' N is the
springboard for scientific exploration, and in the summer months its
airport and three hotels are beehives of activity as mining companies
launch themselves into the deeper barrens in the search of fresh prospects. The developing sea lanes are encouraging not only to Canadian oil
people, but to miners, as well.

The first successful well in Alaska was drilled in 1968 at Prudhoe
Bay, four hundred kilometres north of the Arctic Circle. It sits on North
America's largest oil field, one that is double that of the East Texas Oil
Field (which produces nearly a quarter of the country's output). For the
past four decades Prudhoe has fuelled the Alaskan economy. The state's
eyes are now turned on the nearby Chukchi Sea basin, shared jointly
with Russia. Reserves here are so promising that Shell Oil has already
spent $2.5 billion to establish itself there with a major global operating
centre on offshore Alaska — the "new Gulf of Mexico."

The United States Geological Survey estimates that northeast
Greenland holds up to 31.4 billion barrels offshore of undiscovered oil
and natural gas reserves, an amount on par with Alberta's oil sands. Half
a dozen oil giants are actively studying the economics of extraction in
that highly inhospitable region. Mining operations in Greenland have
long existed, and in the past they focused on cryolite (used in the manufacture of aluminum), lead, and zinc. By the 1980s, the reserves of cryolite had become exhausted, but the extraction of lead and zinc continues.
Today's receding glacial ice is laying bare parts of the country and fresh
mineral deposits are being uncovered, including coal, platinum, palladium (a rare metal used in jewellery, dentistry, and watch-making), and
molybdenum (aircraft parts, electrical contacts, and industrial motors).

Russia is the foremost player in the Arctic. Twenty-two percent of
the country's exports originate in those distant reaches, and the region
accounts for an astonishing 11 percent of the country's GDP. Gas is a

principal commodity — in 2009, Russia provided Europe with a quarter of its natural gas needs, and although much of this originated in the country's underbelly, particularly in the Caspian Sea area, the Arctic was a critical source. But mining is of no less importance — thirty-two major mines are scattered throughout the vast expanse. The Kola Peninsula mines large quantities of alumina, iron ore, mica, and titanium. The world's deepest borehole lies between Murmansk and the Norwegian border — a vertical shaft toward the earth's centre, which is 7.7 miles deep. In Siberia, nearly 1,800 miles from Moscow, stands the mining centre of Norilsk at 69°20' N with a population of three hundred thousand, the Arctic's second-largest city. At one-time it was a Stalinist labour camp where over seventeen thousand prisoners died of harsh working conditions, starvation, and cold — the place is snow-covered over 250 days of the year and average annual temperatures are 14°F (with lows of -60°F not uncommon). Ninety percent of Russia's nickel and 55 percent of its copper are mined here, as well as half the world's supply of palladium, a vital element in the manufacture of catalytic converters. (Norilsk, incidentally, is among the top ten most polluted cities in the world.)

The Arctic shows promise of becoming a cornucopia of raw materials. While miners, oil people, and shippers chortle with satisfaction at the effect global warming is having on the region, the rest of the world weeps. The climatic change our fragile globe is encountering is universally felt, in some places with relatively minimum effect on the geography and ecosystems, and in others with profound consequence. In the Arctic, however, the change is robust and accelerating at a rate double or more to that of the earth's average. In Siberia and Alaska, for example, temperatures in the past half century have risen a by a remarkable 3.5°F, and in some parts shrubs are beginning to sprout on the barren tundra. The great glaciers of western Alaska, some predict, will disappear by 2035.

Our globe has two polar caps, one a continental land mass surrounded by water, and the other a body of water surrounded by land masses. The grounded Antarctic ice is thick, over two kilometres deep in places; the floating Arctic ice is thin, just a few metres thick and therefore significantly quicker in melting. And melt it does: in the past three decades rising temperatures have reduced the areas of summer ice dramatically, as sequences of satellite images shockingly illustrate. In photos taken in September 1980, white summer ice is seen covering an expanse of 3 million square miles; in 2005, the area shrank to 1.9 million, and a mere three years later, to 1.8 million; the Arctic Ocean's summer ice pack today covers a little over a half of its reach three decades ago. Yesterday's white ice is today's black water surface. And here is the rub: 80 percent of the heat from the sun's rays falling onto white ice is reflected back into space, but only 5 percent of rays are reflected by dark water, with the balance being retained. It's a vicious circle — less heat is reflected, temperatures rise, regeneration of ice in winter is injuriously retarded, darker surface increase, less heat reflected. By definition, global warming is a wordwide phenomenon, but in the northern polar region the effect of ice melt accelerates temperature rise causing quickened climatic and ecological change — an effect known as Arctic amplification.

Little wonder that climatologists and environmentalists consider the Arctic "the canary in the global coal mine."[1] The sustainability of the world's present condition may be judged by the welfare of the Arctic — if the caged canary droops or falls dead, it's a signal for the coal miners that gas levels are dangerously high and that the tunnel is no longer safe. That the Arctic ice cap will someday disappear seems a foregone conclusion. It could happen by the end of the century, with one study having it by 2050, and when it does, the canary might well be found belly-up on the floor of its cage.

Some labour under the impression that melting ice caps cause ocean levels to rise. This is as untrue as with the melting process of ice cubes in a glass of water — as the cubes melt, water volume in the glass does not increase. If — better yet, *when* — low-lying places such as the Maldives disappear through flooding, it will not be because of melting ice caps, but through the runoff of melting glaciers. Climatic warming is indeed global, and glaciers everywhere are retreating because of it — as in Antarctica, Alaska, Africa, and Argentina, so in parts of India, the United States, and Switzerland.

But it is the change in the Greenland glacier that gives pause for concern. Satellite imagery show that in some places the ice is noticeably receding, whereas in other spots it appears to be surging forward.

not true
for
land
base
ice
it will
raise
ocean
levels

Taken together, however, it is clear that a reduction in its mass is taking place. A team of twenty-six specialists from eight Arctic countries was brought together in 2004 by the University of Alaska to develop an Arctic Climate Impact Assessment. The report notes that the surface-melt area of the Greenland ice sheet averaged 16 percent from 1979 to 2002, "an area roughly the size of Sweden," It goes on to note that in the twenty-year period prior to the study, global average of sea level rise was 3.2 inches. Some estimates have it that if the enormous Greenland glacier was to melt overnight, the globe's ocean levels would rise in excess of twenty feet. Terrifying to consider which parts of the earth's surface would be affected. Mark Lynas in *Six Degrees* writes

> [T]he geography of the world's coastlines would then look radically different. Miami would disappear entirely, as would most of Manhattan. Central London would be flooded. Bangkok, Mumbai and Shanghai would also lose most of their area. In all half of humanity would have to move to higher ground, leaving landscapes, buildings and monuments that have been central to civilization for over a thousand years to be gradually consumed by the sea.

The good news is that modellers predict that the Greenland ice cap will be long in melting, and the apocalyptic flooding scenario is unlikely to unfold for another thousand years. Walker and King observe in *The Hot Topic*, that in a 2007 study "modellers calculate that it would take a global average warming of a full 4.5°F to push Greenland over the edge, a threshold that we probably still have time to avoid." Insofar as today's 56,000 Greenlanders are concerned, global warming is not altogether unwelcome. Not only does the glacier's retreat present new possibilities for the mining, as already noted, but it unlocks fresh sources of power. The melting ice provides a steady flow of fast-moving water strong enough to be harnessed by turbines and this brings promise of hydroelectric development. In 1993, the first hydro station was opened and today there are three that serve local communities. Fifteen likely sites have been identified for future possible exploitation, with some of them attracting the interest of industries that require large amounts of energy — aluminum and the Internet industry, for example. Before long we might well see the rise of smelters in that Arctic land.

As consideration is given to the effects of climate change, one must appreciate that the science of prediction is imperfect and still in its relative infancy. In any complex scientific picture there will be misrepresentations and mistakes, and the art of climate modelling is riddled with uncertainties and gaps. Like a wind tunnel to aircraft design, no scenario can perfectly reproduce the system being modelled. In the case of climate prediction, however, despite a number of uncertainties, all are producing unequivocal outcomes indicating warming.

Receding ice on water, receding ice on land. But the effect of global warming is impacting Arctic regions well beyond the ice-covered, as millions of square miles of tundra and taiga experience a ground thaw. These lands are covered with permafrost, a layer of frozen earth that remains at 32°F or less year-round without melting. In some parts, such ground is relatively shallow, in others, the depths are profound — at the mouth of Siberia's Lena River a 4,900 foot depth of freeze has been recorded. In some regions its development is relatively recent, in others it's ancient — at Prudhoe Bay, for example, it is over a half million years old. Permafrost thaw is impacting every facet of the Arctic, on its topography, vegetation, animal life, and on native populations, to which we shall return in Chapter 11.

Construction on permafrost is problematic: heat escaping from buildings over time melts the permafrost beneath, resulting in foundations giving way and structures folding or collapsing. Buildings erected on posts, therefore, are not uncommon in the Arctic, thus permitting the circulation of cold air beneath which partially obviates melt. Oil pipelines must also undergo special construction. For oil to flow freely it must be kept at 61°F, and therefore the lines must be erected on supports or, where buried, bound in insulation. The destructive shift of soil has begun to affect entire communities. Dawson City, Yukon, for example, has seen a number of buildings buckle and serious damage sustained to its infrastructure. In 2006, the city increased its annual water and sewer maintenance budget threefold due to permafrost shift. Yakutsk, a Siberian city of 320,000, has been experiencing permafrost shift so badly that one dark prediction has it that by the year 2030 none of its buildings will remain standing. (As an aside: for three consecutive winter months, this city averages a temperature of -42°F, with one monthly average having once been recorded as -98°F).

The effect of permafrost change on the landscape is alarming enough. But of immeasurably greater threat to the Arctic's immediate health and to our planet's sustainability is what's beneath the surface — methane, a greenhouse gas deemed to be twenty times more potent than carbon dioxide. Scientists estimate the amount of methane in storage underground may be in the millions of tons with deposits most clearly defined in Siberia. Until recently, permafrost has effectively capped these deposits, but the thawing has punctured the lid and gas has begun to rise to the surface — bubbles of the stuff are surfacing in the summer lakes of Siberia and in the marshes of northern Sweden. One estimate issued by the Russian Academy of Sciences is that if a mere 10 percent of permafrost disappears, the release of underground gases would be equal to approximately 1.2°F of global warming. A vicious circle: emissions of carbon gasses precipitate warming, warming melts permafrost, disappearance of permafrost releases gases, gases precipitate warming.

And what of animal life? The world's imagination seems focused on the hazards climate change presents to polar bears. Estimates of the world's population of these animals stand at twenty thousand to twenty-five thousand, with 60 percent living in Canada and the remainder scattered in Siberia, Alaska, Greenland, and the Svalbard Islands. As Arctic ice melts, the cause for concern for the future of these noble beasts becomes increasingly undeniable, with the United States government having already declared them an endangered species.

Although the polar bear is a land animal, it spends most of its time in water and it depends on sea ice as a platform for hunting. A male in good health is an avaricious eater and is capable of consuming a hundred pounds of food a day. The ringed seal is its principal fare and the hunt for these smaller mammals carries on not only offshore, but at distances away — and it requires extreme patience. Although a seal is capable of remaining submerged for as long as forty-five minutes, it usually comes up for air every five to fifteen minutes, and this it finds either in areas of open water or through one of the many breathing holes it has bored with the claws on its flippers. The bear's keen sense of smell permits it to seek out the most recently used hole and then the wait begins — sometimes hours or even days. With luck the seal emerges and the catch is made, yielding as much as 150 pounds of dinner.

The concern here is that the platforms from which bears hunt are becoming less stable and diminishing or outright disappearing. Although bears are intrepid swimmers, the widening of gaps between suitably thick floes makes a swim between them longer and riskier — incidences of bear drownings are being noted. The United States Fish and Wildlife Service (USFWS) reports that in the western Hudson Bay region reductions in adult weights of the animals are being found, "correlated with loss of sea ice." In some places, furthermore, it has been noticed that during the summer, bears are moving increasingly inland where often they have difficulty in finding food. Their only recourse is to enter villages to scavenge what they can and this brings them in conflict with humans. Alarm has been raised at the number of animals being shot in the Chukotka area of Siberia.

All said, it should be noted that agreement is not universal on the existing state and long-term prospects of bear populations. Whereas the USFWS found the situation sufficiently dire to bring the animal under the protection of the Endangered Species Act, others take exception, claiming that the bears are not under threat of extinction and they point out that in places such as Davis Strait the numbers are reported as actually increasing.

The awe and romance surrounding these majestic animals makes them the North's headline-grabber. But the walrus is no less affected by the thinning and diminishing ice, and it certainly numbers among nature's more singular creations. Weighing as much as 4,500 pounds, this bulky, bewhiskered marine mammal is universally found in circumpolar regions and has played an important role in native culture. The long, ivory tusks — actually molars — jutting from the corners of the mouth are the animal's distinguishing feature, and it was the hunt for this ivory that motivated many early explorers to venture into Arctic regions. Tusks are common to both sexes, growing as much as a metre long, and are essential to the animal not only for defence against bears and orca whales, their two natural enemies, but as a tool in drawing themselves up onto the floes.

Like the polar bear, the walrus requires ice floes for transport in its migration north. As ice melts in the spring and summer near shorelines and floes move north, herds of walrus hitch rides on them. But with reduction of floes, travel becomes problematic and migration patterns are modified. Ice also is important for adults' feeding. The walrus is a "bottom feeder," living off what it forages on the sea bed — shrimp, crab, clams, tube worms, and other marine life. It therefore prefers shallower waters and, although it is capable of remaining submerged for as long as half an hour, it regains the surface more frequently literally to "take a breath." During the search it requires rest periods, and if land is at a distance, the break is taken on the floes. With retreat of ice, the search for food off-shore becomes more hazardous through lack of resting places.

Additionally, while the mother forges for food below the surface, she deposits her young on the ice — calves take over a year to wean, and even after that they remain attached to their mothers for up to four or five years. Mothers are now found becoming separated from their calves as rapid currents of open waters whisk away the lighter and freer floes; lone pups are found swimming directionless or floating dead. "If walruses and other ice-associated marine mammals cannot adapt to caring for their young in shallow waters without sea-ice available as a resting platform between dives to the sea floor," the Woods Hole Oceanographic Institution reports, "a significant population decline of this species could occur."

One uncommon hazard to the well-being of the walrus should not be overlooked: the risk of stampedes. Walruses are gregarious animals that gather together in herds, sometimes numbering in the thousands. As ice packs are abandoned, the animals increasingly assemble along the shores where they become more vulnerable. A suddenly perceived danger launches a frantic stampede for the water, and as the behemoths rush for the safety of the sea, many of the young are squashed. Polar bears consume walruses, but are cautious of attacking them on a one-to-one basis. Instead they boldly invade a reposing herd, throwing it into panic, and in the dash for the sea many are seriously injured or killed, making easy pickings for the interloper. In 2008, Russian scientists working on the shores of the Bering Sea discovered over four thousand carcasses scattered over a three-kilometre stretch of shoreline: deaths attributed to panic. Although the world's walrus population today is not under immediate threat, there are clear indications that change is in the air.

Climatic changes affecting the Arctic are not all related to the disappearing ocean cover. Subtle and not so subtle changes are also occurring on the tundra that affect virtually all its animal life, chief among which is the caribou — called reindeer in its domesticated state in Eurasia. Huge numbers of these migratory animals are found throughout polar and sub-polar regions — in Canada, Alaska, Siberia, Norway, Greenland, and even in northern reaches of China and Mongolia. During the brief summer they gather together on northern calving grounds in herds numbering in the scores of thousands, and at other times of the year they are found in small groups scattered far and wide.

Climate change is disrupting the caribou's feeding habits and is tipping natural balances. Since the Stone Age these antlered herds numbered in the millions; no longer so, and although in no way are they near being endangered, the numbers are diminishing. In Alaska and the Yukon the so-called Porcupine Herd has dwindled from 178,000 in 1989 to a current estimate of 100,000. Another group, the Bathurst Herd in the Northwest Territories, has decreased even more dramatically — 75 percent since 2006. In the winter of 1996–97 in Russia's northeastern Chukotsk Peninsula, ten thousand reindeer died of starvation due to unusual icing and deep snow packs.

Whereas the unusual feature of the walrus is its molars, that of the caribou is the hoof. The animal's hooves are concave in form with edges that semi-annually take on startling new structures. In summer, when dampness makes the tundra soft, the pads are spongy to provide better traction; in winter these areas harden, becoming bony to allow for firmer grip of the ice and snow. In providing this endowment, nature has given the animal a tool for winter feeding. In summer, caribou rely on grasses, sedges, flowering plants, and leaves of willow and birch. In winter, mosses and lichens are the staple of the diet, and here the hard-edged hoof plays a critical role. The animal's developed sense of smell discerns pockets of snow-covered growth, and by determined pawing and digging with their hard-edged hooves, the food is exposed — a process known as "cratering."

Among the effects climate change is having on caribou, there are three factors which directly or indirectly interact with the animal's feeding. Increased autumnal rainfalls deposit more water on the surface, which quickly freezes and more frequent snowfalls make for deeper ground cover. The desired mosses and lichens thus become tightly lidded, and cratering becomes more difficult. In areas of shallow snow and little icing, it takes the caribou a few minutes to forage the food; in tightly covered conditions cratering might involve a couple of hours of hard work, at double the expenditure of energy. In such circumstances, exhaustion or starvation could overtake the animal.

In the caribou's seasonal cycle, a correlation exists between food sourcing and calving. With the approach of the birthing season in early spring, the animals move north to access newly emerging plant life. The caribou receives its cue for the migration by the increase of daylight hours, whereas the development of plant life evolves as a response to heat. Studies carried out in West Greenland by Danish scientists, for example, report that the temperature in that area has risen 7.2°F over the past few years and this has brought on a remarkable early bloom of flora. But the calving instinct embedded in the caribou for millennia is so firmly rooted in lengthening of days that by the time it does reach the fresh grazing ground it's too late — the growth has already peaked and its full nutritional value has become lost. This phenomenon, called "trophic mismatch," affects caribou reproduction by retarding the buildup of fat in females, which is required to bring it into heat in sufficient time to achieve pregnancy.

And thirdly, a factor to which many of us can relate to directly — caribou face the problem of mosquitoes, flies, and other aggravating insects. Nothing new in such pests tormenting animals, but with warming their numbers are increasing and the harassment is greatly exacerbated. This is particularly true in areas of the Arctic where wind velocity is low and summer temperatures rise above 55°F. Caribou are expending increased amounts of energy in coping with the aggravation — often in crazed, debilitating runs of escape, energy that is lost to foraging and fattening up for winter. Studies of herds in northern Canada and Alaska show decreases in female body fat, and since there is a direct correlation between body fat and spring calving, birthrates are decreasing — attributable not only to lessening quantity and quality of nutrition but to summertime harassment by insects.

A study of global herds by University of Alberta in 2009 makes what it calls a "dramatic revelation" — the world's caribou population has plunged 60 percent in the past thirty years. A variety of threads have come together to cause this disturbing state of affairs: rising temperatures, melting permafrost, trophic mismatch, lengthening wildfire seasons — this plus human encroachment, particularly with expansion of pipelines, roads, and hydro corridors, all of which affect migratory patterns. Alarmists plead for the animal to be placed on the endangered species list — a premature call, perhaps, but one that might legitimately resonate within the next few decades.

The bear, the walrus, the caribou — but so also, the Arctic fox, wolf, and hare, musk ox, and the lemming. All fauna, be it herbivore or carnivore, is facing changing conditions to the habitat. Not just the larger animals and fish, but microscopic forms, as well — algae, water fleas, insect larva, invertebrate crustaceans ... the organisms at the bottom of the ecosystem and food chain. In 2005, an international sixteen-member team assessed fifty-five lakes in Canada, Norway, Finland, and Russia and found that such organisms are undergoing changes in diversity, and it concluded that the possibility is low of finding an Arctic water environment that has not undergone change through global warming. No different than in other parts of the globe, but in the Arctic the rate of development is markedly faster — the canary in the coalminer's tunnel.

As changes occur in circumpolar land masses and fresh waters, so changes are also developing beneath the seas. Global warming and human intrusion affects the ocean's animal life ... and its currents. The creature most conspicuous in this regard is the whale, believed to be the

largest known mammal ever to have lived, with the blue whale developing lengths of 115 feet and weights of 150 tons. There are two orders
of these animals: the toothless baleen which feeds on plankton filtered
through a tough elastic hair-like construction within its mouth, and the
sharp-toothed whale, which relies principally on fish and squid. The former includes humpbacks, the blue and the gray, while the latter includes
sperm whales, pilot whales, beluga, and orca, otherwise known as "killer
whale" for its readiness to feed on seals, walrus, and even other whales.

Commercial whaling has been taking place in the Arctic since the
early seventeenth century when whale meat, whalebone, ambergris, and
particularly whale oil were in demand.[2] Estimates have it that within the
first half of the twentieth century, over two million of these animals were
hunted down worldwide, with stocks in Arctic regions suffering particularly severely. The International Whaling Commission (IWC) formed in
1986 by whaling nations has imposed a universal moratorium on the
hunt, though allowing aboriginal people to carry on and permitting the
occasional kill for scientific study. Environmentalists are quick to point
out that ever since IWC was founded, Japan has continued in the commercial hunt of the animal under the guise of "scientific study." More
alarming still is that Iceland openly re-engaged in commercial hunting
in 2006, in spite of any agreement.   *Also Norway?*

Commercial hunting is but one threat to whales. The World Wildlife
Federation (WWF) lists a series of other potentially lethal hazards, foremost of which is underwater pollution. The same toxic pollutants that
sully the air find their way underwater, and, distributed by currents,
they are as harmful to sea life as atmospheric pollution is to land life.
Expansion of oil-related activity — construction, extraction, and transport to markets — is a conspicuous threat not only to whales, but to
the overall health of the Arctic. The 1989 *Exxon Valdez* accident off the
Alaskan coast and the 2010 sinking of the BP drilling rig in the Gulf of
Mexico illustrate dramatically the destructive effect escaping oil has not
only on animal life, but on human habitation. To contemplate a *Valdez* or
Gulf of Mexico situation unfolding in the Arctic is mind-boggling.

But oil pollution is not the only concern — another, less dramatic,
factor endangering whales is noise pollution. The whale's survival over

the ages is largely attributable to its highly developed sense of hearing. In murky or pitch-black waters the search for food is directed by sound — a built-in sonarlike arrangement within the whale's ears permits it "to see" its prey, be it swarms of krill or something more substantial. Sensitive ears pick up the din of large ships' propellers as far as a mile away, and, if great enough, the animal risks disorientation sufficient to strand itself unwittingly on a shoreline and possibly to die. Injurious sound emanates not only from tankers and cargo ships, but from a variety of other sources: scouting submarines, low-frequency waves used in underwater exploration, seismic surveys by oil companies, underwater security detection systems, acoustic weapon testing, and the like. Incidences of beached whales with ear damage are becoming more frequent. Seismic surveys of offshore oil and gas carried out off Russia's Pacific coast near Sakhalin have excluded gray whales from their primary feeding habitat. Noise pollution should not be disregarded as a factor in endangerment of whales.

Let us return now to the Greenland glacial melt and the effect it has on ocean waters. The possibility of inundations through the melt is disturbing enough, but there is another aspect to the melt, a supplementary source of climate change to a localized region of the globe. The relatively temperate climates of Ireland, the British islands, and Western Europe are delivered by the Gulf Stream, the powerful current circling the Atlantic. It picks up the warm, saline surface waters of the Caribbean and pushes them north, then veers east and hugs the European coasts. There it is given a push by cold dense Nordic waters flowing south, which propels the stream along the Atlantic's east side, eventually to complete its cyclical passage off the western hemisphere — a conveyer belt, as it were. It is the Gulf Stream that allows strawberries to grow in Norway and palm trees in parts of Britain. (And consider that Oslo is nearly at the same latitude as Churchill, Manitoba, and London, the same as Irkutsk, Siberia, where the average January temperature is -59°F).

The concerning news is that the Greenland glacial melt is pouring vast quantities of fresh water into the saline ocean and this is beginning to have a disruptive effect on the Gulf Stream's natural progress. The stream's movement is largely propelled by the natural interaction of cold, salty water with warmer, less saline water. Scientists have long been concerned that a freshening of the salt water would disrupt that interaction and shut down the conveyer belt, and this is what is beginning to happen. The developing flow of fresh glacial water is pouring into the Norwegian and Greenland Seas and mixing with the Gulf Stream.

British scientists monitoring Gulf Stream waters over the years reported in 2004 that less warm water was flowing north from the Caribbean and less cold water was flowing south from the Arctic, a phenomenon that puts into jeopardy the force of the conveyor belt. Although a United Nations study finds it highly unlikely that the conveyor belt will slow down in our century, longer-term prospects are questionable. If the Gulf Stream weakens sufficiently, the relatively temperate climate of Western Europe stands to be affected and an overall cooling will take place. It is possible that someday in the future a family on the Cornwall coast will wake up to find that the palm trees growing in the front yard have been displaced by a grove of birches.

The lead organization monitoring global climate change is the International Panel of Climate Change (IPCC), established by the United Nations in 1988. Over the years it has issued four in-depth assessments of the situation, the most recent one in 2007, which was authored by six hundred scientific researchers from forty countries. Before being made public, 620 experts studied the findings, followed by representatives from 113 countries reviewing the final text. It's as credible a document as one might find despite the flurry of excitement caused in early 2010 by the discovery of certain errors that crept into it, which concerned the rate of melt of the Himalayan glacier — "glaciergate," climate skeptics called it. But just as the organization in this instance was criticized for poorly worded or poorly sourced claims, so it is criticized for being too conservative inasmuch as it reflects a consensus view of a diversity of contributors and nations.

It would be well to reflect on some sobering points raised in the organization's 2007 assessment report. Cold days, cold nights, and frost events have become less frequent, while hot days, hot nights, and heat waves have become more frequent. In the period spanning 1995 to 2006, eleven of the twelve years were the warmest since 1850 when instrumental record began. In the six-year period of 2001 to 2007, there has been a 2.5°F increase in the average global temperature of the past hundred years, and "average Arctic temperatures increased at almost twice the global average rate." As for sea levels, in the forty-two year period of 1961 to 2003, the average annual rate of rise was .07 inches, with the last ten years of those years being .5 inches (The report does caution that "it is unclear whether this as a long-term trend or a variability.")

The assessment report concludes with the following: "Most of the increase of global temperature since the mid-20th century is very likely due to the observed increase of anthropogenic gas contributors … warming of the climate system is unequivocal." Since Arctic amplification accelerates the process, developments in the Arctic may be viewed as a possible preview of things to come.

II

People and Politics

IN 1294, THE INTREPID Marco Polo journeyed into the far reaches of the sprawling Mongol Empire where he spent time in the court of Kublai Khan. In his account of that visit, he wrote: "… beyond the most distant part of the territory of those Tartars … there is another region which extends to the utmost bounds of the north, and it is called the Region of Darkness, because during most part of winter months the sun is invisible …"[1]

Polo goes on to tell of the people living in that polar region, as described by his hosts: "The men of this country are well made and tall, but of pallid complexion. They are not united under the government of a king or prince, and they live without any established laws or usages, in the manner of brute creatures. Their intellects also are dull, and they have an air of stupidity." We are told, however, that the Mongols were impressed by the hunting skills of these seemingly backward polar natives, who "catch vast multitudes of ermines, martens, foxes and other creatures of that kind, the furs of which are more delicate, and consequently more valuable than found in those districts inhabited by the tartars." (And which the Tartars took every occasion to steal or barter for worthless trinkets.) Polo's report is one of the earliest European accounts of encounters with natives of Arctic regions.

What of these people today? Who are they and how are they dispersed over the vast northern expanses? It is estimated that approximately 404,000 indigenous peoples live above the Artic Circle — two-thirds in the western half and one-third in the eastern. The population numbers in the United States, Canada, and Greenland are clearly defined with the respective figures at 130,000, 65,000, and 46,200. The Eurasian numbers are more difficult to come by because of the high degree of assimilation, but the approximate figures for Russia, Norway, and Sweden-Finland are 79,200, 57,000 and 27,000. If one were to add the non-native European inhabitants, the figure would rise by 97 percent for a grand total of Arctic population of 3.4 million, with two-thirds living in Russia.

A tenuous commonality exists between the indigenous of the circumpolar north. The population falls within two definable categories, those that inhabit the taiga year-round or travel between taiga and tundra, and those living in coastal areas. Within each grouping are divisions and sub-divisions — in Russia alone anthropologists have identified nineteen ethnic groups, delineated principally by language. The major divisions, however, are the *Sami* (or Lapps) of Scandinavia, Finland, and extreme northwest Russia; the *Nenets* (or Samoyeds) and *Yakuts* of central Siberia; the *Chukchi* of northeastern Siberia; the *Aleuts* of Alaska and Bering Strait; and the so-called *Eskimoan* division, which sub-divides into two groups — the *Yupik* of western Alaska and the *Inuit* of Canada, Greenland, and north coastal Alaska.

Initial contact with Europeans invariably proved disastrous for Arctic natives, just as it had for indigenous peoples in other parts of the globe. Encroachment above all brought new diseases which immune systems could not withstand and thousands died of smallpox, influenza, measles, diphtheria, or other sicknesses. Greenland in the Middle Ages, it will be recalled, suffered disastrously from the ravages wrought by disease-bearing Scandinavians. In Kamchatka of the seventeenth century and in other northeast parts of Siberia, the same story — in the Magadan region, for example, two-thirds of the inhabitants died of smallpox. In eastern Canada, early whalers from Britain and France infected the Inuit with smallpox and diphtheria and thousands perished. In the nineteenth century, American whalers wrought havoc along the Alaskan coastline by bringing in not only a raft of contagious diseases, but by introducing the natives to alcohol — losses of populations were as high as 50 percent in places. Following the arrival of Russian fur traders in the Bering

Straits area, the Aleuts suffered population losses estimated to have been 80 percent.

The tale of European encroachment into the Eurasian Arctic differs from that of the western Arctic for reasons of a head start, geography, and assimilation. At the time that Frobisher was making initial European contacts with the Inut, Slavs and Vikings had already been trading with the indigenous of Siberia and Scandinavia for over two hundred years. Early explorers and traders who pressed into those northern parts were favored by river networks that facilitated two-way exchanges. Segments of the Northeast Passage, furthermore, had been navigated long before any salt-water access into North America's interior opened up. From the early eighteenth century, the northward flow of civilization within Siberia progressed spectacularly compared to that of the western Arctic, not only because Russians by then were more familiar with the Arctic, but because the departure points for the northward bound were closer and more developed. In Siberia, they started from northern towns founded by Cossacks in the seventeenth century — Turkhansk at 65°49' N, for example, established in 1607, or Irkutsk, Siberia's capital city, founded in 1652. In Canada and Alaska, the early springboards for Arctic penetration were from European ports and later from isolated outposts of the three major fur concerns — Hudson's Bay Company, North West Company, and Russian-American Company. Transportation facilities in Siberia, be they by water, land, or air, are and have always been more extensively developed than in North America.

Russian settlement of Arctic regions predates movement into Siberia by a long shot. As early as 1429, the first monks arrived to Solovki Islands, an archipelago on the White Sea at 65°N, and here they established a monastery that grew spectacularly, eventually becoming considered by many as "the spiritual heart of Russia." Hunters and traders quickly followed in the footsteps of "the holy ones," and trading posts and tiny hamlets soon dotted parts of the White Sea region. As hunters and traders penetrated farther and farther into Siberia, others followed, electing freely to settle in those far reaches (in time to be joined by multitudes of prisoners and exiles). By the 1660s, thousands of schismatic sect called Old Believers quit European Russia and migrated into those distant parts to escape persecution, unwilling to accept decreed church reforms or to forego established rites. Many of these new arrivals found themselves not only living side by side with the natives, but intermarrying with them. Assimilation of local populations seemed natural and inevitable in the early Arctic development of Eurasia.

In the western Arctic, the record of assimilation was and is significantly different from the Eurasian experience. To understand the slower rate of assimilation in the Canadian Arctic, one must more completely appreciate the country's peculiar geography and demography. Or rather, *unique* geography. Canada is the world's second-largest country. It is the only country that fronts three oceans and its coastline is the longest of any nation. Its east–west stretch is virtually the same as the north–south distance — from St. John's, Newfoundland, to Victoria, British Columbia, it's 3,150 miles east–west; from Alert, Nunavut to Windsor, Ontario, it's 2,815 miles. Above the country's north mainland lies the Canadian Arctic Archipelago, an area of 550,000 square miles — more than twice the size of Texas — within which are scattered 36,563 islands, mostly uninhabited.

Demographically, the spread of Canadian population can only be considered bizarre. It's a country of just under 34 million — ranking thirty-ninth in the world — with three-quarters living within a narrow one-hundred-mile band above the United States. Its three northern territories, Yukon, Northwest Territories, and Nunavut, account for 40 percent of the country's size, yet with 108,000 inhabitants they are home to a mere one-third of one percent of the population. Populated Canada may be likened to a horizontal Chile, but narrower and longer. Given the enormous distances and sparse population, plus difficulties of transportation and communication posed by harsh climate and topography, it's understandable why European encroachment into Arctic reaches was long in coming.

The first Europeans arriving in western Arctic in early seventeenth century were independent Russian and English fur traders. All too soon they were edged out by the dominating fur companies whose small trading posts throughout the region beckoned native hunters. Trade with "the white man" flourished, but the businesslike exchanges were void of social or cultural intercourse. Hunters and traders lived separate lives according to their ways with little or no assimilation, and thus it substantially continued into the mid-nineteenth century. In the second half of the century, an increased stream of Europeans flowed into various corners of the Arctic, triggering profound transformations to the societal structures of the Alaskan Yupik and Canadian and Greenland Inuit.

As noted, it was the early whalers who were largely responsible for the introduction of disease and alcohol among native populations. With the American takeover of Alaska, the whaling industry burgeoned and local labour was required to help run operations. For their services, the natives received payment in guns, ammunition, manufactured items, southern foodstuffs, and liquor. While the Yupiks indiscriminately killed caribou with their newly acquired firearms to feed the whalers, the whalers combed the waters for bowheads, and hunters slaughtered the walrus. Enormous numbers of animals were killed — one estimate has it that by 1880, fourteen thousand bowheads had been taken and over one hundred thousand walruses slaughtered. By the turn of the century, stocks had become virtually exhausted and the hunters disappeared. The unemployed Yupik continued on their severely depleted hunting grounds, ravaged by disease and alcohol and depending on "shopfood." This lamentable sequence was substantially duplicated by the Canadian Inuit, particularly those living along Cumberland Sound, Hudson Bay, and the Mackenzie Delta.

On the heels of departing whalers, missionaries arrived — Presbyterians and Evangelicals into Alaska, Catholics and Anglicans into the Canadian North, and Moravians into Greenland. The cause of these enthusiasts was held in common: to bring the word of God to the pathetically deprived people, to free them from the shackles of superstition and in the process to draw them into the civilized way of the home country. As one early Danish missionary postulated, "the poor Greenlander shall have learned to know the worship of God, as their Creator and Redeemer, then they shall likewise learn to acknowledge and honour a Christian Sovereign as their King and Ruler ..."[2] Although much good was achieved by the missionaries in the areas of education and health, the net impact of their efforts was ruinous for native ways.

Priests and pastors displaced shamans, thereby depriving the communities of the influence of those eminent, generally wise and knowledgeable leaders. Christian Inuit found themselves being pulled away from their heathen brothers and sisters and gulfs opened between the propertied and less-propertied. The concepts of community ownership, of community action, and even of community were irrevocably shaken. Ancient customs such as polygamy, wife-exchange, taboos, and even hunting on Sundays faded away. Blood feuds were ended as was the dispatch of individuals for antisocial behavior.

And then in the twentieth century, came the Cold War with all its tensions between the United States and the Soviet Union. A protective barrier was deemed necessary to guard America from a sudden transpolar air attack. In 1954, President Eisenhower authorized the construction of the Distant Early Warning Line (DEW line), a string of sixty-three radar bases spanning a 6,300-mile length of the Arctic from the Aleutians to

A radar instillation in northern Canada, one of a chain of such establishments in the Distant Early Warning system, established during the Cold War in defence of a surprise attack by the Soviet Union.

Courtesy of United States Air Force. Photographer: Tech. Sgt. Donald L. Wetterman.

Baffin Island in a line 250 to three hundred miles north of the Arctic Circle. By the time the project was completed three years later, an influx of more than twenty-five thousand engineers, technicians, and military had flooded these areas. The bilateral agreement establishing the DEW stipulated that Canadians would be employed in the actual construction of the sites with the United States bearing the costs. Although thousands of workers were airlifted from the south, a portion of labour fell to the Inuit, who received training for specific tasks.

No sooner had DEW begun its task of surveillance than the advent of ICBMs and missile-carrying submarines made it obsolete, a short-lived existence, indeed. Work began on dismantling the sites and here again the Inuit were involved. It had been a costly venture for Uncle Sam — from the start of construction in 1954 to the completion of its close-down in 1992, an estimated $900 million had been expended. The impact of those frenzied years of activity on the Inuit in the further loss of their traditional ways and culture should not be underestimated. With establishment of airfields and improved water transport, easier access was had to southern foodstuffs and household goods, to new building materials and mechanized equipment, and to communication with the world.

Native people and non-native learned more of one another as scores of new arrivals from the south flowed into Arctic settlements. Freshly arrived government administrators managed, the preachers preached, physicians healed, entrepreneurs bought and sold, and teachers taught.

Not surprising, then, that the process of Inuit transformation took hold and that it continues to develop. Snow houses and fur tents have been forsaken in favour of timber and prefabricated homes. Sleds and kayaks have given way to skidoos and outboard motors; caribou and sealskin to wool, synthetics, and duffel; story-telling to television and the Internet. A way of life that evolved over millennia has been trans-formed in a matter of decades and the Inuit emerged into a new world order not of their making and at an enormous social cost, an order not necessarily to universal approval or benefit. One native leader speaks of the fearful possibility of "having to completely reinvent what it means to be an Inuit."[3]

In achieving the 2007 submarine triumph at the North Pole, Artur Chilingarov was satisfied that Russia had taken possession of that northern region. A hundred years earlier, however, a Canadian Arctic mariner, Joseph-Elzéar Bernier from L'Islet, Quebec, on board Canadian Coast Guard ship *Arctic*, erected on his own initiative a plaque at Winter Harbour at McClure Strait. It read:

> This Memorial
> is
> erected to commemorate
> The taking possession for the
> DOMINION OF CANADA
> Of the whole
> ARCTIC ARCHIPELAGO
> Lying to the north of America
> From long. 60°W to 141°W,
> Upto latitude 90°N.
> Winter Hbr. Melville Island
> C.G.S. Arctic, July 1st 1909
> J.E. Bernier, Commander

Not only was Bernier formally laying claim to the vast territory of the archipelago, but also to all that lay up to that ultimate polar dot. The Canadians and then the Russians, two stakeholders defining claims that together encompass three-quarters of the Arctic. Then the other Arctic coastal nations: United States, Denmark, and Norway, each with their own jurisdictional claims and vested interests. Shunting aside the dominant issue of climate change, the absorbing question causing international angst today is: who owns what in the Arctic?

History records scores of territorial or jurisdictional disputes and most wars are rooted in such quarrels. In today's world, over two hundred territorial disputes are ongoing — Golan Heights, Falkland Islands, Kashmir, and Gibraltar, for example. (Perhaps the two most comical ones are Rock Island, an extinct volcanic protrusion of 8,500 square feet,

Canadian Coast Guard vessel approaches the barren Hans Island, lying in the narrow channel between Greenland and Ellesmere Island. A negotiated settlement of the Danish-Canadian dispute over the island's ownership appears imminent. One possibility under consideration is a joint ownership, with half the island going to Denmark and the other to Canada. Such a solution gives rise to the intriguing possibility that Canada would then share a common border with the European Union, just as Russia does.

which juts out of the North Atlantic, claimed by *four* nations — the United Kingdom, Ireland, Denmark, and Iceland. The other is a strip of roadway called *Passetto di Borgo*, ten feet by two hundred, claimed by the Vatican City and Italy.) The Arctic does not escape territorial disputes. Denmark and Canada, for example, both lay claim to the tiny barren Hans Island situated between Greenland and Ellesmere Island. In 1984, Denmark's minister for Greenland planted his nation's flag and in a lightedhearted move he left behind a bottle of cognac with the note, "Welcome to the Danish island." A decade later, Denmark followed up more seriously on the minister's visit by dispatching a group of warships on manoeuvres around the island. The Canadian press had a field day with the news, offering such tongue-in-cheek headlines as "Canada Being Invaded," and "Danish Massing Troops on Canadian Territory." Later that same year, the situation intensified when over 180 Canadian troops took over Hans Island and held military exercises, complete with aircraft, helicopters, and a frigate. And when Canada's Foreign Minister Bill Graham visited the island in 2005, an immediate objection was raised by the Danish foreign ministry — "We consider Hans Island to be part of Danish territory and will therefore hand over complaint about the Canadian minister's unannounced visit." Long-standing friends as the two countries are, the dispute no doubt will find peaceful resolution, although with unconfirmed reports of nearby oil reserves the negotiations are unlikely to be held lightly over that Danish bottle of cognac. The two nations might follow the example of the Norwegians and Russians who in April 2010 amicably settled a forty-year conflict over a 68,000-square-mile maritime area with promising oil reserves — the disputed area was equally divided.

On the other side of the Arctic Ocean, the United States and Canada are at odds over two issues. First, a dispute over the division of the Beaufort Sea. The Canadians hold that the territorial boundary is an extension of the 141° parallel that delineates the Yukon–Alaska border, a line that has been in effect since 1903. The United States takes the position that the boundary is a line perpendicular to the coast where the 141° parallel meets the sea. The difference between the two positions creates an 8,100-square-mile wedge of disputed waters, beneath which are potential oil reserves.

The other dispute is more consequential, carrying international implications. It concerns the Northwest Passage. As global warming brings its changes to the Arctic landscape, the viability of the long-coveted route becomes more real; the icy setting for Amundsen's successful traverse over a century ago has altered dramatically. In 1969, the specially reinforced American supertanker, the *Manhattan*, navigated the passage without incident, accompanied by the Canadian icebreaker, *Sir John A. Macdonald*. In 1984, the Swedish vessel *Linblad Explorer*, carrying ninety passengers was the first cruise ship to pass through the waterway, and since then a succession of other ships and adventurous yachtsmen have also completed the journey. As for secretive nuclear submarine traffic, there is no accounting of numbers, but it is clear that a subsurface passage from the Atlantic to the Pacific has its attractions.

The crux of the territorial dispute lies in Canada's contention that the archipelago through which these vessels passed is its sovereign territory, which under international law is subject to the 1982 United Nations Convention of the Law of the Sea (UNCLOS), ratified by 158 countries. By a concept dating back to the seventeenth century, a nation held sovereignty over a coastline belt of three nautical miles — anything beyond that limit was considered international water open to all without hindrance. UNCLOS extended that baseline to twelve miles (with provision being made for the right of foreign vessels to make non-stop "innocent passages" under certain specific conditions). Additionally, the convention provided for a two-hundred-mile extension from the baseline as an Exclusive Economic Zone (EEZ), by which the coastal nation has sole rights to natural resources lying therein.

Canada claims the EEZ over the entire Arctic Archipelago and therefore sovereignty over the Northwest Passage by reason of historic title. It thus asserts its right to regulate activity and enforce its own law therein. The United States, supported by other maritime nations, views the passage as an international strait, a corridor linking two major bodies of water, like the straits of Magellan, Hormuz, Malacca, and the Bosporus. In 2009, a presidential directive unequivocally declared, "The Northwest Passage is a strait used for international navigation."

For Canadians, the issue of jurisdiction over the passage is important for reasons of control. First and foremost, the fragile ecology must be protected from environmental damage, and secondly, there must be overseeing of ships flying flags of convenience that cloak their true origins and their owners from accountability.

As drilling and trans-Arctic shipment of gas and oil develops the danger of oil spills loom threateningly — oil takes decades to disperse and degrade in frigid waters. The cleanup of the 1989 *Exxon Valdez* NEVER spill in comparatively warm waters and that of the devastating 2010 BP COMPLETED disaster in the Gulf of Mexico in temperate waters were horrendously expensive and lengthy processes, and the toll on animal life and human habitation was reprehensible.

Imagine a replay of the BP catastrophe in the Beaufort Sea or in Davis Strait. The expense and effort of bringing equipment and manpower to such remote places to cope with a spill is unimaginable. The *Exxon Valdez* spill was confined to a relatively small coastline area, principally within Prince William Sound. If a spill such as that occurred within the complex system of strong Arctic Ocean currents, it would have far-reaching international consequences. The damage sustained to the highly specialized and easily disrupted food chains — from algae and bacteria to mammals and people — would be calamitous. Whereas the Gulf of Mexico disaster brought profound economic and emotional distress to the population and animal life, a similar disaster in the Arctic would most likely terminate a way of life for the affected inhabitants.

A commercial sea lane has already been established for fast delivery of goods from Murmansk to Churchill, which connects by rail with the heartland of North America. As maritime traffic becomes heavier, not only will environmental issues increase exponentially, but security concerns will come to the fore. As Michael Byers points out in *Who Owns the Arctic?*, one might well anticipate "rogue states and terrorist groups using the Northwest Passage to traffic in weapons of mass destruction, equipment for enriching nuclear isotopes, and missiles. Unlikely as these risks might seem at first, it is not difficult to imagine a captain of this sort of cargo choosing an ice-free, under-policed Northwest Passage over a closely scrutinized Panama Canal."[4]

China, Japan, and Korea cast covetous eyes upon budding polar routes, not only for transport of Siberian and Beaufort Sea oil and gas purchases, but for transpolar communication with North American east-coast ports and European markets. A cargo vessel transporting goods from Yokohama to Boston through the Northwest Passage, rather than taking the Panama Canal route, can cut the distance by a quarter, saving time, fuel, and money. China has invested heavily in Alberta tar sands, and with easy access to the sea port at Churchill on the Hudson Bay, the spectre of tankers regularly plying Arctic waters becomes more real.

A suggestion has been made that nuclear-powered submarines might transport liquid gas under the polar cap. In Russia, construction of a floating nuclear power station to provide energy is in progress and there is talk of a possible fleet of such stations eventually delivering energy across that country's Arctic.

As these lines are being written, exploration is well underway of laying a fibre-optic cable between London and Tokyo by way of the Passage. The ice melt "opens up the construction window to actually do something like this without the need of heavy icebreakers," explains a spokesman for ArcticLink, as the venture is called (at an estimated cost of $1.2 billion). All this in the interest of quicker transmission time, critical to the financial world where milliseconds count in executing trades.

The magnitude of environmental and security issues in the Northwest Passage are undeniable. Little wonder that Canada takes the position it does on sovereignty over those Arctic waters, particularly as UNCLOS environmental regulations governing international straits are less stringent than its own. The American contention that the Passage falls under international jurisdiction is also meritorious. No doubt agreement on the matter will eventually be reached by Ottawa and Washington, and the same spirit of collaboration will prevail, which brought about the 1817 Rush-Bagot Agreement, demilitarizing the Great Lakes, and also in the establishment of the St. Lawrence Seaway. For the moment, the two neighbours appear content in agreeing to disagree. Russia has kept a low profile in all this, for what's applicable to the Northwest Passage may be equally applicable to the Northern Sea Route.

The issue of Arctic navigation is real enough, but more burning is the question of who owns the ocean's seabed. Article 76 of UNCLOS gives a coastal state right to claim ownership of its "extended continental shelf," even if it stretches beyond the twelve-mile Exclusive Economic Zone. A nation, therefore, that can successfully define its continental shelf can lay claim to sovereign rights of its seabed riches. If USGC estimates of the Arctic oil and gas reserves that lie beneath the ocean floor are correct, then the continental shelf issue becomes of vital interest to all the players.

What then is "continental shelf"? Simply put, it is the gently sloping land that lies submerged around the edges of a continent that extends from the shoreline out to what is called the "continental break." At this point, the land noticeably drops, causing the waters above to become much deeper, an occurrence that with few exceptions is uniform around the world at approximately 460 feet. According to Article 76, Byers explains, a nation "may claim rights over an 'extended continental shelf,' beyond the EEZ, if the depth and shape of the seabed and the thickness of underlying sediments indicate a 'natural prolongation' of the shelf closer to shore." He goes on to note that nations making claims have two options in defining maximum limits: "either 350 nautical miles from shore, or 100 nautical miles beyond the point where the depth of the water reaches 2,500 metres. Again, the coastal state can choose whichever limit or combination of limits works best for it." It's a given that with such options being proffered that nations will define claims most advantageous to themselves, irrespective of overlap with others.

A special commission was established by the United Nations, reporting to UNCLOS, to receive supporting documentation from coastal states related to seabed claims. In 2001 Russia made a formal such submission in which it claimed a large part of the Arctic, including the North Pole. Within the country's continental shelf, the Russians asserted, lay the Mendeleev Ridge and the by-far larger and more significant Lomonosov Ridge, both extensions of its continental sovereign territory. The Lomonosov Ridge extends 1,125 miles from the Anzhu Islands, an archipelago off Siberia's northeast coast at approximately 76°N, over the central part of the Arctic Ocean, to Ellesmere Island of the Canadian Arctic Archipelago. In 2002, the UN commission neither accepted nor rejected Russia's submission, returning it with the request for additional geological evidence.

Meanwhile, Denmark argued that the Lomonsov Ridge is an extension of Greenland; Norway has made its own submission to UNCLOS and the United States has launched ambitious mapping work to determine the extent of Alaska's continental shelf.

Claim and counter-claim: it all appears conflicting, but, in fact, the five nations have banded together to seek harmonious resolutions to the issues by making the decision to map the entire Arctic seabed. Oceanographers continue exploring the ocean floor's sediments and rock formations with sonar and seismic sensors, and slowly the meticulous undertaking is taking shape. Eventually the completed work, with all the supporting documentation, will be submitted to UNCLOS, which will then have the task of adjudication. Once the territorial claims have been fixed, the platforms and rigs of the oil giants will move in and the face of the ocean's surface may be expected to change dramatically. Until then it remains the nearly the pristine wilderness of the ages.

On one hand, diminishing ice cover, melting permafrost, and environmental conditions threaten the lives and traditions of many circumpolar communities. On the other hand, the prospect of an ice-free Arctic opens possibility for global trade routes, economic development, and Arctic prosperity. As Charles Emmerson points out in *The Future History of the Arctic*, "Putting value judgments aside, the consequences of global warming in the Arctic will involve both tragedy and success, destruction and innovation, risk and opportunity, and for better or worse, losers and winners. What is certain is that a static vision of the Arctic is unsustainable in an era of rapid change and shifting climate."[5]

Soon alas — perhaps in the lifetime of some of my younger readers — the Arctic sublime, the place that "God had secreted all for himself," will be but a wondrous memory. And, in the words of Stefansson, it will look more like "a commonplace country… like Michigan or Switzerland."

Then the sweet songs of the fair-voiced Arctic Siren will beguile no more, silenced forever.

Acknowledgements

FOR THEIR ASSISTANCE AND unfailing courtesy, I owe particular thanks to the staffs of The Bodleian Library, Oxford — particularly that of the Duke Humphrey Room — and the Toronto Reference Library. I wish also to thank the personnel of the Robarts Library of the University of Toronto and the Library of the City of New York. I acknowledge the helpful assistance of United States Naval Archives, Washington, D.C.; the Arctic and Antarctic Research Institute, St. Petersburg (Russia); and the Arctic Institute of North America, Calgary. Thanks also to Google Books for providing Internet access to thousands of rare books, and to the Wikimedia Foundation for the helpful material it makes available to the public on Wikipedia.

My profound gratitude to Professor Franklyn Griffiths, University of Toronto and Senior Fellow, Peace and Conflict Studies; and to Dr. Stanislav Shmelev of the Environmental Change Institute, Oxford University, for their helpful critique and insights on aspects of the final two chapters. And to Cameron MacLeod Jones for the production of the illustrative maps — impressive work indeed for a fifteen-year-old. And finally, thanks to my agent Bill Hanna of Acacia House Publishing Services and to his wife, Frances, for their support in this work — the idea for the book was Bill's in the first place. Memories continue unflagging of two individuals now deceased who introduced me to the Arctic: businessman Otto Kredl, with whom I travelled into the extreme North, and George W. Jacobsen, the Arctic pioneer and founder of the Jacobsen-McGill Arctic Research Centre on Axel Heiberg, who was my mentor on that remarkable tour of discovery.

Notes

Introduction — The Arctic: Who Is She?

1. George Kennon, *Tent Life in Siberia* (G.P. Putnam's Sons: New York, 1882), 276.

1 — Earliest Explorations

1. J.R.S. Sterrett, *The Geography of Strabo, Vol. I* (London: Loeb Classical Library, 1917), 261.

2. Paul Simpson-Housley, *The Arctic: Enigmas and Myths* (Toronto: Dundurn Press, 1996), 24.

3. Jeannette Mirsky, *To the Arctic!* (Chicago: University of Chicago Press, 1970), 18.

4. Finn Gad, *The History of Greenland, Vol. I* (London: C. Hurst & Co., 1970), 19.

5. *Ibid.*, 26

6. H.A.L. Fisher, *A History of Europe* (London: Eyre and Spottiswoode, 1955), 374.

2 — Eastern Thrusts to Cathay

1. Jeannette Mirsky, *To the Arctic!* (Chicago: University of Chicago Press, 1970), 26.

2. G.B. Parks, *Richard Hakluyt and the English Voyages*, Publication #10 (New York: American Geographical Society, 1928), 56.

3. Richard Vaughan, *The Arctic: A History* (Stroud, UK: Sutton Publishing, 1994), 56.

4. *Ibid.*, 27.

5. J. Hamel, *England and Russia:Comprising the Voyages of Tradescant the Elder and Others* (London: Frank Cass &Co. Ltd., 1965), 87.

6. L.H. Neatby, *Discovery in Russian and Siberian Waters* (Athens, OH: Ohio University Press, 1973), 10.

7. J. Hamel, 100.

8. J. Watts De Peyster, *The Dutch at the North Pole and the Dutch in Main* (New York: New York Historical Society, 1857), 10.

9. Richard Vaughan, 60.

10. Gerrit De Veer, *The Three Voyages of William Barents to the Arctic* (London: The Hakluyt Society, 1876), 25.

11. *Ibid.*, 63.

12. L.H. Neatby, 22.

13. A small town north of Amsterdam.

14. A large wine cask capable of holding 150 gallons.

15. An astrolabe is a primitive instrument used in determining latitudes, in bygone days essential for navigation.

3 — First Western Thrusts

1. "The Voyage of John Cabot to America" (*www.chroniclesofamerica. com/sea-dogs/voyage_of_john_cabot_to_america.htm*).

2. The continuation of Cabot's commission is amusing in its language

and naïveté: "... and as many mariners or men as they will have with them in the saide shippes, upon their owne proper costs and charges, to seeke out, discover, and finde, whatsoever Iles, Countreyes, Regions, or Provinces, of the Heathennes and Infidelles, whatsoever they bee, and in what part of the worlde soever they bee, which before this time have been unknowen to all Christians."

3. In 1583, Gilbert set sail for America in five ships, and, having arrived to Newfoundland, he claimed the land in the name of Her Majesty, thus laying the foundation of the British Empire. Of the voyage's greater significance is the motivation it gave to Humphrey's half brother, Sir Walter Raleigh, who commanded one of Gilbert's ships, to undertake the eventual Roanoke expeditions that led to the founding in Virginia of the first English colony in North America.

4. John Campbell, *The Naval History of Great Britain* (London: Baldwin & Co, 1818), 396.

5. A pinnace is a boat that is usually carried on board a larger ship. In Frobisher's day they were equipped with full rigging and held ready for inshore work. The one accompanying him, however, sailed "on its own bottom" rather than being carried on the decks of the *Gabriel*.

6. John Barrow, *A Chronological History of Voyages into the Arctic Regions* (1818; reprint, London: John Murray, 1971), 82.

7. Richard Coelinson, *The Three Voyages of Martin Frobisher* (London: The Hakluyt Society, 1867), 189.

4 — First Western Thrusts

1. Henry S. Burrage, *Rosier's Relation of Waymouth's Voyage to the Coast of Main* (Portland: Gorges Society, 1887), 17.

2. G.M. Asher, ed., *Henry Hudson the Navigator. The Original Documents in which his Career is Recorded* (London: The Haklyut Society, 1860), 152.

3. The correct name for this seasonal plant is *spoonwart*, a flowering green containing large quantities of vitamin C. The vitamin is essential

for battling scurvy, the dreaded disease that strikes those who do not regularly consume fruit or green plants.

4. It was a Northern custom to create food caches in strategic places as emergency stores for hunters travelling far from home.

5. A shallop was a ship's single-mast boat, twenty to thirty feet in length, six feet in breadth, for use in navigating within shallow waters. It was frequently carried in pieces on the deck and assembled when required.

5 — A Dane at Hudson Bay

1. C.A.A. Gosch, ed., *Danish Arctic Expedition, 1605–1620* (London: The Hakluyt Society, 1847), 8.

2. During the Napoleonic Wars, the Royal Navy made compulsory a daily dose of lime juice for all its personnel at sea — hence "Limey," the pejorative for Englishman.

3. Samuel de Champlain, *Voyages du Sieur de Champlain* (1613; reprint, Toronto: The Champlain Society, 1971), 147.

4. Clement Markham, *The Voyages of William Baffin, 1612–1622* (London: The Hakluyt Society, 1881), 114.

5. Miller Christy, *The Voyages of Captain Luke Foxe in Search of the Northwest Passage* (London: 1894), 222.

6 — Russians in the Arctic

1. L.H. Neatby, *Discovery in Russian and Siberian Waters* (Athens, OH: Ohio University Press, 1973), 56.

2. F.A. Golder, *Bering's Voyages* (American Geographical Society: New York, 1922), 13.

3. The peninsula has 160 volcanoes, the highest one reaching 15,600 feet. Today, twenty-nine of these are active, some spewing mile-high columns of ashes. The cluster of volcanoes is a UNESCO World

Heritage Site. (Kamchatka, incidentally, averages an annual precipitation of 110 inches.)

4. Bruce Lincoln, W., *The Conquest of a Continent* (New York: Random House, 1994), 104.

5. Yuri Semyonov, *Siberia: Its Conquest and Development* (Montreal: International Publishers, 1968), 173.

6. *Ibid.*, 170.

7. Raymond Fisher, *The Voyage of Semen Dezhnev* (London: The Hakluyt Society, 1981), 1.

8. David Roberts, *Four Against the Arctic* (New York: Simon & Schuster, 2003), 122.

9. *Ibid.*, 93.

10. Adolf Nordenskiöld, *Voyage of the Vega Round Asia and Europe. Vol. I* (London: Macmillian & Co., 1885), 428.

11. F.A. Golder, *Russian Expansion of the Pacific, 1641–1850* (Gloucester: Peter Smith, 1960), 282.

12. Pierre Le Roy, "A Narrative of the Singular Adventures of Four Russian Sailors," in *An Account of the New Northern Archipelago Lately Discovered by the Russians in the Seas of Kamtschatka and Anadir* by J. von Staehlin (London: C. Heydinger, 1774), 12.

13. David Roberts, 27.

14. *Ibid.*, 288.

7 — The Franklin Tragedy

1. Jeannette Mirsky, *To the Arctic!* (Chicago: University of Chicago Press, 1970), 114.

2. John Richardson, *Arctic Ordeal: the Journal of John Richardson* (Montreal: McGill-Queen's University Press, 1984), 231.

3. *Ibid.*, 150.

4. Scott Cookman notes in *Iceblink* that since the *Terror* participated in the attack on Fort McHenry during the War of 1812, it's quite likely that "the bombs bursting in air" in the American national anthem were fired from its decks.

5. "Official Report on the Franklin Expedition," *Arctic Expedition* (London: House of Commons, April 13, 1848), 332.

6. Owen Beattie and J. Geiger, *Frozen in Time* (Saskatoon: Western Producer Prairie Books, 1987), 17.

7. Scott Cookman, *Ice Blink* (Toronto: John Wiley & Sons, 2000), 80.

8. *Ibid.*, 99

9. Jeannette Mirsky, 133.

10. In the years 1819–25 Sir William Parry lead three expeditions in search of the Northwest Passage and had passed through these waters. It will be recalled that Parry was Barrow's first choice to command the expedition ultimately entrusted to Franklin.

11. Scott Cookman, 161.

12. Owen Beattie and J. Geiger, 123.

13. F.L. McClintock, *A Narrative of the Discovery of the Fate of Sir John J. Franklin* (Edmonton: Hurtig Publishers, 1972).

14. Kenneth McGoogan, *Fatal Passage: the Untold Story of John Rae* (New York: HarperCollins Publishers: 2001), 237.

15. J. Rae, *Narrative of an Expedition to the Shores of the Arctic Sea, 1846–1847* (London: T. & W. Boone, 1850).

16. Owen Beattie and J. Geiger, 59.

17. Anne Keenleyside, "The Final Days of the Franklin Expedition: New Skeletal Evidence," *Arctic* Vol. 50, No. 1 (March 1997), 36. Keenleyside also lists nine femurs and tibia having high levels of lead.

8 — Americans of the Arctic

1. Albert A Woodman, *Lincoln and the Russians* (New York: The World Publishing Company, 1952), 377.

2. Alexander Tarsaidze, *Czars and Presidents* (New York: Obolensky and McDowell, 1958), 239.

3. *Ibid.*, 236.

4. George Kennon, *Tent Life in Siberia* (G.P. Putnam's Sons: New York, 1882), 422.

5. Like his diplomat nephew, Kennan held an abiding interest in Russia, its people, culture, and policies. In subsequent trips to that country, he came to know it well and soon became a vocal critic of its government. He made a brilliant career as a sought-after lecturer and acclaimed journalist. Whereas the name of George Kennan, the diplomat, is well known to the contemporary world whose immediate history he helped to shape, his uncle is all but forgotten, a "posthumous misfortune" as one admirer put it, and today no more than a footnote in history, a shadow to his nephew.

6. Bennett founded a French edition of his paper, *The Paris Herald*, forerunner of *The International Herald Tribune*.

7. Edward Ellsberg, *Hell on Ice: the Saga of the "Jeannette"* (New York: Dodd, Mead &Co, 1938), 18.

9 — The Scandinavians

1. Whalebone quickly developed into a popular byproduct of the hunt. Scoresby in *An Account of the Arctic Regions,* quotes one 1807 patent taken out for the adoption of whalebone: "hats, caps and bonnets for men and women; harps for harping or cleansing corn or grain; and also the bottoms of sieves and riddles; and girths for horse; and also cloth for webbing, fit for making into hats, caps &c; and for the backs and seats of chairs; sofas, gigs, and other similar carriages and things; and for the bottom of beds; and also whalebone reeds for weavers."

2. Adolf Nordenskiöld, *Voyage of the Vega Round Asia and Europe* (London: Macmillian & Co., 1885), 231.

3. *Ibid.*, 394.

4. Shortly after this despairing note, the greatly relieved De Long received word that Nordenskiöld had safely passed the winter and was continuing on his journey. De Long was now free to pursue his appointed mission without distraction.

5. Raymond Fisher, *The Voyage of Semen Dezhnev* (London: The Hakluyt Society, 1981), 562.

6. Jeannette Mirsky, *To the Arctic!* (Chicago: University of Chicago Press, 1970), 200.

7. A non sequitur: Nansen's thesis, *The Structure and Combination of Histological Elements of the Central Nervous System*, became a classic.

8. Fridtjof Nansen, *The First Crossing of Greenland* (London: Longmans, Green, 1890), 189.

9. One of Nansen's inventions was a certain bottle that was capable of collecting a sample from a specific depth and retrieving it without compromise of waters from other levels.

10. Charles Emmerson, *The Future History of the Arctic* (New York: Public Affairs, 2010), 13.

11. Roald Amundsen, *The South Pole: an Account of the Norwegian Antarctic Expedition in the "Fram," 1910–12* (London: John Murray, 1912), 437.

12. Vilhjalmur Stefansson, *The Friendly Arctic: The Story of Five Years in Polar Regions* (London: MacMillan, 1922), 377.

13. Richard Vaughan, *The Arctic: A History* (Stroud, UK: Sutton Publishing, 1994), 234.

10 — Canary in the Cage

1. Scott G. Borgerson, "The Arctic Meltdown: the Economic and Security Implications of Global Warming," *Foreign Affairs* (March/April, 2008), 77.

2. Whalebone is in fact baleen — that hair-like material within the mouth — which in pre-plastic days found use as corset stays and parasol ribs. Ambergris, a substance from the intestine of sperm whales, at one time or another was used in the mixing of perfumes, incense and medication, and in the Middle Ages was worn around the neck in the conviction that it wards off Black Death.

11 — People and Politics

1. Thomas Wright, ed. *The Travels of Marco Polo the Venetian* (London: Henry G. Bohn, 1854), 449.

2. Richard Vaughan, *The Arctic: A History* (Stroud, UK: Sutton Publishing, 1994), 278.

3. Franklyn Griffiths, "Camels in the Arctic?" *The Walrus* (November 2007): 48.

4. Michael Byers, *Who Owns the Arctic? Understanding Sovereignty Disputes in the North* (Toronto: Douglas & McIntyre, 2009), 60.

5. Charles Emmerson, *The Future History of the Arctic* (New York: Public Affairs, 2010), 150.

Bibliography

Amundsen, Roald. *"The New Passage": Being the Record of the Voyage of Exploration of the Ship "Gjøa."* London: Archibald Constable, 1906.

Amundsen, Roald. *The South Pole: an Account of the Norwegian Antarctic Expedition in the "Fram," 1910–12.* London: John Murray, 1912.

Asher, G.M., ed. *Henry Hudson the Navigator. The Original Documents in which his Career is Recorded.* London: The Haklyut Society, 1860.

Barrow, John. *A Chronological History of Voyages into the Arctic Regions.* 1818. Reprint, London: John Murray, 1971.

Beattie, Owen and J. Geiger. *Frozen in Time.* Saskatoon: Western Producer Prairie Books, 1987.

Beerling, David. *The Emerald Planet: How Plants Changed Earth's History.* Oxford: Oxford University Press, 2007.

Bone, Robert M. *The Geography of the Canadian North.* Toronto: Oxford University Press, 1992.

Borgerson, Scott G. "The Arctic Meltdown: the Economic and Security Implications of Global Warming." *Foreign Affairs* (March/April, 2008).

Brandt, Anthony. *The North Pole: A Narrative History.* Washington: National Geographic Society, 2005.

Bumstead, J.M. *The Peoples of Canada: a Pre-Confederation History.* Oxford University Press: Toronto, 1992.

Burrage, Henry S. *Rosier's Relation of Waymouth's Voyage to the Coast of Main*. Portland: Gorges Society, 1887.

Byers, Michael. *Who Owns the Arctic? Understanding Sovereignty Disputes in the North*. Toronto: Douglas & McIntyre, 2009.

Campbell, John. *The Naval History of Great Britain*. London: Baldwin & Co, 1818.

Christy, Miller. *The Voyages of Captain Luke Foxe in Search of the Northwest Passage*. London, 1894.

Coelinson, Richard. *The Three Voyages of Martin Frobisher*. London: The Hakluyt Society, 1867.

Cookman, Scott. *Ice Blink*. Toronto: John Wiley & Sons, 2000.

De Champlain, Samuel. *Voyages du Sieur de Champlain*. 1613. Reprint, Toronto: The Champlain Society, 1971.

De Long, Emma, ed. *The Voyage of the Jeannette: the Ship and Ice Journals of George Washington De Long*. New York: Houghton, Mifflin & Co. 1883.

De Peyster, J. Watts. *The Dutch at the North Pole and the Dutch in Main*. New York: New York Historical Society, 1857.

De Ponctins, Contran. *Kabloona*. Chicago: Time-Life Books, 1965.

De Veer, Gerrit. *The Three Voyages of William Barents to the Arctic*. London: The Hakluyt Society, 1876.

Dictionary of Canadian Biography (*www.biographi.ca*).

Duffy, R. Quinn. *The Road to Nunavut: the Progress of the Eastern Arctic Inuit since the Second World War*. Montreal: McGill-Queen's University Press, 1988.

Ellsberg, Edward. *Hell on Ice: the Saga of the "Jeannette."* New York: Dodd, Mead &Co, 1938.

Emmerson, Charles. *The Future History of the Arctic*. New York: Public Affairs, 2010.

Ferguson, Michael A.D. "Arctic Tundra Caribou and Climatic Change." *Geoscience Canada* 23(4).

Fisher, H.A.L. *A History of Europe*. London: Eyre and Spottiswoode, 1955.

Fisher, Raymond. *The Voyage of Semen Dezhnev*. London: The Hakluyt Society, 1981.

Fitzburgh, W.W. & Jacqueline Olin. *Archeology of the Frobisher Voyages*. Washington: Smithsonian Institute Press, 1993.

Foxe, Thomas. *The Strange and Dangerous Voyage of Captaine Thomas James and his intended discouvery of the northwest passage*. London: John Leggatt, 1633.

Franklin, John. *Narrative of a Journey to the Shores of the Polar Sea*. Vancouver: Douglas & McIntyre, 2000.

Gad, Finn. *The History of Greenland, Vol. I*. London: C. Hurst & Co., 1970.

Gilder, W.H. *Schwatka's Search*. New York: Abercrombie & Finch, 1972.

Golovnen, A. and G. Osherenko. *Siberian Survival: the Nenets and Their Story*. Ithaca: Cornell University Press, 1999.

Golder, F.A. *Russian Expansion of the Pacific, 1641–1850*. Gloucester: Peter Smith, 1960.

___. *Bering's Voyages*. American Geographical Society: New York, 1922.

Gosch, C.A.A. *Scandinavia's First Great Polar Explorer*.

Gosch, C.A.A., ed. *Danish Arctic Expedition, 1605–1620*. London: The Hakluyt Society, 1847.

Graf, Miller. *Arctic Journeys: A History of Exploration*. New York: Peter Lang, 1992.

Griffiths, Franklyn. *Politics of the Northwest Passage*. Montreal: McGill-Queens University Press, 1987.

Griffiths, Franklyn. "Camels in the Arctic?" *The Walrus* (November 2007).

Guttridge, L.F. *Icebound: the Jeannette Expedition's Quest for the North Pole*. Annapolis: Naval Institute Press, 1986.

Hamel, J. *England and Russia; Comprising the Voyages of Tradescant the Elder and Others*. London: Frank Cass & Co. Ltd., 1965.

Hansen, Thornkeld. *North West to Hudson Bay: the Life and Times of Jens Munk*. London: Collins, 1970.

Hunter, Douglas. *God's Mercies: Rivalry and Betrayal and the Dream of Discovery*. Toronto: Doubleday Canada, 2007.

"Impacts of a Warming Globe." *Arctic Climate Impact Assessment*. Cambridge: Cambridge University Press, 2004.

International Panel of Climate Change. *Climate Change, 2007: the Fourth Assessment Report*. New York: The United Nations, 2007.

Keenleyside, Anne. "The Final Days of the Franklin Expedition: New Skeletal Evidence." *Arctic* Vol. 50, No. 1 (March 1997).

Kennon, George. *Tent Life in Siberia*. New York: G.P. Putnam's Sons, 1882.

Kenyon, Walter. *Arctic Argonauts*. Waterloo: Penumbrian Press, 1990.

Kimble, G.H.T. and Dorothy Good. *Geography of the Northlands*. New York: The American Geographical Society, 1955.

Krogh, Knud J. *Viking Greenland*. Copenhagen: The National Museum, 1967.

Labévière, Eichard and François Thual. *La Bataille du Grand Nord a Commencé*. Paris: Perrin, 2008.

Le Roy, Pierre. "A Narrative of the Singular Adventures of Four Russian Sailors." *An Account of the New Northern Archipelago Lately Discovered by the Russians in the Seas of Kamtschatka and Anadir*. J. von Staehlin. London: C. Heydinger, 1774.

Lincoln, W. Bruce. *The Conquest of a Continent*. New York: Random House, 1994.

Lusin, G.P. and V.V. Vasiliev. "The Kola Peninsula: Geography, History and Resources." *Arctic* 47 (1997).

Lynas, Mark. *Six Degrees: Our Future on a Hotter Planet*. London: Harper Perennial, 2008.

Malcolm, Jay R. "The Demise of an Ecosystem: Arctic Wildlife in a Changing Climate." Washington: *World Wildlife Fund Report*, 1995.

Bibliography

Mancall, Peter C. *Fatal Journey.* New York: Basic Books, 2009.

Markham, Clement. *The Voyages of William Baffin, 1612-1622.* London: The Hakluyt Society, 1881.

Markov, Sergey N. *Podvig Semyona Dezhneva.* Moscow: 1948.

McGhee, Robert. *The Last Imaginary Place: a Human History of the Arctic World.* Ottawa: Canadian Museum of Civilization, 2004.

McClintock, F.L. *A Narrative of the Discovery of the Fate of Sir John J. Franklin.* Edmunton: Hurtig Publishers, 1972.

McGoogan, Kenneth. *Fatal Passage: the Untold Story of John Rae.* New York: HarperCollins Publishers, 2001.

Mirsky, Jeannette. *To the Arctic!* Chicago: University of Chicago Press, 1970.

Mowat, Farley. *Ordeal by Ice: the Search for the Northwest Passage.* Toronto: McClelland & Stewart, 1989.

Nansen, Fridtjof. *The First Crossing of Greenland.* London: Longmans, Green, 1890.

Nansen, Fridtjof. *Farthest North.* London: Archibald Constable, 1897.

Neatby, L.H. *Discovery in Russian and Siberian Waters.* Athens, OH: Ohio University Press, 1973.

Nordenskiöld, Adolf. *Voyage of the Vega Round Asia and Europe.* London: Macmillian & Co., 1885.

"Official Report on the Franklin Expedition." *Arctic Expedition.* London: House of Commons, April 13, 1848.

Parks, G.B. *Richard Hakluyt and the English Voyages.* Publication #10. New York: American Geographical Society, 1928.

Pollack, Henry. *A World Without Ice.* New York: The Penguin Group, 2009.

Powys, Lewelyn. *Henry Hudson.* London: John Lane Ltd., 1927.

Rae, J. *Narrative of an Expedition to the Shores of the Arctic Sea, 1846-1847.* London: T. & W. Boone, 1850.

Rasmussen, Knud. *Across Arctic America: Narrative of the Fifth Thule Expedition.* New York: G.P. Putnam's Sons, 1927.

Richardson, John. *Arctic Ordeal: the Journal of John Richardson.* Montreal: McGill-Queen's University Press, 1984.

Roberts, David. *Four Against the Arctic.* New York: Simon & Schuster, 2003.

Quinn, David B. *New American World: a Documentary History of North America to 1612.* New York: Arno Press, 1979.

Quinn, David B. *Sir Humphrey Gilbert and Newfoundland.* New York: P.F. Collier and Son, 1910.

Scorseby, W. *An Account of the Arctic Regions.* New York: Archibald Constable, 1969.

Semyonov, Yuri. *Siberia: Its Conquest and Development.* Montreal: International Publishers, 1968.

Shelikhov, G.I. and I.K. Nikolai. "Severnoi Amerike v XVII–XIX Vekakh: Sbornik Materialov." Moscow: Geograficheskoe Obschestvo SSSR, 1987.

Simpson-Housley, Paul. *The Arctic: Enigmas and Myths.* Toronto: Dundurn Press, 1996.

Slezkine, Yuri. *Arctic Mirrors: Russia and the Small Peoples of the North.* Ithaca: Cornell University Press, 1994.

Stefansson, Vilhjalmur. *The Friendly Arctic: The Story of Five Years in Polar Regions.* London: MacMillan, 1922.

Stefansson, Vilhjamur. *My Life with the Eskimo.* New York: Macmillan Co., 1945.

Sterrett, J.R.S. *The Geography of Strabo.* Vol I. London: Loeb Classical Library, 1917.

Vaughan, Richard. *The Arctic: A History.* Stroud, UK: Sutton Publishing, 1994.

Victor, Paul-Emile. *Man and the Conquest of the Poles.* New York: Simon & Schuster, 1963.

Bibliography

Wilkinson, Doug. *Arctic Fever: The Search for the Northwest Passage.* Toronto: Clarke, Irwin & Co, 1971.

Williams, Glyn. *Arctic Labyrinth: the Quest for the Northwest Passage.* Toronto: Penguin Group, 2009.

Williams, Heathcote. *Whale Nation.* New York: Harmony Books, 1988.

Walker, Gabrielle and Sir David King. *The Hot Topic.* London: Bloomsbury, 2008.

Woodman, Albert A. *Lincoln and the Russians.* New York: The World Publishing Company, 1952.

Wozencraft, W.C. and D.E. Wilson, eds. *Mammal Species of the World.* Baltimore: Johns Hopkins University Press, 2005.

Wright, Thomas, ed. *The Travels of Marco Polo the Venetian.* London: Henry G. Bohn, 1854.

Ziker, John P. *Peoples of the Tundra.* Prospect Heights: Waleland Press, 2002.

Index